Servlet and JSP

A Tutorial

Budi Kurniawan

Servlet and JSP : A Tutorial
Copyright © 2012 by Budi Kurniawan
First Edition: March 2012

ISBN: 978-0-9808396-2-3

Printed in the United States of America
Book and Cover Designer: Mona Setiadi

Technical Reviewer: Paul Deck
Indexer: Chris Mayle

Trademarks
Oracle and Java are registered trademarks of Oracle and/or its affiliates.
UNIX is a registered trademark of The Open Group.
Microsoft Internet Explorer is either a registered trademark or a trademark of Microsoft Corporation in The United States and/or other countries.
Apache is a trademark of The Apache Software Foundation.
Firefox is a registered trademark of the Mozilla Foundation.
Google is a trademark of Google, Inc.

Throughout this book the printing of trademarked names without the trademark symbol is for editorial purpose only. We have no intention of infringement of the trademark.

Warning and Disclaimer
Every effort has been made to make this book as accurate as possible. The author and the publisher shall have neither liability nor responsibility to any person or entity with respect to any loss or damages arising from the information in this book.

Table of Contents

Introduction

Welcome to *Servlet and JSP: A Tutorial*. This book covers Servlet 3.0 and JSP 2.2.

Java Servlet technology, or Servlet for short, is the underlying technology for developing web applications in Java. Sun Microsystems released it in 1996 to compete with the Common Gateway Interface (CGI), the then standard for generating dynamic content on the web. The main problem with the CGI was the fact that it spawned a new process for every HTTP request. This made it difficult to write scalable CGI programs because creating a process took a lot of CPU cycles. A servlet, on the other hand, is much faster than a CGI program because a servlet stays in memory after serving its first request, waiting for subsequent requests.

Since the day Servlet emerged, a number of Java-based web frameworks have been developed to help programmers write web applications more rapidly. These frameworks let you focus on the business logic and spend less time writing boilerplate code. However, you still have to understand the nuts and bolts of Servlet. And JavaServer Pages (JSP), which was later released to make writing servlets easier. You may be using a great framework like Struts 2, Spring MVC, or JavaServer Faces. However, without excellent knowledge of Servlet and JSP, you won't be able to code effectively and efficiently. Servlets, by the way, are Java classes that run on a servlet container. A servlet container or servlet engine is like a web server but has the ability to generate dynamic contents, not only serve static resources.

Servlet 3.0, the current version, is defined in Java Specification Request (JSR) 315 (http://jcp.org/en/jsr/detail?id=315). It requires Java Standard Edition 6 or later. JSP 2.2 is specified in JSR 245 (http://jcp.org/en/jsr/detail?id=245). This book assumes you know Java and object-oriented programming. If you're new to Java, I recommend my own *Java 7: A Beginner's Tutorial (Third Edition)*, ISBN 978-0-9808396-1-6.

The next sections of this introduction discuss servlet/JSP application architecture, the HTTP protocol, and the content of each chapter in this book.

Servlet/JSP Application Architecture

A servlet is a Java program. A servlet application consists of one or more servlets. A JSP page is translated and compiled into a servlet.

A servlet application runs inside a servlet container and cannot run on its own. A servlet container passes requests from the user to the servlet application and responses from the servlet application back to the user. Most servlet applications include at least several JSP pages. As such, it's more appropriate to use the term "servlet/JSP application" to refer to a Java web application than to leave JSP out.

Web users use a web browser such as Internet Explorer, Mozilla Firefox, or Google Chrome to access servlet applications. A web browser is referred to as a web client. Figure I.1 shows the architecture of a servlet/JSP application.

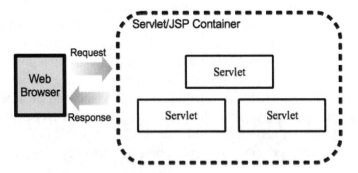

Figure I.1: Servlet/JSP application architecture

The web server and the web client communicate in a language they both are fluent in: the Hypertext Transfer Protocol (HTTP). Because of this, a web server is also called an HTTP server. HTTP is covered in more detail in the next section.

A servlet/JSP container is a special web server that can process servlets as well as serve static contents. In the past, people were more comfortable running a servlet/JSP container as a module of an HTTP server such as the Apache HTTP Server because an HTTP server was considered more robust than a servlet/JSP container. In this scenario the servlet/JSP container would be tasked with generating dynamic contents and the HTTP server with serving static resources. Today servlet/JSP containers are considered mature and widely deployed without an HTTP server. Apache Tomcat and Jetty are the most popular servlet/JSP containers and are free and open-source. You can download them from http://tomcat.apache.org and http://jetty.codehaus.org, respectively.

Servlet and JSP are two of a multitude of technologies defined in the Java Enterprise Edition (EE). Other Java EE technologies include Java Message Service (JMS), Enterprise JavaBeans (EJB), JavaServer Faces (JSF), and Java Persistence. The complete list of technologies in the Java EE version 6 (the current version) can be found here.

```
http://www.oracle.com/technetwork/java/javaee/tech/index.html
```

To run a Java EE application, you need a Java EE container, such as GlassFish, JBoss, Oracle WebLogic, and IBM WebSphere. You can deploy a servlet/JSP application in a Java EE container, but a servlet/JSP container is sufficient and is more lightweight than a Java EE container. Tomcat and Jetty are not Java EE containers, so they cannot run EJB or JMS.

The Hypertext Transfer Protocol (HTTP)

The HTTP protocol enables web servers and browsers to exchange data over the Internet or an intranet. The World Wide Web Consortium (W3C), an international community that develops standards, is responsible for revising and maintaining this protocol. The first version of HTTP was HTTP 0.9, which was then replaced by HTTP 1.0. Superseding HTTP 1.0 is HTTP 1.1, the current version. HTTP 1.1 is defined in the W3C's Request

for Comments (RFC) 2616, which can be downloaded from
http://www.w3.org/Protocols/HTTP/1.1/rfc2616.pdf.

A web server runs 24x7 waiting for HTTP clients (normally web
browsers) to connect to it and ask for resources. In HTTP it is always the
client that initiates a connection, a server is never in a position to contact a
client. To locate a resource, an Internet user clicks a link that contains a
Uniform Resource Locator (URL) or enter one in the Location box of
his/her browser. Here are two examples of URLs:

```
http://google.com/index.html

http://facebook.com/index.html
```

The first part of the URLs is **http**, which identifies the protocol. Not all
URLs use HTTP. For instance, these two URLs are valid even though they
are not HTTP-based URLs:

```
mailto:joe@example.com

ftp://marketing@ftp.example.org
```

In general a URL has this format:

```
protocol://[host.]domain[:port][/context][/resource][?query string]
```

or

```
protocol://IP address[:port][/context][/resource][?query string]
```

The parts in square brackets are optional, therefore a URL can be as simple
as http://yahoo.ca or http://192.168.1.9. An Internet Protocol (IP) address,
by the way, is a numerical label assigned to a computer or another device. A
computer may host more than one domain, so multiple domains can have
the same IP address. In other words, instead of typing http://google.com,
you can use its IP address: http://209.85.143.99. To find out what the IP
address of a domain is, use the **ping** program on your computer console:

```
ping google.com
```

An IP address is hard to remember, so people prefer to use a domain. And,
did you know that you can't buy example.com and example.org because
they are reserved for documentation purpose?

The host part may be present and identify a totally different location on the Internet or an intranet. For instance, http://yahoo.com (no host) brings you to a different location than http://mail.yahoo.com (with a host). Over the years www has been the most popular host name and become the default. Normally, http://www.*domainName* is mapped to http://*domainName*.

80 is the default port of HTTP. Therefore, if a web server runs on port 80, you don't need the port number to reach the server. Sometimes, however, a web server doesn't run on port 80 and you need to type the port number. For example, Tomcat by default runs on port 8080, so you need to supply the port number:

```
http://localhost:8080
```

localhost is a reserved name typically used to refer to the local computer, i.e. the same computer the web browser is running on.

The context part in a URL refers to the application name, but this is also optional. A web server can run multiple contexts (applications) and one of them can be configured to be the default context. To request a resource in the default context, you skip the context part in a URL.

Finally, a context can have one or more default resources (ordinarily index.html or index.htm or default.htm). A URL without a resource name is considered to identify a default resource. Of course, if more than one default resource exists in a context, the one with the highest priority will always be returned when a client does not specify a resource name.

After a resource name comes one or more query string. A query string is a key/value pair that can be passed to the server to be processed. You'll learn more about query strings in the next chapters.

The following subsections discuss HTTP requests and responses in more detail.

HTTP Requests

An HTTP request consists of three components:

- Method—Uniform Resource Identifier (URI)—Protocol/Version

- Request headers
- Entity body

Here is a sample HTTP request:

```
POST /examples/default.jsp HTTP/1.1
Accept: text/plain; text/html
Accept-Language: en-gb
Connection: Keep-Alive
Host: localhost
User-Agent: Mozilla/5.0 (Macintosh; U; Intel Mac OS X 10.5; en-US;
➡rv:1.9.2.6) Gecko/20100625 Firefox/3.6.6
Content-Length: 30
Content-Type: application/x-www-form-urlencoded
Accept-Encoding: gzip, deflate

lastName=Blanks&firstName=Mike
```

The method—URI—protocol version appears as the first line of the request.

```
POST /examples/default.jsp HTTP/1.1
```

Here **POST** is the request method, **/examples/default.jsp** the URI, and **HTTP/1.1** the Protocol/Version section.

An HTTP request can use one of the many request methods specified in the HTTP standards. HTTP 1.1 supports seven request types: GET, POST, HEAD, OPTIONS, PUT, DELETE, and TRACE. GET and POST are the most commonly used in Internet applications.

The URI specifies an Internet resource. It is usually interpreted as being relative to the server's root directory. Thus, it should always begin with a forward slash /. A Uniform Resource Locator (URL) is actually a type of URI (See http://www.ietf.org/rfc/rfc2396.txt).

In an HTTP request, the request header contains useful information about the client environment and the entity body of the request. For instance, it may contain the language the browser is set for, the length of the entity body, and so on. Each header is separated by a carriage return/linefeed (CRLF) sequence.

Between the headers and the entity body is a blank line (CRLF) that is important to the HTTP request format. The CRLF tells the HTTP server where the entity body begins. In some Internet programming books, this CRLF is considered the fourth component of an HTTP request.

In the previous HTTP request, the entity body is simply the following line:

```
lastName=Blanks&firstName=Mike
```

The entity body can easily be much longer in a typical HTTP request.

HTTP Responses

Similar to an HTTP request, an HTTP response also consists of three parts:

- Protocol—Status code—Description
- Response headers
- Entity body

The following is an example of an HTTP response:

```
HTTP/1.1 200 OK
Server: Apache-Coyote/1.1
Date: Thu, 5 Jan 2012 13:13:33 GMT
Content-Type: text/html
Last-Modified: Wed, 4 Jan 2012 13:13:12 GMT
Content-Length: 112

<html>
<head>
<title>HTTP Response Example</title>
</head>
<body>
Welcome to Brainy Software
</body>
</html>
```

The first line of the response header is similar to the first line of the request header. It tells you that the protocol used is HTTP version 1.1, and that the request succeeded (200 is the success code).

The response headers contain useful information similar to the headers in an HTTP request. The entity body of the response is the HTML content of the response itself. The headers and the entity body are separated by a sequence of CRLFs.

Status code 200 is only issued if the web server was able to find the resource requested. If a resource cannot be found or the request cannot be understood, the server sends a different request code. For instance, 401 is the status code for an unauthorized access and 405 indicates that the HTTP method is not allowed. For a complete list of HTTP status codes, refer to this online document.

```
http://www.w3.org/Protocols/rfc2616/rfc2616-sec10.html
```

About This Book

This section presents an overview of each chapter.

Chapter 1, "Servlets" introduces the Servlet API and presents several simple servlets. This chapter focuses on two of the four Java packages in the Servlet API, the **javax.servlet** and **javax.servlet.http** packages.

Chapter 2, "Session Management" discusses session tracking or session management, a very important topic in web application development due to the statelessness of HTTP. This chapter explores four techniques for retaining states: URL rewriting, hidden fields, cookies, and the **HTTPSession** objects.

JavaServer Pages (JSP) is a technology that complements Servlet. Chapter 3, "JavaServer Pages" covers the JSP syntax, including its directives, scripting elements, and actions.

Chapter 4, "The Expression Language" explains one of the most important features added in JSP 2.0, the Expression Language (EL). The EL aims to make it possible to author script-free JSP pages and can help you write shorter and more effective JSP pages. In this chapter you will learn to use the EL to access JavaBeans and scoped objects.

Chapter 5, "JSTL" explains the most important libraries in the JavaServer Pages Standard Tag Library (JSTL), a collection of custom tag libraries for solving common problems such as iterating over a map or collection, conditional testing, XML processing, and even database access and data manipulation.

Most of the time you will use JSTL to access scoped objects and perform other tasks in your JSP pages. However, for more specific tasks, you may need to write your own custom tags. Chapter 6, "Writing Custom Tags" teaches you how to do that.

Chapter 7, "Tag Files" discusses tag files, a new feature in JSP 2.0 that makes writing custom actions simpler. This chapter covers several aspects of writing custom tags using tag files only.

Chapter 8, "Listeners" talks about event-driven programming in Servlet. It discusses the event classes and listener interfaces that come with the Servlet API and shows how to write listeners and use them in servlet/JSP applications.

Chapter 9, "Filters" covers filters, which are web objects that intercept requests. This chapter discusses the Filter API that includes the **Filter**, **FilterConfig**, and **FilterChain** interfaces as well as shows how to write filters by implementing the **Filter** interface.

Chapter 10, "Application Design" explains the Model 2 Architecture, the recommended architecture for all but the simplest Java web applications. Several examples are given to illustrate different components in Model 2 applications.

Chapter 11, "File Upload" shows how to make use of the Servlet 3 file upload feature and what can be done on the client side to improve user experience.

Chapter 12, "File Download" explains how to send a resource to the browser programmatically.

The Servlet API comes with classes for wrapping servlet requests and responses. In Chapter 13, "Decorating Requests and Responses" you learn how to use the Decorator pattern and these classes to change the behavior of servlet requests and responses.

Chapter 14, "Asynchronous Processing" discusses a new feature in Servlet 3.0 for processing asynchronous operations. This feature is especially useful when your servlet/JSP application is a very busy one with one or more long-running operations. This feature works by assigning those operations to a new thread and thereby releasing the request processing thread back to the pool, ready to serve another request.

Chapter 15, "Security" explains how to secure a Java web application both declaratively and programmatically. Four main security topics discussed are authentication, authorization, confidentiality, and data integrity.

Chapter 16, "Deployment" talks about the deployment process of a servlet/JSP application and discusses the elements in the deployment descriptor.

Chapter 17, "Dynamic Registration and Servlet Container Initializers" is about two new features in Servlet 3. Dynamic registration is useful for dynamically registering web objects without application restart. And, framework developers will surely love the servlet container initializer.

Chapter 18, "Introduction to Struts 2" introduces Struts 2 as an MVC framework. It explains the basic components and configuration of Struts 2 and presents a simple application.

Appendix A, "Tomcat" explains how to install and configure Tomcat and run it in multiple operating systems.

Appendix B, "Servlet and JSP Annotations" lists all annotations that can be used to configure a web object, such as a servlet, a listener, or a filter. These annotations are a new feature in Servlet 3 that makes the deployment descriptor optional.

Appendix C, "SSL Certificates" explains how you can generate a private/public key pair using the KeyTool program and have a trusted authority sign the public key as a digital certificate.

Downloading the Sample Applications

You can download the zipped sample applications used in this book from this web page.

```
http://books.brainysoftware.com/download
```

Choosing a Framework

After you finish this book and master Servlet and JSP, it is a good idea to pick and learn at least one web framework. There are many excellent frameworks freely available. Struts 2, JavaServer Faces, Spring MVC, and Google Web Toolkit are all recommended. A framework solves common problems in servlet/JSP development and shorten development time.

You may want to check your favorite job sites to find out which frameworks are currently in high demand.

Chapter 1
Servlets

Servlet is the main technology for developing servlets. Understanding the Servlet API is your gateway to becoming a formidable Java web developer. It is imperative that you be familiar with each of the over seventy types defined in the Servlet API. Seventy may sound a lot but it's not hard if you learn one at a time.

This chapter introduces the Servlet API and teaches you how to write your first servlet.

Servlet API Overview

The Servlet API comes in four Java packages. The packages are as follows.

- **javax.servlet**. Contains classes and interfaces that define the contract between a servlet and a servlet container.
- **javax.servlet.http**. Contains classes and interfaces that define the contract between an HTTP servlet and a servlet container.
- **javax.servlet.annotation**. Contains annotations to annotate servlets, filters, and listeners. It also specifies metadata for annotated components.
- **javax.servlet.descriptor**. Contains types that provide programmatic access to a web application's configuration information.

This chapter focuses on members of **javax.servlet** and **javax.servlet.http**.

The javax.servlet Package

Figure 1.1 shows the main types in **javax.servlet**.

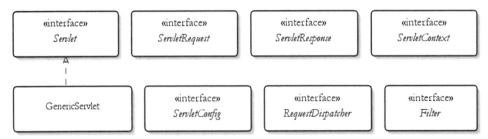

Figure 1.1: Prominent members of javax.servlet

At the center of Servlet technology is **Servlet**, an interface that all servlet classes must implement either directly or indirectly. You implement it directly when you write a servlet class that implements **Servlet**. You implement it indirectly when you extend a class that implements this interface.

The **Servlet** interface defines a contract between a servlet and the servlet container. The contract boils down to the promise by the servlet container to load the servlet class into memory and call specific methods on the servlet instance. There can only be one instance for each servlet type in an application.

A user request causes the servlet container to call a servlet's **service** method, passing an instance of **ServletRequest** and an instance of **ServletResponse**. The **ServletRequest** encapsulates the current HTTP request so that servlet developers do not have to parse and manipulate raw HTTP data. The **ServletResponse** represents the HTTP response for the current user and makes it easy to send response back to the user.

For each application the servlet container also creates an instance of **ServletContext**. This object encapsulates the environment details of the context (application). There is only one **ServletContext** for each context. For each servlet instance, there is also a **ServletConfig** that encapsulates the servlet configuration.

Let's first look at the **Servlet** interface. Other interfaces mentioned above will be explained in the other sections of this chapter.

Servlet

The **Servlet** interface defines these five methods.

```
void init(ServletConfig config) throws ServletException

void service(ServletRequest request, ServletResponse response)
        throws ServletException, java.io.IOException

void destroy()

java.lang.String getServletInfo()

ServletConfig getServletConfig()
```

Note that the convention for writing a Java method signature is to use the fully-qualified name for types that are not in the same package as the type containing the method. As such, in the signature of the **service** method **javax.servlet.ServletException**, which is in the same package as **Servlet**, is written without the package information whereas **java.io.Exception** is written fully.

init, **service**, and **destroy** are lifecycle methods. The servlet container invokes these three methods according to these rules.

- **init**. The servlet container invokes this method the first time the servlet is requested. This method is not called at subsequent requests. You use this method to write initialization code. When invoking this method, the servlet container passes a **ServletConfig**. Normally, you will assign the **ServletConfig** to a class level variable so that this object can be used from other points in the servlet class.
- **service**. The servlet container invokes this method each time the servlet is requested. You write the code that the servlet is supposed to do here. The first time the servlet is requested, the servlet container calls the **init** method and the **service** method. For subsequent requests, only **service** is invoked.
- **destroy**. The servlet container invokes this method when the servlet is about to be destroyed. This occurs when the application is unloaded or when the servlet container is being shut down. Normally, you write clean-up code in this method.

The other two methods in **Servlet** are non-life cycle methods: **getServletInfo** and **getServletConfig**.

- **getServletInfo**. This method returns the description of the servlet. You can return any string that might be useful or even **null**.
- **getServletConfig**. This method returns the **ServletConfig** passed by the servlet container to the **init** method. However, in order for **getServletConfig** to return a non-null value, you must have assigned the **ServletConfig** passed to the **init** method to a class level variable. **ServletConfig** is explained in the section "ServletConfig" in this chapter.

An important point to note is thread safety. A servlet instance is shared by all users in an application, so class-level variables are not recommended, unless they are read-only or members of the **java.util.concurrent.atomic** package.

The next section, "Writing A Basic Servlet Application," shows how you can write a **Servlet** Implementation.

Writing A Basic Servlet Application

Writing a servlet application is surprisingly easy. All you have to do is create a directory structure and place your servlet classes in a certain directory. In this section you'll learn how to write a simple servlet application named **app01a**. Initially it will contain one servlet, **MyServlet**, which sends a greeting to the user.

You need a servlet container to run your servlets. Tomcat, an open source servlet container, is available free of charge and runs on any platform where Java is available. You should now read Appendix A and install Tomcat if you have not done so.

Writing and Compiling the Servlet Class

After making sure you have a servlet container on your local machine, the next step is to write and compile a servlet class. The servlet class for this example, **MyServlet**, is given in Listing 1.1. By convention, the name of a servlet class is suffixed with **Servlet**.

Listing 1.1: The MyServlet class

```
package app01a;
import java.io.IOException;
import java.io.PrintWriter;
import javax.servlet.Servlet;
import javax.servlet.ServletConfig;
import javax.servlet.ServletException;
import javax.servlet.ServletRequest;
import javax.servlet.ServletResponse;
import javax.servlet.annotation.WebServlet;

@WebServlet(name = "MyServlet", urlPatterns = { "/my" })
public class MyServlet implements Servlet {

    private transient ServletConfig servletConfig;

    @Override
    public void init(ServletConfig servletConfig)
            throws ServletException {
        this.servletConfig = servletConfig;
    }

    @Override
    public ServletConfig getServletConfig() {
        return servletConfig;
    }

    @Override
    public String getServletInfo() {
        return "My Servlet";
    }

    @Override
    public void service(ServletRequest request,
            ServletResponse response) throws ServletException,
            IOException {
        String servletName = servletConfig.getServletName();
        response.setContentType("text/html");
        PrintWriter writer = response.getWriter();
        writer.print("<html><head></head>"
                + "<body>Hello from " + servletName
```

```
        + "</body></html>");
    }

    @Override
    public void destroy() {
    }
}
```

The first thing that you may notice when reading the code in Listing 1.1 is this annotation.

```
@WebServlet(name = "MyServlet", urlPatterns = { "/my" })
```

The **WebServlet** annotation type is used to declare a servlet. You can name the servlet as well as tell the container what URL invokes the servlet. The **name** attribute is optional and, if present, ordinarily given the name of the servlet class. What's important is the **urlPatterns** attribute, which is also optional but almost always present. In **MyServlet**, **urlPattern** tells the container that the **/my** pattern should invoke the servlet.

Note that a URL pattern must begin with a forward slash.

The servlet's **init** method is called once and sets the private transient **servletConfig** variable to the **ServletConfig** object passed to the method.

```
    private transient ServletConfig servletConfig;

    @Override
    public void init(ServletConfig servletConfig)
            throws ServletException {
        this.servletConfig = servletConfig;
    }
```

You only have to assign the passed **ServletConfig** to a class variable if you intend to use the **ServletConfig** from inside your servlet.

The **service** method sends the String "Hello from MyServlet" to the browser. **service** is invoked for every incoming HTTP request that targets the servlet.

To compile the servlet, you have to include the types in the Servlet API in your class path. Tomcat comes with the **servlet-api.jar** file that packages members of the **javax.servlet** and **javax.servlet.http** packages. The jar file is located in the **lib** directory under Tomcat's installation directory.

Application Directory Structure

A servlet application must be deployed in a certain directory structure.
Figure 1.2 shows the directory structure for this application.

Figure 1.2: The application directory

The **app01a** directory at the top of the structure is the application directory.
Under the application directory is a **WEB-INF** directory. It in turn has two
subdirectories:

- **classes**. Your servlet classes and other Java classes must reside here.
  The directories under classes reflect the class package. In Figure 1.2
  there is one class deployed, **app01a.MyServlet**.
- **lib**. Deploy jar files required by your servlet application here. The
  Servlet API jar file does not need to be deployed here because the
  servlet container already has a copy of it. In this application, the **lib**
  directory is empty. An empty **lib** directory may be deleted.

A servlet/JSP application normally has JSP pages, HTML files, image files,
and other resources. These should go under the application directory and are
often organized in subdirectories. For instance, all image files can go to an
image directory, all JSP pages to **jsp**, and so on.

Any resource you put under the application directory is directly
accessible to the user by typing the URL to the resource. If you want to
include a resource that can be accessed by a servlet but not accessible to the
user, put it under **WEB-INF**.

Now, deploy the application to Tomcat. With Tomcat, one way to
deploy an application is by copying the application directory to the
webapps directory under Tomcat installation. You can also deploy an
application by editing the **server.xml** file in Tomcat's **conf** directory or

deploying an XML file separately in order to avoid editing **server.xml**. Other servlet containers may have different deployment rules. Please refer to Appendix A for details on how to deploy a servlet/JSP application to Tomcat.

The recommended method for deploying a servlet/JSP application is to deploy it as a war file. A war file is a jar file with **war** extension. You can create a war file using the **jar** program that comes with the JDK or tools like WinZip. You can then copy the war file to Tomcat's **webapps** directory. When you start or restart Tomcat, Tomcat will extract the war file automatically. Deployment as a war file will work in all servlet containers. You'll learn more on deployment in Chapter 16, "Deployment."

Invoking the Servlet

To test your first servlet, start or restart Tomcat and direct your browser to the following URL (assuming Tomcat is configured to listen on port 8080, its default port):

```
http://localhost:8080/app01a/my
```

The output should be similar to Figure 1.3.

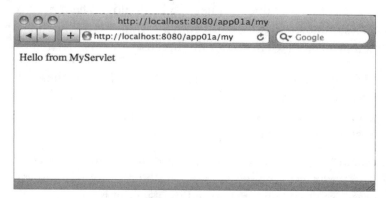

Figure 1.3: Response from MyServlet

Congratulations. You just wrote your first servlet application.

ServletRequest

For every HTTP request, the servlet container creates an instance of **ServletRequest** and passes it to the servlet's **service** method. The **ServletRequest** encapsulates information about the request.

These are some of the methods in the **ServletRequest** interface.

```
public int getContentLength()
```
Returns the number of bytes in the request body. If the length is not known, this method returns -1.

```
public java.lang.String getContentType()
```
Returns the MIME type of the request body or null if the type is not known.

```
public java.lang.String getParameter(java.lang.String name)
```
Returns the value of the specified request parameter.

```
public java.lang.String getProtocol()
```
Returns the name and version of the protocol of this HTTP request.

getParameter is the most frequently used method in **ServletRequest**. A common use of this method is to return the value of an HTML form field. You'll learn how you can retrieve form values in the section "Working with Forms" later in this chapter.

getParameter can also be used to get the value of a query string. For example, if a servlet is invoked using this URI

```
http://domain/context/servletName?id=123
```

you can retrieve the value of **id** from inside your servlet using this statement:

```
String id = request.getParameter("id");
```

Note that **getParameter** returns null if the parameter does not exist.

In addition to **getParameter**, you can also use **getParameterNames**, **getParameterMap**, and **getParameterValues** to retrieve form field names and values as well as query strings. See the section "HttpServlet" for examples of how to use these methods.

ServletResponse

The **javax.servlet.ServletResponse** interface represents a servlet response. Prior to invoking a servlet's **service** method, the servlet container creates a **ServletResponse** and pass it as the second argument to the **service** method. The **ServletResponse** hides the complexity of sending response to the browser.

One of the methods defined in **ServletResponse** is the **getWriter** method, which returns a **java.io.PrintWriter** that can send text to the client. By default, the **PrintWriter** object uses ISO-8859-1 encoding.

When sending response to the client, most of the time you send it as HTML. You are therefore assumed to be familiar with HTML.

Note
There is also another method that you can use to send output to the browser: **getOutputStream**. However, this method is for sending binary data, so in most cases you will use **getWriter** and not **getOutputStream**. See Chapter 12, "File Download" for instructions on how to send binary content.

Before sending any HTML tag, you should set the content type of the response by calling the **setContentType** method, passing "text/html" as an argument. This is how you tell the browser that the content type is HTML. Most browsers by default render a response as HTML in the absence of a content type. However, some browsers will display HTML tags as plain text if you don't set the response content type.

You have used **ServletResponse** in **MyServlet** in Listing 1.1. You'll see it used in other applications in this chapter and next chapters.

ServletConfig

The servlet container passes a **ServletConfig** to the servlet's **init** method when the servlet container initializes the servlet. The **ServletConfig** encapsulates configuration information that you can pass to a servlet through **@WebServlet** or the deployment descriptor. Every piece of information so passed is called an initial parameter. An initial parameter has two components: key and value.

To retrieve the value of an initial parameter from inside a servlet, call the **getInitParameter** method on the **ServletConfig** passed by the servlet container to the servlet's **init** method. The signature of **getInitParameter** is as follows.

```
java.lang.String getInitParameter(java.lang.String name)
```

In addition, the **getInitParameterNames** method returns an **Enumeration** of all initial parameter names:

```
java.util.Enumeration<java.lang.String> getInitParameterNames()
```

For example, to retrieve the value of a **contactName** parameter, use this.

```
String contactName = servletConfig.getInitParameter("contactName");
```

On top of **getInitParameter** and **getInitParameterNames**, **ServletConfig** offers another useful method, **getServletContext**. Use this method to retrieve the **ServletContext** from inside a servlet. See the section "ServletContext" later in this chapter for discussion on this object.

As an example of **ServletConfig**, let's add a servlet named **ServletConfigDemoServlet** to **app01a**. The new servlet is given in Listing 1.2.

Listing 1.2: The ServletConfigDemoServlet class

```
package app01a;
import java.io.IOException;
import java.io.PrintWriter;
import javax.servlet.Servlet;
import javax.servlet.ServletConfig;
import javax.servlet.ServletException;
import javax.servlet.ServletRequest;
import javax.servlet.ServletResponse;
import javax.servlet.annotation.WebInitParam;
import javax.servlet.annotation.WebServlet;

@WebServlet(name = "ServletConfigDemoServlet",
    urlPatterns = { "/servletConfigDemo" },
    initParams = {
        @WebInitParam(name="admin", value="Harry Taciak"),
```

```
            @WebInitParam(name="email", value="admin@example.com")
    }
)
public class ServletConfigDemoServlet implements Servlet {
    private transient ServletConfig servletConfig;

    @Override
    public ServletConfig getServletConfig() {
        return servletConfig;
    }

    @Override
    public void init(ServletConfig servletConfig)
            throws ServletException {
        this.servletConfig = servletConfig;
    }

    @Override
    public void service(ServletRequest request,
            ServletResponse response)
            throws ServletException, IOException {
        ServletConfig servletConfig = getServletConfig();
        String admin = servletConfig.getInitParameter("admin");
        String email = servletConfig.getInitParameter("email");
        response.setContentType("text/html");
        PrintWriter writer = response.getWriter();
        writer.print("<html><head></head><body>" +
                "Admin:" + admin +
                "<br/>Email:" + email +
                "</body></html>");
    }

    @Override
    public String getServletInfo() {
        return "ServletConfig demo";
    }

    @Override
    public void destroy() {
    }
}
```

As you can see in Listing 1.2, you pass two initial parameters (**admin** and **email**) to the servlet in the **initParams** attribute in **@WebServlet**:

```
@WebServlet(name = "ServletConfigDemoServlet",
```

```
    urlPatterns = { "/servletConfigDemo" },
    initParams = {
        @WebInitParam(name="admin", value="Harry Taciak"),
        @WebInitParam(name="email", value="admin@example.com")
    }
)
```

You can invoke **ServletConfigDemoServlet** using this URL:

`http://localhost:8080/app01a/servletConfigDemo`

The result should be similar to that in Figure 1.4.

Figure 1.4: ServletConfigDemoServlet in action

Alternatively, you can pass initial parameters in the deployment descriptor. Utilizing the deployment descriptor for this purpose is easier than using **@WebServlet** since the deployment descriptor is a text file and you can edit it without recompiling the servlet class.

The deployment descriptor is discussed in the section "Using the Deployment Descriptor" later in this chapter and in Chapter 16, "Deployment."

ServletContext

The **ServletContext** represents the servlet application. There is only one context per web application. In a distributed environment where an application is deployed simultaneously to multiple containers, there is one **ServletContext** object per Java Virtual Machine.

You can obtain the **ServletContext** by calling the **getServletContext** method on the **ServletConfig**.

The **ServletContext** is there so that you can share information that can be accessed from all resources in the application and to enable dynamic registration of web objects. The former is done by storing objects in an internal **Map** within the **ServletContext**. Objects stored in **ServletContext** are called attributes.

The following methods in **ServletContext** deal with attributes:

```
java.lang.Object getAttribute(java.lang.String name)

java.util.Enumeration<java.lang.String> getAttributeNames()

void setAttribute(java.lang.String name, java.lang.Object object)

void removeAttribute(java.lang.String name)
```

Examples on these methods are given in Chapter 8, "Listeners." Using **ServletContext** to register web objects dynamically is discussed in Chapter 17, "Dynamic Registration and Servlet Container Initializers."

GenericServlet

The preceding examples showed how to write servlets by implementing the **Servlet** interface. However, did you notice that you had to provide implementations for all the methods in **Servlet**, even though some of them did not contain code? In addition, you needed to preserve the **ServletConfig** object into a class level variable.

Fortunately, the **GenericServlet** abstract class comes to the rescue. In keeping with the spirit of easier code writing in object-oriented programming, **GenericServlet** implements both **Servlet** and **ServletConfig** and perform the following tasks:

- Assign the **ServletConfig** in the **init** method to a class level variable so that it can be retrieved by calling **getServletConfig**.

- Provide default implementations of all methods in the **Servlet** interface.
- Provide methods that wrap the methods in the **ServletConfig**.

GenericServlet preserves the **ServletConfig** object by assigning it to a class level variable **servletConfig** in the **init** method. Here is the implementation of **init** in **GenericServlet**.

```
public void init(ServletConfig servletConfig)
        throws ServletException {
    this.servletConfig = servletConfig;
    this.init();
}
```

However, if you override this method in your class, the **init** method in your servlet will be called instead and you have to call **super.init(servletConfig)** to preserve the **ServletConfig**. To save you from having to do so, **GenericServlet** provides a second **init** method, which does not take arguments. This method is called by the first **init** method after **ServletConfig** is assigned to **servletConfig**:

```
public void init(ServletConfig servletConfig)
        throws ServletException {
    this.servletConfig = servletConfig;
    this.init();
}
```

This means, you can write initialization code by overriding the no-argument **init** method and the **ServletConfig** will still be preserved by the **GenericServlet** instance.

The **GenericServletDemoServlet** class in Listing 1.3 is a rewrite of **ServletConfigDemoServlet** in Listing 1.2. Note that the new servlet extends **GenericServlet** instead of implementing **Servlet**.

Listing 1.3: The GenericServletDemoServlet class

```
package app01a;
import java.io.IOException;
import java.io.PrintWriter;
import javax.servlet.GenericServlet;
import javax.servlet.ServletConfig;
import javax.servlet.ServletException;
```

```
import javax.servlet.ServletRequest;
import javax.servlet.ServletResponse;
import javax.servlet.annotation.WebInitParam;
import javax.servlet.annotation.WebServlet;

@WebServlet(name = "GenericServletDemoServlet",
    urlPatterns = { "/generic" },
    initParams = {
        @WebInitParam(name="admin", value="Harry Taciak"),
        @WebInitParam(name="email", value="admin@example.com")
    }
)
public class GenericServletDemoServlet extends GenericServlet {

    private static final long serialVersionUID = 62500890L;

    @Override
    public void service(ServletRequest request,
            ServletResponse response)
            throws ServletException, IOException {
        ServletConfig servletConfig = getServletConfig();
        String admin = servletConfig.getInitParameter("admin");
        String email = servletConfig.getInitParameter("email");
        response.setContentType("text/html");
        PrintWriter writer = response.getWriter();
        writer.print("<html><head></head><body>" +
                "Admin:" + admin +
                "<br/>Email:" + email +
                "</body></html>");
    }
}
```

As you can see, by extending **GenericServlet** you do not need to override methods that you don't plan to change. As a result, you have cleaner code. In Listing 1.3, the only method overridden is the **service** method. Also, there is no need to preserve the **ServletConfig** yourself.

Invoke the servlet using this URL and the result should be similar to that of **ServletConfigDemoServlet**.

```
http://localhost:8080/app01a/generic
```

Even though **GenericServlet** is a nice enhancement to Servlet, it is not something you use frequently, however, as it is not as advanced as

HttpServlet. **HttpServlet** is the real deal and used in real-world applications. It is explained in the next section, "HTTP Servlets."

HTTP Servlets

Most, if not all, servlet applications you write will work with HTTP. This means, you can make use of the features offered by HTTP. The **javax.servlet.http** package is the second package in the Servlet API that contains classes and interfaces for writing servlet applications. Many of the types in **javax.servlet.http** override those in **javax.servlet**.

Figure 1.5 shows the main types in **javax.servlet.http**.

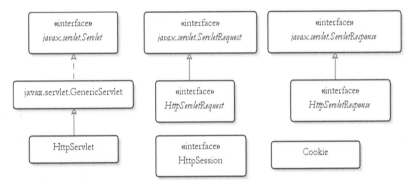

Figure 1.5: The more important members of javax.servlet.http

HttpServlet

The **HttpServlet** class overrides the **javax.servlet.GenericServlet** class. When using **HttpServlet**, you will also work with the **HttpServletRequest** and **HttpServletResponse** objects that represent the servlet request and the servlet response, respectively. The **HttpServletRequest** interface extends **javax.servlet.ServletRequest** and **HttpServletResponse** extends **javax.servlet.ServletResponse**.

HttpServlet overrides the **service** method in **GenericServlet** and adds another **service** method with the following signature:

```
protected void service(HttpServletRequest request,
    HttpServletResponse response)
    throws ServletException, java.io.IOException
```

The difference between the new **service** method and the one in **javax.servlet.Servlet** is that the former accepts an **HttpServletRequest** and an **HttpServletResponse**, instead of a **ServletRequest** and a **ServletResponse**.

The servlet container, as usual, calls the original **service** method in **javax.servlet.Servlet**, which in **HttpServlet** is written as follows:

```
public void service(ServletRequest req, ServletResponse res)
    throws ServletException, IOException {
    HttpServletRequest request;
    HttpServletResponse response;
    try {
        request = (HttpServletRequest) req;
        response = (HttpServletResponse) res;
    } catch (ClassCastException e) {
        throw new ServletException("non-HTTP request or response");
    }
    service(request, response);
}
```

The original **service** method downcasts the request and response objects from the servlet container to **HttpServletRequest** and **HttpServletResponse**, respectively, and call the new **service** method. The downcasting is always successful because the servlet container always passes an **HttpServletRequest** and an **HttpServletResponse** when calling a servlet's **service** method, to anticipate the use of HTTP. Even if you are implementing **javax.servlet.Servlet** or extending **javax.servlet.GenericServlet**, you can downcast the servlet request and servlet response passed to the **service** method to **HttpServletRequest** and **HttpServletResponse**, respectively.

The new **service** method in **HttpServlet** then examines the HTTP method used to send the request (by calling **request.getMethod**) and call one of the following methods: **doGet**, **doPost**, **doHead**, **doPut**, **doTrace**, **doOptions**, and **doDelete**. Each of the seven methods represents an HTTP method. **doGet** and **doPost** are the most often used. As such, you rarely need to override the **service** methods anymore. Instead, you override **doGet** or **doPost** or both **doGet** and **doPost**.

To summarize, there are two features in **HttpServlet** that you do not find in **GenericServlet**:

- Instead of the **service** method, you will override **doGet**, **doPost**, or both of them. In rare cases, you will also override any of these methods: **doHead**, **doPut**, **doTrace**, **doOptions**, **doDelete**.
- You will work with **HttpServletRequest** and **HttpServletResponse**, instead of **ServletRequest** and **ServletResponse**.

HttpServletRequest**HttpServletRequest** represents the servlet request in the HTTP environment. It extends the **javax.servlet.ServletRequest** interface and adds several methods. Some of the methods added are as follows.

`java.lang.String getContextPath()`
Returns the portion of the request URI that indicates the context of the request.

`Cookie[] getCookies()`
Returns an array of **Cookie** objects.

`java.lang.String getHeader(java.lang.String name)`
Returns the value of the specified HTTP header.

`java.lang.String getMethod()`
Returns the name of the HTTP method with which this request was made.

`java.lang.String getQueryString()`
Returns the query string in the request URL.

`HttpSession getSession()`
Returns the session object associated with this request. If none is found, creates a new session object.

`HttpSession getSession(boolean create)`
Returns the current session object associated with this request. If none is found and the create argument is **true**, create a new session object.

You will learn to use these methods in the chapters to come.

HttpServletResponse

HttpServletResponse represents the servlet response in the HTTP environment. Here are some of the methods defined in it.

`void addCookie(Cookie cookie)`
> Adds a cookie to this response object.

`void addHeader(java.lang.String name, java.lang.String value)`
> Adds a header to this response object.

`void sendRedirect(java.lang.String location)`
> Sends a response code that redirects the browser to the specified location.

You will learn these methods further in the next chapters.

Working with HTML Forms

A web application almost always contains one or more HTML forms to take user input. You can easily send an HTML form from a servlet to the browser. When the user submits the form, values entered in the form elements are sent to the server as request parameters.

The value of an HTML input field (a text field, a hidden field, or a password field) or text area is sent to the server as a string. An empty input field or text area sends an empty string. As such, **ServletRequest.getParameter** that takes an input field name never returns null.

An HTML select element also sends a string to the header. If none of the options in the select element is selected, the value of the option that is displayed is sent.

A multiple-value select element (a select element that allows multiple selection and is indicated by **<select multiple>**) sends a string array and has to be handled by **ServletRequest.getParameterValues**.

A checkbox is a bit extraordinary. A checked checkbox sends the string "on" to the server. An unchecked checkbox sends nothing to the server and **ServletRequest.getParameter(*fieldName*)** returns null.

Radio buttons send the value of the selected button to the server. If none of the buttons is selected, nothing is sent to the server and **ServletRequest.getParameter(***fieldName***)** returns null.

If a form contains multiple input elements with the same name, all values will be submitted and you have to use **ServletRequest.getParameterValues** to retrieve them. **ServletRequest.getParameter** will only return the last value.

The **FormServlet** class in Listing 1.4 demonstrates how to work with an HTML form. Its **doGet** method sends an order form to the browser. Its **doPost** method retrieves the values entered and prints them. This servlet is part of the **app01b** application.

Listing 1.4: The FormServlet class

```
package app01b;
import java.io.IOException;
import java.io.PrintWriter;
import java.util.Enumeration;
import javax.servlet.ServletException;
import javax.servlet.annotation.WebServlet;
import javax.servlet.http.HttpServlet;
import javax.servlet.http.HttpServletRequest;
import javax.servlet.http.HttpServletResponse;

@WebServlet(name = "FormServlet", urlPatterns = { "/form" })
public class FormServlet extends HttpServlet {
    private static final long serialVersionUID = 54L;
    private static final String TITLE = "Order Form";

    @Override
    public void doGet(HttpServletRequest request,
            HttpServletResponse response)
            throws ServletException, IOException {
        response.setContentType("text/html");
        PrintWriter writer = response.getWriter();
        writer.println("<html>");
        writer.println("<head>");
        writer.println("<title>" + TITLE + "</title></head>");
        writer.println("<body><h1>" + TITLE + "</h1>");
        writer.println("<form method='post'>");
        writer.println("<table>");
        writer.println("<tr>");
```

```
writer.println("<td>Name:</td>");
writer.println("<td><input name='name'/></td>");
writer.println("</tr>");
writer.println("<tr>");
writer.println("<td>Address:</td>");
writer.println("<td><textarea name='address' "
        + "cols='40' rows='5'></textarea></td>");
writer.println("</tr>");
writer.println("<tr>");
writer.println("<td>Country:</td>");
writer.println("<td><select name='country'>");
writer.println("<option>United States</option>");
writer.println("<option>Canada</option>");
writer.println("</select></td>");
writer.println("</tr>");
writer.println("<tr>");
writer.println("<td>Delivery Method:</td>");
writer.println("<td><input type='radio' " +
        "name='deliveryMethod'"
        + " value='First Class'/>First Class");
writer.println("<input type='radio' " +
        "name='deliveryMethod' "
        + "value='Second Class'/>Second Class</td>");
writer.println("</tr>");
writer.println("<tr>");
writer.println("<td>Shipping Instructions:</td>");
writer.println("<td><textarea name='instruction' "
        + "cols='40' rows='5'></textarea></td>");
writer.println("</tr>");
writer.println("<tr>");
writer.println("<td> </td>");
writer.println("<td><textarea name='instruction' "
        + "cols='40' rows='5'></textarea></td>");
writer.println("</tr>");
writer.println("<tr>");
writer.println("<td>Please send me the latest " +
        "product catalog:</td>");
writer.println("<td><input type='checkbox' " +
        "name='catalogRequest'/></td>");
writer.println("</tr>");
writer.println("<tr>");
writer.println("<td> </td>");
writer.println("<td><input type='reset'/>" +
        "<input type='submit'/></td>");
writer.println("</tr>");
writer.println("</table>");
```

```java
        writer.println("</form>");
        writer.println("</body>");
        writer.println("</html>");
    }

    @Override
    public void doPost(HttpServletRequest request,
            HttpServletResponse response)
            throws ServletException, IOException {
        response.setContentType("text/html");
        PrintWriter writer = response.getWriter();
        writer.println("<html>");
        writer.println("<head>");
        writer.println("<title>" + TITLE + "</title></head>");
        writer.println("</head>");
        writer.println("<body><h1>" + TITLE + "</h1>");
        writer.println("<table>");
        writer.println("<tr>");
        writer.println("<td>Name:</td>");
        writer.println("<td>" + request.getParameter("name")
                + "</td>");
        writer.println("</tr>");
        writer.println("<tr>");
        writer.println("<td>Address:</td>");
        writer.println("<td>" + request.getParameter("address")
                + "</td>");
        writer.println("</tr>");
        writer.println("<tr>");
        writer.println("<td>Country:</td>");
        writer.println("<td>" + request.getParameter("country")
                + "</td>");
        writer.println("</tr>");
        writer.println("<tr>");
        writer.println("<td>Shipping Instructions:</td>");
        writer.println("<td>");
        String[] instructions = request
                .getParameterValues("instruction");
        if (instructions != null) {
            for (String instruction : instructions) {
                writer.println(instruction + "<br/>");
            }
        }
        writer.println("</td>");
        writer.println("</tr>");
        writer.println("<tr>");
```

```
            writer.println("<td>Delivery Method:</td>");
            writer.println("<td>"
                    + request.getParameter("deliveryMethod")
                    + "</td>");
            writer.println("</tr>");
            writer.println("<tr>");
            writer.println("<td>Catalog Request:</td>");
            writer.println("<td>");
            if (request.getParameter("catalogRequest") == null) {
                writer.println("No");
            } else {
                writer.println("Yes");
            }
            writer.println("</td>");
            writer.println("</tr>");
            writer.println("</table>");
            writer.println("<div style='border:1px solid #ddd;" +
                        "margin-top:40px;font-size:90%'>");

            writer.println("Debug Info<br/>");
            Enumeration<String> parameterNames = request
                    .getParameterNames();
            while (parameterNames.hasMoreElements()) {
                String paramName = parameterNames.nextElement();
                writer.println(paramName + ": ");
                String[] paramValues = request
                        .getParameterValues(paramName);
                for (String paramValue : paramValues) {
                    writer.println(paramValue + "<br/>");
                }
            }
            writer.println("</div>");
            writer.println("</body>");
            writer.println("</html>");
        }
    }
```

You can invoke the **FormServlet** by using this URL:

```
http://localhost:8080/app01b/form
```

The invoked **doGet** method sends this HTML form to the browser.

```
<form method='post'>
<input name='name'/>
<textarea name='address' cols='40' rows='5'></textarea>
```

```
<select name='country'>");
    <option>United States</option>
    <option>Canada</option>
</select>
<input type='radio' name='deliveryMethod' value='First Class'/>
<input type='radio' name='deliveryMethod' value='Second Class'/>
<textarea name='instruction' cols='40' rows='5'></textarea>
<textarea name='instruction' cols='40' rows='5'></textarea>
<input type='checkbox' name='catalogRequest'/>
<input type='reset'/>
<input type='submit'/>
</form>
```

The form's method is set to **post** to make sure the HTTP POST method is used when the user submits the form. Its **action** attribute is missing, indicating that the form will be submitted to the same URL used to request it.

Figure 1.6 shows an empty order form.

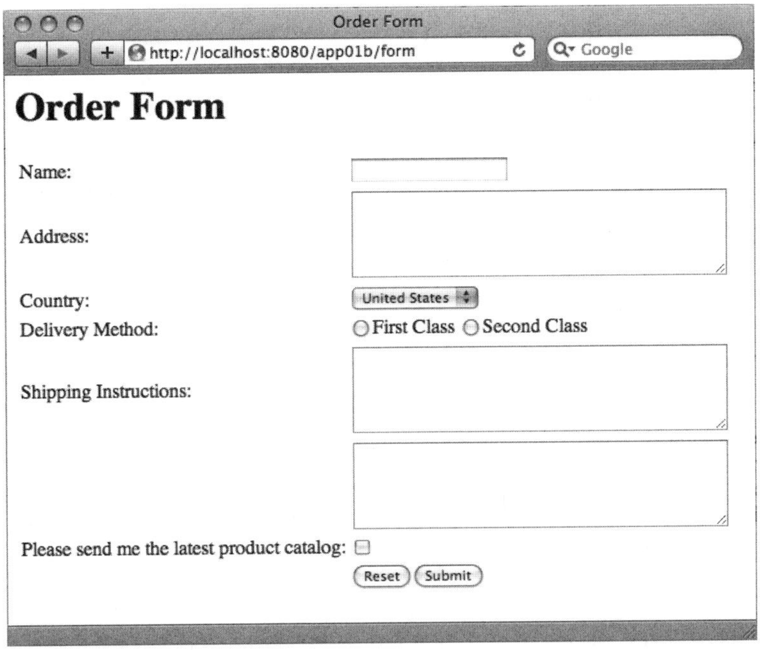

Figure 1.6: An empty Order form

Now, fill in the form and click the Submit button. The values you entered in the form will be sent to the server using the HTTP POST method and this will invoke the servlet's **doPost** method. As a result, you'll see the values printed as shown in Figure 1.7.

Figure 1.7: The values entered into the Order form

Using the Deployment Descriptor

As you can see in the previous examples, writing and deploying a servlet application is easy. One aspect of deployment is configuring the mapping of your servlet with a path. In the examples, you mapped a servlet with a path by using the **WebServlet** annotation type.

Using the deployment descriptor is another way of configuring a servlet application and the deployment descriptor is discussed in detail in Chapter 16, "Deployment." The deployment descriptor is always named **web.xml** and located under the **WEB-INF** directory. In this chapter I show you how to create a servlet application named **app01c** and write a **web.xml** file for it.

The **app01c** has two servlets, **SimpleServlet** and **WelcomeServlet**, and a deployment descriptor to map the servlets. Listings 1.5 and 1.6 show **SimpleServlet** and **WelcomeServlet**, respectively. Note that the servlet classes are not annotated **@WebServlet**. The deployment descriptor is given in Listing 1.7.

Listing 1.5: The unannotated SimpleServlet class

```
package app01c;
import java.io.IOException;
import java.io.PrintWriter;
import javax.servlet.ServletException;
import javax.servlet.http.HttpServlet;
import javax.servlet.http.HttpServletRequest;
import javax.servlet.http.HttpServletResponse;

public class SimpleServlet extends HttpServlet {
    private static final long serialVersionUID = 8946L;

    @Override
    public void doGet(HttpServletRequest request,
            HttpServletResponse response)
            throws ServletException, IOException {
        response.setContentType("text/html");
        PrintWriter writer = response.getWriter();
        writer.print("<html><head></head>" +
                "<body>Simple Servlet</body></html>");
    }
}
```

Listing 1.6: The unannotated WelcomeServlet class

```
package app01c;
import java.io.IOException;
import java.io.PrintWriter;
import javax.servlet.ServletException;
import javax.servlet.http.HttpServlet;
import javax.servlet.http.HttpServletRequest;
import javax.servlet.http.HttpServletResponse;

public class WelcomeServlet extends HttpServlet {
    private static final long serialVersionUID = 27126L;

    @Override
    public void doGet(HttpServletRequest request,
```

```
            HttpServletResponse response)
            throws ServletException, IOException {
        response.setContentType("text/html");
        PrintWriter writer = response.getWriter();
        writer.print("<html><head></head>"
                + "<body>Welcome</body></html>");
    }
}
```

Listing 1.7: The deployment descriptor

```
<?xml version="1.0" encoding="ISO-8859-1"?>
<web-app xmlns="http://java.sun.com/xml/ns/javaee"
    xmlns:xsi="http://www.w3.org/2001/XMLSchema-instance"
    xsi:schemaLocation="http://java.sun.com/xml/ns/javaee
    http://java.sun.com/xml/ns/javaee/web-app_3_0.xsd"
    version="3.0">

    <servlet>
        <servlet-name>SimpleServlet</servlet-name>
        <servlet-class>app01c.SimpleServlet</servlet-class>
        <load-on-startup>10</load-on-startup>
    </servlet>

    <servlet-mapping>
        <servlet-name>SimpleServlet</servlet-name>
        <url-pattern>/simple</url-pattern>
    </servlet-mapping>


    <servlet>
        <servlet-name>WelcomeServlet</servlet-name>
        <servlet-class>app01c.WelcomeServlet</servlet-class>
        <load-on-startup>20</load-on-startup>
    </servlet>

    <servlet-mapping>
        <servlet-name>WelcomeServlet</servlet-name>
        <url-pattern>/welcome</url-pattern>
    </servlet-mapping>
</web-app>
```

There are many advantages of using the deployment descriptor. For one,
you can include elements that have no equivalent in **@WebServlet**, such as

the **load-on-startup** element. This element loads the servlet at application start-up, rather than when the servlet is first called. Using **load-on-startup** means the first call to the servlet will take no longer than subsequent calls. This is especially useful if the **init** method of the servlet takes a while to complete.

Another advantage of using the deployment descriptor is that you don't need to recompile your servlet class if you need to change configuration values, such as the servlet path.

In addition, you can pass initial parameters to a servlet and edit them without recompiling the servlet class.

The deployment descriptor also allows you to override values specified in a servlet annotation. A **WebServlet** annotation on a servlet that is also declared in the deployment descriptor will have no effect. However, annotating a servlet not in the deployment descriptor in an application with a deployment descriptor will still work. This means, you can have annotated servlets and declare servlets in the deployment descriptor in the same application.

Figure 1.8 presents the directory structure of **app01c**. The directory structure does not differ much from that of **app01a**. The only difference is that **app01c** has a **web.xml** file (the deployment descriptor) in the **WEB-INF** directory.

Figure 1.8: Directory structure of app01c with deployment descriptor

Now that **SimpleServlet** and **WelcomeServlet** are declared in the deployment descriptor, you can use these URLs to access them:

```
http://localhost:8080/app01c/simple
http://localhost:8080/app01c/welcome
```

For more information on deployment and the deployment descriptor, refer to Chapter 16, "Deployment."

Summary

Servlet technology is part of the Java EE. All servlets run in a servlet container, and the contract between the container and the servlets takes the form of the **javax.servlet.Servlet** interface. The **javax.servlet** package also provides the **GenericServlet** abstract class that implements **Servlet**. This is a convenient class that you can extend to create a servlet. However, most modern servlets will work in the HTTP environment. As such, subclassing the **javax.servlet.http.HttpServlet** class makes more sense. The **HttpServlet** class itself is a subclass of **GenericServlet**.

Chapter 2
Session Management

Session management or session tracking is a very important topic in web application development. This is due to the fact that HTTP, the language of the web, is stateless. A web server by default does not know if an HTTP request comes from a first time user or from someone who has visited it before.

For example, a webmail application requires its users to log in before they can check their emails. However, once a user types in the correct user name and password, the application should not prompt the user to log in again to access different parts of the application. The application needs to remember which users have successfully logged in. In other words, it must be able to manage user sessions.

This chapter explores four techniques you can use to retain states: URL rewriting, hidden fields, cookies, and the **HttpSession** objects. The samples presented in this chapter are part of the **app02a** application.

URL Rewriting

URL rewriting is a session tracking technique whereby you add a token or multiple tokens as a query string to a URL. The token is generally in key=value format:

```
url?key-1=value-1&key-2=value-2 ... &key-n=value-n
```

Note that the URL and the tokens are separated by a question mark. Two tokens are separated by an ampersand character (&).

URL rewriting is suitable if the tokens do not have to be carried around across too many URLs. The drawbacks of using URL rewriting include

- URLs are limited to some 2,000 characters in some web browsers.
- Values are transferable to the next resources only if there are links to insert values. In addition, you cannot easily append values to links in static pages.
- URL rewriting requires work on the server side. All links must carry the values and this would present a challenge if there are many links in a page.
- Certain characters, such as the space, the ampersand character (&), and the question mark must be encoded.
- Information appended to a URL is clearly visible, a situation that is not always preferred.

Because of these limitations, URL rewriting is only suitable if the information that needs to be retained does not span too many pages and the information is not sensitive.

As an example, the **Top10Servlet** class in Listing 2.1 is a servlet that shows the ten most favorite tourist attractions in London and Paris. The information is shown in two pages. The first page shows the first five attractions in a selected city and the second page the second five. The servlet uses URL rewriting to track the selected city and the page number. It extends **HttpServlet** and is invoked using the **/top10** URL pattern.

Listing 2.1: Top10Servlet class

```
package app02a.urlrewriting;
import java.io.IOException;
import java.io.PrintWriter;
import java.util.ArrayList;
import java.util.List;
import javax.servlet.ServletException;
import javax.servlet.annotation.WebServlet;
import javax.servlet.http.HttpServlet;
import javax.servlet.http.HttpServletRequest;
import javax.servlet.http.HttpServletResponse;

@WebServlet(name = "Top10Servlet", urlPatterns = { "/top10" })
public class Top10Servlet extends HttpServlet {
    private static final long serialVersionUID = 987654321L;

    private List<String> londonAttractions;
    private List<String> parisAttractions;
```

```java
@Override
public void init() throws ServletException {
    londonAttractions = new ArrayList<String>(10);
    londonAttractions.add("Buckingham Palace");
    londonAttractions.add("London Eye");
    londonAttractions.add("British Museum");
    londonAttractions.add("National Gallery");
    londonAttractions.add("Big Ben");
    londonAttractions.add("Tower of London");
    londonAttractions.add("Natural History Museum");
    londonAttractions.add("Canary Wharf");
    londonAttractions.add("2012 Olympic Park");
    londonAttractions.add("St Paul's Cathedral");

    parisAttractions = new ArrayList<String>(10);
    parisAttractions.add("Eiffel Tower");
    parisAttractions.add("Notre Dame");
    parisAttractions.add("The Louvre");
    parisAttractions.add("Champs Elysees");
    parisAttractions.add("Arc de Triomphe");
    parisAttractions.add("Sainte Chapelle Church");
    parisAttractions.add("Les Invalides");
    parisAttractions.add("Musee d'Orsay");
    parisAttractions.add("Montmarte");
    parisAttractions.add("Sacre Couer Basilica");
}

@Override
public void doGet(HttpServletRequest request,
        HttpServletResponse response) throws ServletException,
        IOException {

    String city = request.getParameter("city");
    if (city != null &&
            (city.equals("london") || city.equals("paris"))) {
        // show attractions
        showAttractions(request, response, city);
    } else {
        // show main page
        showMainPage(request, response);
    }
}

private void showMainPage(HttpServletRequest request,
```

```java
        HttpServletResponse response) throws ServletException,
        IOException {
    response.setContentType("text/html");
    PrintWriter writer = response.getWriter();
    writer.print("<html><head>" +
            "<title>Top 10 Tourist Attractions</title>" +
            "</head><body>" +
            "Please select a city:" +
            "<br/><a href='?city=london'>London</a>" +
            "<br/><a href='?city=paris'>Paris</a>" +
            "</body></html>");
}

private void showAttractions(HttpServletRequest request,
        HttpServletResponse response, String city)
        throws ServletException, IOException {

    int page = 1;
    String pageParameter = request.getParameter("page");
    if (pageParameter != null) {
        try {
            page = Integer.parseInt(pageParameter);
        } catch (NumberFormatException e) {
            // do nothing and retain default value for page
        }
        if (page > 2) {
            page = 1;
        }
    }
    List<String> attractions = null;
    if (city.equals("london")) {
        attractions = londonAttractions;
    } else if (city.equals("paris")) {
        attractions = parisAttractions;
    }
    response.setContentType("text/html");
    PrintWriter writer = response.getWriter();
    writer.println("<html><head>" +
            "<title>Top 10 Tourist Attractions</title>" +
            "</head><body>");
    writer.println("<a href='top10'>Select City</a> ");
    writer.println("<hr/>Page " + page + "<hr/>");

    int start = page * 5 - 5;
    for (int i = start; i < start + 5; i++) {
        writer.println(attractions.get(i) + "<br/>");
```

```
        }
        writer.print("<hr style='color:blue'/>" +
                "<a href='?city=" + city +
                "&page=1'>Page 1</a>");
        writer.println("  <a href='?city=" + city +
                "&page=2'>Page 2</a>");
        writer.println("</body></html>");
    }
}
```

The **init** method, which is invoked once when the first user requests the servlet, populates two class-level **Lists**, **londonAttractions** and **parisAttractions**, with ten tourist sites each.

The **doGet** method, which is invoked in every request, checks if the URL contains the request parameter **city** and if its value is either "london" or "paris." Based on the value of this parameter, the method calls either **showAttractions** or **showMainPage**.

```
        String city = request.getParameter("city");
        if (city != null &&
                (city.equals("london") || city.equals("paris"))) {
            // show attractions
            showAttractions(request, response, city);
        } else {
            // show main page
            showMainPage(request, response);
        }
```

Initially, a user would call the servlet without a request parameter and **showMainPage** would be invoked. It is a simple method that sends two hyperlinks to the browser, each with an embedded token city=*cityName*. The user would see the screen like that shown in Figure 2.1. The user can now select a city.

If you open the page source, you'll see the following HTML tags inside the body tag:

```
Please select a city:<br/>
<a href='?city=london'>London</a><br/>
<a href='?city=paris'>Paris</a>
```

Figure 2.1: The initial screen of Top10Servlet

Of special interest is the value of the **href** attribute of the **a** tags, which includes a question mark followed by the token **city=london** or **city=paris**. Any relative URL, that is one without the protocol part, will be considered relative to the URL of the current page. In other words, if you click one of the hyperlinks on the page, either

```
http://localhost:8080/app02a/top10?city=london
```

or

```
http://localhost:8080/app02a/top10?city=paris
```

will be sent to the server.

Upon the user clicking one of the hyperlinks the **doGet** method will detect the presence of a **city** request parameter and direct control to the **showAttractions** method, which then examines the URL to see if it contains a **page** request parameter. If no **page** request parameter is present or if its value cannot be converted to a number, then 1 is assumed and the method sends the first five attractions in the selected city. Figure 2.2 shows what the screen looks like if London has been chosen.

In addition to the city attractions, **showAttractions** also sends three hyperlinks: Select City, Page 1, and Page 2. Select City calls the servlet without a request parameter. Page 1 and Page 2 contain two tokens, city and page:

```
http://localhost:8080/app02a/top10?city=cityName&page=pageNumber
```

Figure 2.2: The first page of Top 10 London attractions

If you selected London and then click Page 2, you'll send this URL to the server that appends two key/value tokens:

```
http://localhost:8080/app02a/top10?city=london&page=2
```

You'll get the second five of Top 10 London attractions, shown in Figure 2.3.

Figure 2.3: The second page of Top 10 London attractions

This example showed how URL rewriting was used to embed a city so that the server would know what to display in Page 2.

Hidden Fields

Using hidden fields to retain states is similar to employing the URL rewriting technique. Instead of appending values to the URL, however, you put them in hidden fields within an HTML form. When the user submits the form, the values in the hidden fields are also passed to the server. Hidden fields are only suitable if your page contains a form or you can add one to it. The advantage of this technique over URL rewriting is you can pass much more characters to the server and no character encoding is necessary. Like URL rewriting, however, this technique is only good if the information to be passed doesn't need to span many pages.

The servlet in Listing 2.3 shows how you can use hidden fields to update customer information. The **Customer** class models a customer and is given in Listing 2.2.

Listing 2.2: The Customer class

```
package app02a.hiddenfields;
public class Customer {
    private int id;
    private String name;
    private String city;

    public int getId() {
        return id;
    }
    public void setId(int id) {
        this.id = id;
    }
    public String getName() {
        return name;
    }
    public void setName(String name) {
        this.name = name;
    }
    public String getCity() {
        return city;
    }
    public void setCity(String city) {
        this.city = city;
    }
}
```

Listing 2.3: The CustomerServlet class

```java
package app02a.hiddenfields;
import java.io.IOException;
import java.io.PrintWriter;
import java.util.ArrayList;
import java.util.List;
import javax.servlet.ServletException;
import javax.servlet.annotation.WebServlet;
import javax.servlet.http.HttpServlet;
import javax.servlet.http.HttpServletRequest;
import javax.servlet.http.HttpServletResponse;

/*
 * Not thread-safe. For illustration purpose only
 */
@WebServlet(name = "CustomerServlet", urlPatterns = {
        "/customer", "/editCustomer", "/updateCustomer"})
public class CustomerServlet extends HttpServlet {
    private static final long serialVersionUID = -20L;

    private List<Customer> customers = new ArrayList<Customer>();

    @Override
    public void init() throws ServletException {
        Customer customer1 = new Customer();
        customer1.setId(1);
        customer1.setName("Donald D.");
        customer1.setCity("Miami");
        customers.add(customer1);

        Customer customer2 = new Customer();
        customer2.setId(2);
        customer2.setName("Mickey M.");
        customer2.setCity("Orlando");
        customers.add(customer2);
    }

    private void sendCustomerList(HttpServletResponse response)
            throws IOException {
        response.setContentType("text/html");
        PrintWriter writer = response.getWriter();
        writer.println("<html><head><title>Customers</title></head>"
                + "<body><h2>Customers </h2>");
        writer.println("<ul>");
```

```
        for (Customer customer : customers) {
            writer.println("<li>" + customer.getName()
                    + "(" + customer.getCity() + ") ("
                    + "<a href='editCustomer?id=" + customer.getId()
                    + "'>edit</a>)");
        }
        writer.println("</ul>");
        writer.println("</body></html>");

    }

    private Customer getCustomer(int customerId) {
        for (Customer customer : customers) {
            if (customer.getId() == customerId) {
                return customer;
            }
        }
        return null;
    }

    private void sendEditCustomerForm(HttpServletRequest request,
            HttpServletResponse response) throws IOException {
        response.setContentType("text/html");
        PrintWriter writer = response.getWriter();
        int customerId = 0;
        try {
            customerId =
                    Integer.parseInt(request.getParameter("id"));
        } catch (NumberFormatException e) {
        }
        Customer customer = getCustomer(customerId);

        if (customer != null) {
            writer.println("<html><head>"
                    + "<title>Edit Customer</title></head>"
                    + "<body><h2>Edit Customer</h2>"
                    + "<form method='post' "
                    + "action='updateCustomer'>");
            writer.println("<input type='hidden' name='id' value='"
                    + customerId + "'/>");
            writer.println("<table>");
            writer.println("<tr><td>Name:</td><td>"
                    + "<input name='name' value='" +
                    customer.getName().replaceAll("'", "&#39;")
                    + "'/></td></tr>");
            writer.println("<tr><td>City:</td><td>"
```

```
                    + "<input name='city' value='" +
                    customer.getCity().replaceAll("'", "&#39;")
                    + "'/></td></tr>");
        writer.println("<tr>"
                    + "<td colspan='2' style='text-align:right'>"
                    + "<input type='submit' value='Update'/></td>"
                    + "</tr>");
        writer.println("<tr><td colspan='2'>"
                    + "<a href='customer'>Customer List</a>"
                    + "</td></tr>");
        writer.println("</table>");
        writer.println("</form></body>");
    } else {
        writer.println("No customer found");
    }

}
@Override
public void doGet(HttpServletRequest request,
        HttpServletResponse response)
        throws ServletException, IOException {
    String uri = request.getRequestURI();
    if (uri.endsWith("/customer")) {
        sendCustomerList(response);
    } else if (uri.endsWith("/editCustomer")) {
        sendEditCustomerForm(request, response);
    }
}


@Override
public void doPost(HttpServletRequest request,
        HttpServletResponse response)
        throws ServletException, IOException {
    // update customer
    int customerId = 0;
    try {
        customerId =
                Integer.parseInt(request.getParameter("id"));
    } catch (NumberFormatException e) {
    }
    Customer customer = getCustomer(customerId);
    if (customer != null) {
        customer.setName(request.getParameter("name"));
        customer.setCity(request.getParameter("city"));
    }
```

```
            sendCustomerList(response);
    }
}
```

The **CustomerServlet** class extends **HttpServlet** and is mapped to three URL patterns: **/customer**, **/editCustomer**, and **/updateCustomer**. The first two patterns will invoke the servlet's **doGet** method and **/updateCustomer** the **doPost** method.

/customer is the entry point to this small application. It lists the customers in the class-level **customers List** populated by the **init** method. (In a real-world application, you'd likely get customer information from a database). See Figure 2.4.

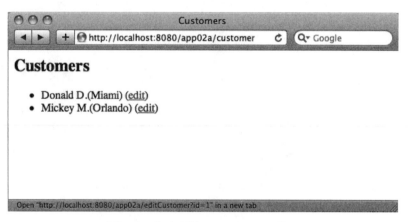

Figure 2.4: The customer list

As you can see in Figure 2.4, each customer comes with an **edit** link. The **href** attribute of each one of these links is directed to **/editCustomer? id=*customerId***. Upon receiving **/editCustomer**, the servlet sends a customer edit form like the one in Figure 2.5.

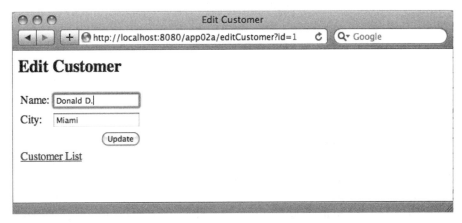

Figure 2.5: The Edit Customer form

If you click the first customer, the servlet will send this **form** tag that includes a hidden field:

```
<form method='post' action='updateCustomer'>
<input type='hidden' name='id' value='1'/>
<table>
    <tr><td>Name:</td>
    <td><input name='name' value='Donald DC.'/></td>
</tr>
<tr>
    <td>City:</td><td><input name='city' value='Miami'/></td>
</tr>
<tr>
    <td colspan='2' style='text-align:right'>
        <input type='submit' value='Update'/>
    </td>
</tr>
<tr>
    <td colspan='2'><a href='customer'>Customer List</a></td>
</tr>
</table>
</form>
```

Notice the hidden field in the form? It contains the customer id so that when the form is submitted, the server knows which customer is being edited.

It's worth mentioning that the form uses the post method so that when it's submitted, the browser will use the HTTP POST method and invoke the servlet's **doPost** method.

Cookies

URL rewriting and hidden fields are only suitable for retaining information that does not need to span many pages. If the information needs to be carried over more than a few pages, the two techniques become harder to implement because you have to manage the information for every page. Fortunately, cookies can tackle what URL rewriting and hidden fields are not capable of handling.

A cookie is a small piece of information that is passed back and forth between the web server and the browser automatically. Cookies are suitable for information that needs to span many pages. Because cookies are embedded as HTTP headers, the process of transferring them is handled by the HTTP protocol. Apart from that, you can make a cookie live as long or as short as you want. A web browser is expected to support up to twenty cookies per web server.

The downside of cookies is a user can refuse to accept cookies by changing his/her browser settings.

To use cookies, you need to be familiar with the **javax.servlet.http.Cookie** class as well as a couple of methods in the **HttpServletRequest** and **HttpServletResponse** interfaces.

To create a cookie, pass a name and a value to the **Cookie** class's constructor:

```
Cookie cookie = new Cookie(name, value);
```

For example, to create a language selection cookie, write this.

```
Cookie languageSelectionCookie = new Cookie("language", "Italian");
```

After you create a **Cookie**, you can set its **domain**, **path**, and **maxAge** properties. The **maxAge** property is of special interest because it determines when a cookie is to expire.

To send a cookie to the browser, call the **add** method on the
HttpServletResponse:

```
httpServletResponse.addCookie(cookie);
```

The browser sends back the cookies it received from a web server when the
former sends another HTTP request to the same resource or a different
resource in the same server.

Cookies can also be created and deleted on the client side using
JavaScript, however this is beyond the scope of this book.

To access a cookie sent by the browser, use the **getCookies** method on
the **HttpServletRequest**. This method returns a **Cookie** array or null if no
cookie is found in the request. To find a cookie by a certain name, you have
to iterate over the array. For example, here is how you read a cookie named
maxRecords.

```
Cookie[] cookies = request.getCookies();
Cookie maxRecordsCookie = null;
if (cookies != null) {
    for (Cookie cookie : cookies) {
        if (cookie.getName().equals("maxRecords")) {
            maxRecordsCookie = cookie;
            break;
        }
    }
}
```

Unfortunately, there's no **getCookieByName** method to make retrieving
cookies simpler. And sadly, there is no method for deleting a cookie either.
To delete a cookie, you need to create an identically-named cookie, set its
maxAge property to 0, and add the new cookie to the
HttpServletResponse. Here is how to delete a cookie called **userName**:

```
Cookie cookie = new Cookie("userName", "");
cookie.setMaxAge(0);
response.addCookie(cookie);
```

As an example of how to use cookies in session management, consider the
PreferenceServlet class in Listing 2.4. This servlet allows the user to
change the values of four cookies to set display settings for other servlets in
the same application.

Listing 2.4: The PreferenceServlet Class

```java
package app02a.cookie;
import java.io.IOException;
import java.io.PrintWriter;
import javax.servlet.ServletException;
import javax.servlet.annotation.WebServlet;
import javax.servlet.http.Cookie;
import javax.servlet.http.HttpServlet;
import javax.servlet.http.HttpServletRequest;
import javax.servlet.http.HttpServletResponse;

@WebServlet(name = "PreferenceServlet",
        urlPatterns = { "/preference" })
public class PreferenceServlet extends HttpServlet {
    private static final long serialVersionUID = 888L;

    public static final String MENU =
            "<div style='background:#e8e8e8;"
            + "padding:15px'>"
            + "<a href='cookieClass'>Cookie Class</a>  "
            + "<a href='cookieInfo'>Cookie Info</a>  "
            + "<a href='preference'>Preference</a>" + "</div>";

    @Override
    public void doGet(HttpServletRequest request,
            HttpServletResponse response) throws ServletException,
            IOException {
        response.setContentType("text/html");
        PrintWriter writer = response.getWriter();
        writer.print("<html><head>" + "<title>Preference</title>"
                + "<style>table {" + "font-size:small;"
                + "background:NavajoWhite }</style>"
                + "</head><body>"
                + MENU
                + "Please select the values below:"
                + "<form method='post'>"
                + "<table>"
                + "<tr><td>Title Font Size: </td>"
                + "<td><select name='titleFontSize'>"
                + "<option>large</option>"
                + "<option>x-large</option>"
                + "<option>xx-large</option>"
                + "</select></td>"
                + "</tr>"
                + "<tr><td>Title Style & Weight: </td>"
```

```
            +"<td><select name='titleStyleAndWeight' multiple>"
            + "<option>italic</option>"
            + "<option>bold</option>"
            + "</select></td>"
            + "</tr>"
            + "<tr><td>Max. Records in Table: </td>"
            + "<td><select name='maxRecords'>"
            + "<option>5</option>"
            + "<option>10</option>"
            + "</select></td>"
            + "</tr>"
            + "<tr><td rowspan='2'>"
            + "<input type='submit' value='Set'/></td>"
            + "</tr>"
            + "</table>" + "</form>" + "</body></html>");

}

@Override
public void doPost(HttpServletRequest request,
        HttpServletResponse response) throws ServletException,
        IOException {

    String maxRecords = request.getParameter("maxRecords");
    String[] titleStyleAndWeight = request
            .getParameterValues("titleStyleAndWeight");
    String titleFontSize =
            request.getParameter("titleFontSize");
    response.addCookie(new Cookie("maxRecords", maxRecords));
    response.addCookie(new Cookie("titleFontSize",
            titleFontSize));

    // delete titleFontWeight and titleFontStyle cookies first
    // Delete cookie by adding a cookie with the maxAge = 0;
    Cookie cookie = new Cookie("titleFontWeight", "");
    cookie.setMaxAge(0);
    response.addCookie(cookie);

    cookie = new Cookie("titleFontStyle", "");
    cookie.setMaxAge(0);
    response.addCookie(cookie);

    if (titleStyleAndWeight != null) {
        for (String style : titleStyleAndWeight) {
            if (style.equals("bold")) {
```

```
            response.addCookie(new
                    Cookie("titleFontWeight", "bold"));
        } else if (style.equals("italic")) {
            response.addCookie(new Cookie("titleFontStyle",
                    "italic"));
        }
    }
}

response.setContentType("text/html");
PrintWriter writer = response.getWriter();
writer.println("<html><head>" + "<title>Preference</title>"
        + "</head><body>" + MENU
        + "Your preference has been set."
        + "<br/><br/>Max. Records in Table: " + maxRecords
        + "<br/>Title Font Size: " + titleFontSize
        + "<br/>Title Font Style & Weight: ");

// titleStyleAndWeight will be null if none of the options
// was selected
if (titleStyleAndWeight != null) {
    writer.println("<ul>");
    for (String style : titleStyleAndWeight) {
        writer.print("<li>" + style + "</li>");
    }
    writer.println("</ul>");
}
writer.println("</body></html>");
    }
}
```

The **doGet** method of **PreferenceServlet** sends a form that contains several input fields as shown in Figure 2.6.

There are three links above the form (Cookie Class, Cookie Info, and Preference) to navigate to other servlets in the same application. I'll explain Cookie Class and Cookie Info slightly later.

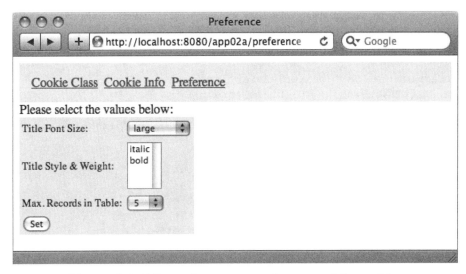

Figure 2.6: Managing user preference with cookies

When the user submits the form, the **doPost** method of **PreferenceServlet** is invoked. The **doPost** method creates these cookies: **maxRecords**, **titleFontSize**, **titleFontStyle**, and **titleFontWeight**, overriding any previous value of the same cookie. It then sends the user-selected values to the browser.

You can invoke **PreferenceServlet** with this URL

```
http://localhost:8080/app02a/preference
```

The **CookieClassServlet** class in Listing 2.5 and the **CookieInfoServlet** class in Listing 2.6 use the cookies set by **PreferenceServlet** to format their contents. The **CookieClassServlet** servlet writes the properties of the **Cookie** class in an HTML list. The number of items in the list is determined by the value of the **maxRecords** cookie that the user can set using **PreferenceServlet**.

Listing 2.5: The CookieClassServlet Class

```
package app02a.cookie;
import java.io.IOException;
import java.io.PrintWriter;
import javax.servlet.ServletException;
import javax.servlet.annotation.WebServlet;
```

```
import javax.servlet.http.Cookie;
import javax.servlet.http.HttpServlet;
import javax.servlet.http.HttpServletRequest;
import javax.servlet.http.HttpServletResponse;

@WebServlet(name = "CookieClassServlet",
        urlPatterns = { "/cookieClass" })
public class CookieClassServlet extends HttpServlet {
    private static final long serialVersionUID = 837369L;

    private String[] methods = {
            "clone", "getComment", "getDomain",
            "getMaxAge", "getName", "getPath",
            "getSecure", "getValue", "getVersion",
            "isHttpOnly", "setComment", "setDomain",
            "setHttpOnly", "setMaxAge", "setPath",
            "setSecure", "setValue", "setVersion"
    };

    @Override
    public void doGet(HttpServletRequest request,
            HttpServletResponse response) throws ServletException,
            IOException {

        Cookie[] cookies = request.getCookies();
        Cookie maxRecordsCookie = null;
        if (cookies != null) {
            for (Cookie cookie : cookies) {
                if (cookie.getName().equals("maxRecords")) {
                    maxRecordsCookie = cookie;
                    break;
                }
            }
        }

        int maxRecords = 5; // default
        if (maxRecordsCookie != null) {
            try {
                maxRecords = Integer.parseInt(
                        maxRecordsCookie.getValue());
            } catch (NumberFormatException e) {
                // do nothing, use maxRecords default value
            }
        }

        response.setContentType("text/html");
```

```
        PrintWriter writer = response.getWriter();
        writer.print("<html><head>" + "<title>Cookie Class</title>"
                + "</head><body>"
                + PreferenceServlet.MENU
                + "<div>Here are some of the methods in " +
                        "javax.servlet.http.Cookie");
        writer.print("<ul>");

        for (int i = 0; i < maxRecords; i++) {
            writer.print("<li>" + methods[i] + "</li>");
        }
        writer.print("</ul>");
        writer.print("</div></body></html>");
    }
}
```

The **CookieInfoServlet** class reads the values of the **titleFontSize**, **titleFontWeight**, and **titleFontStyle** cookies to write the following CSS style to the browser, where x, y, and z are the values of the aforementioned cookies.

```
.title {
    font-size: x;
    font-weight: y;
    font-style: z;
}
```

This style is used by a **div** element to format the text "Session Management with Cookies:".

Listing 2.6: The CookieInfoServlet Class

```
package app02a.cookie;
import java.io.IOException;
import java.io.PrintWriter;
import javax.servlet.ServletException;
import javax.servlet.annotation.WebServlet;
import javax.servlet.http.Cookie;
import javax.servlet.http.HttpServlet;
import javax.servlet.http.HttpServletRequest;
import javax.servlet.http.HttpServletResponse;

@WebServlet(name = "CookieInfoServlet", urlPatterns =
        { "/cookieInfo" })
public class CookieInfoServlet extends HttpServlet {
```

```java
private static final long serialVersionUID = 3829L;

@Override
public void doGet(HttpServletRequest request,
        HttpServletResponse response) throws ServletException,
        IOException {

    Cookie[] cookies = request.getCookies();
    StringBuilder styles = new StringBuilder();
    styles.append(".title {");
    if (cookies != null) {
        for (Cookie cookie : cookies) {
            String name = cookie.getName();
            String value = cookie.getValue();
            if (name.equals("titleFontSize")) {
                styles.append("font-size:" + value + ";");
            } else if (name.equals("titleFontWeight")) {
                styles.append("font-weight:" + value + ";");
            } else if (name.equals("titleFontStyle")) {
                styles.append("font-style:" + value + ";");
            }
        }
    }
    styles.append("}");
    response.setContentType("text/html");
    PrintWriter writer = response.getWriter();
    writer.print("<html><head>" + "<title>Cookie Info</title>"
            + "<style>" + styles.toString() + "</style>"
            + "</head><body>" + PreferenceServlet.MENU
            + "<div class='title'>"
            + "Session Management with Cookies:</div>");
    writer.print("<div>");

    // cookies will be null if there's no cookie
    if (cookies == null) {
        writer.print("No cookie in this HTTP response.");
    } else {
        writer.println("<br/>Cookies in this HTTP response:");
        for (Cookie cookie : cookies) {
            writer.println("<br/>" + cookie.getName() + ":"
                    + cookie.getValue());
        }
    }
    writer.print("</div>");
    writer.print("</body></html>");
}
```

```
}
```

You can invoke **CookieClassServlet** using this URL

```
http://localhost:8080/app02a/cookieClass
```

You can invoke the **CookieInfoServlet** servlet by directing your browser to this URL:

```
http://localhost:8080/app02a/cookieInfo
```

Figures 2.7 and 2.8 shows the results of **CookieClassServlet** and **CookieInfoServlet**, respectively.

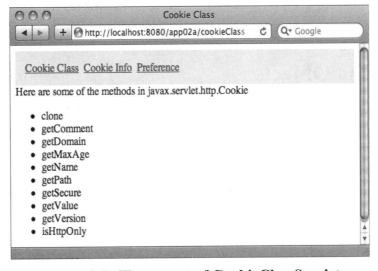

Figure 2.7: The output of CookieClassServlet

Figure 2.8: The output of CookieInfoServlet

HttpSession Objects

Of all the session tracking techniques, **HttpSession** objects are the most powerful and the most versatile. A user can have zero or one **HttpSession** and can only access his/her own **HttpSession**.

An **HttpSession** is created automatically when a user first visits a site. You retrieve a user's **HttpSession** by calling the **getSession** method on the **HttpServletRequest**. There are two overloads of **getSession**:

```
HttpSession getSession()

HttpSession getSession(boolean create)
```

The no-argument **getSession** method returns the current **HttpSession** or creates and returns one if none exists. **getSession(false)** returns the current **HttpSession** is one exists or null if none exists. **getSession(true)** returns the current **HttpSession** if one exists or creates a new one if none does. **getSession(true)** is the same as **getSession()**.

The **setAttribute** method of **HttpSession** puts a value in the **HttpSession**. Its signature is as follows:

```
void setAttribute(java.lang.String name, java.lang.Object value)
```

Note that unlike in URL rewriting, hidden fields and cookies, a value put in an **HttpSession** is stored in memory. As such, you should only store the smallest possible objects in it and not too many of them. Even though modern servlet containers can move objects in **HttpSession**s to secondary storage when it's about to run out of memory, this would be a performance drag. Therefore, be careful what you store in them.

A value added to an **HttpSession** does not have to be a **String** but can be any Java object as long as its class implements **java.io.Serializable**, so that the stored object can be serialized to a file or a database when the servlet container thinks it's necessary to do so, such as when the container almost runs out of memory. You can still store non-serializable objects in an **HttpSession**, however if the servlet container ever attempts to serialize them, it will fail and throw an exception.

The **setAttribute** method expects a different name for a different object. If you pass an attribute name that has been previously used, the name will be disassociated from the old value and associated with the new value.

You can retrieve an object stored in an **HttpSession** by calling the **getAttribute** method on the **HttpSession**, passing an attribute name. The signature of this method is as follows:

```
java.lang.Object getAttribute(java.lang.String name)
```

Another useful method in **HttpSession** is **getAttributeNames**, which returns an **Enumeration** for iterating all attributes in an **HttpSession**.

```
java.util.Enumeration<java.lang.String> getAttributeNames()
```

Note that values stored in an **HttpSession** are not sent to the client side, unlike the other session management techniques. Instead, the servlet container generates a unique identifier for every **HttpSession** it creates and sends this identifier as a token to the browser, either as a cookie named **JSESSIONID** or by appending it to URLs as a **jsessionid** parameter. On subsequent requests, the browser sends back the token to the server, allowing the server to tell which user is making the request. Whichever way the servlet container chooses to transmit session identifiers, it happens automatically in the background without you having to make an effort.

You can retrieve an **HttpSession**'s identifier by calling the **getId** method on the **HttpSession**.

```
java.lang.String getId()
```

There is also an **invalidate** method defined in **HttpSession**. This method forces the session to expire and unbinds all objects bound to it. By default, an **HttpSession** expires after some period of user inactivity. You can configure the session timeout for the whole application through the session-timeout element in the deployment descriptor (See Chapter 16, "Deployment.") For example, setting this value to 30 makes all session objects expire thirty minutes after the user's last visit. If this element is not configured, the timeout will be determined by the servlet container.

In most cases, you would want to destroy unused **HttpSession** instances before their expiration times if you could to free up some memory.

You can call the **getMaxInactiveInterval** method to find out how long more an **HttpSession** will live after the user's last visit. This method returns the number of seconds left. The **setMaxInactiveInterval** method allows you to set a different value for session timeout for an individual **HttpSession**.

```
void setMaxInactiveInterval(int seconds)
```

Passing 0 to this method causes the **HttpSession** to never expire. Generally this is a bad idea since the heap space taken by the **HttpSession** will never be released until the application is unloaded or the servlet container shuts down.

As an example, examine the **ShoppingCartServlet** class in Listing 2.9. This servlet features a small online store with four products. It allows the user to add products to a shopping cart and view its content. The servlet uses the **Product** class in Listing 2.7 and the **ShoppingItem** class in Listing 2.8. **Product** defines four properties (**id**, **name**, **description**, and **price**) and **ShoppingItem** contains a **quantity** and a **Product**.

Listing 2.7: The Product class

```
package app02a.httpsession;
public class Product {
    private int id;
    private String name;
```

```
    private String description;
    private float price;

    public Product(int id, String name, String description, float
        price) {
        this.id = id;
        this.name = name;
        this.description = description;
        this.price = price;
    }

    // get and set methods not shown to save space
}
```

Listing 2.8: The ShoppingItem class

```
package app02a.httpsession;
public class ShoppingItem {
    private Product product;
    private int quantity;

    public ShoppingItem(Product product, int quantity) {
        this.product = product;
        this.quantity = quantity;
    }

    // get and set methods not shown to save space
}
```

Listing 2.9: The ShoppingCartServlet class

```
package app02a.httpsession;
import java.io.IOException;
import java.io.PrintWriter;
import java.text.NumberFormat;
import java.util.ArrayList;
import java.util.List;
import java.util.Locale;

import javax.servlet.ServletException;
import javax.servlet.annotation.WebServlet;
import javax.servlet.http.HttpServlet;
import javax.servlet.http.HttpServletRequest;
import javax.servlet.http.HttpServletResponse;
import javax.servlet.http.HttpSession;
```

```
@WebServlet(name = "ShoppingCartServlet", urlPatterns = {
        "/products", "/viewProductDetails",
        "/addToCart", "/viewCart" })
public class ShoppingCartServlet extends HttpServlet {
    private static final long serialVersionUID = -20L;
    private static final String CART_ATTRIBUTE = "cart";

    private List<Product> products = new ArrayList<Product>();
    private NumberFormat currencyFormat = NumberFormat
            .getCurrencyInstance(Locale.US);

    @Override
    public void init() throws ServletException {
        products.add(new Product(1, "Bravo 32' HDTV",
                "Low-cost HDTV from renowned TV manufacturer",
                159.95F));
        products.add(new Product(2, "Bravo BluRay Player",
                "High quality stylish BluRay player", 99.95F));
        products.add(new Product(3, "Bravo Stereo System",
                "5 speaker hifi system with iPod player",
                129.95F));
        products.add(new Product(4, "Bravo iPod player",
                "An iPod plug-in that can play multiple formats",
                39.95F));
    }

    @Override
    public void doGet(HttpServletRequest request,
            HttpServletResponse response) throws ServletException,
            IOException {
        String uri = request.getRequestURI();
        if (uri.endsWith("/products")) {
            sendProductList(response);
        } else if (uri.endsWith("/viewProductDetails")) {
            sendProductDetails(request, response);
        } else if (uri.endsWith("viewCart")) {
            showCart(request, response);
        }
    }

    @Override
    public void doPost(HttpServletRequest request,
            HttpServletResponse response) throws ServletException,
            IOException {
        // add to cart
        int productId = 0;
```

```
    int quantity = 0;
    try {
        productId = Integer.parseInt(
                request.getParameter("id"));
        quantity = Integer.parseInt(request
                .getParameter("quantity"));
    } catch (NumberFormatException e) {
    }

    Product product = getProduct(productId);
    if (product != null && quantity >= 0) {
        ShoppingItem shoppingItem = new ShoppingItem(product,
                quantity);
        HttpSession session = request.getSession();
        List<ShoppingItem> cart = (List<ShoppingItem>) session
                .getAttribute(CART_ATTRIBUTE);
        if (cart == null) {
            cart = new ArrayList<ShoppingItem>();
            session.setAttribute(CART_ATTRIBUTE, cart);
        }
        cart.add(shoppingItem);
    }
    sendProductList(response);
}

private void sendProductList(HttpServletResponse response)
        throws IOException {
    response.setContentType("text/html");
    PrintWriter writer = response.getWriter();
    writer.println("<html><head><title>Products</title>" +
            "</head><body><h2>Products</h2>");
    writer.println("<ul>");
    for (Product product : products) {
        writer.println("<li>" + product.getName() + "(" 
                + currencyFormat.format(product.getPrice())
                + ") (" + "<a href='viewProductDetails?id="
                + product.getId() + "'>Details</a>)");
    }
    writer.println("</ul>");
    writer.println("<a href='viewCart'>View Cart</a>");
    writer.println("</body></html>");

}

private Product getProduct(int productId) {
```

```java
        for (Product product : products) {
            if (product.getId() == productId) {
                return product;
            }
        }
        return null;
    }

    private void sendProductDetails(HttpServletRequest request,
            HttpServletResponse response) throws IOException {
        response.setContentType("text/html");
        PrintWriter writer = response.getWriter();
        int productId = 0;
        try {
            productId = Integer.parseInt(
                    request.getParameter("id"));
        } catch (NumberFormatException e) {
        }
        Product product = getProduct(productId);

        if (product != null) {
            writer.println("<html><head>"
                    + "<title>Product Details</title></head>"
                    + "<body><h2>Product Details</h2>"
                    + "<form method='post' action='addToCart'>");
            writer.println("<input type='hidden' name='id' "
                    + "value='" + productId + "'/>");
            writer.println("<table>");
            writer.println("<tr><td>Name:</td><td>"
                    + product.getName() + "</td></tr>");
            writer.println("<tr><td>Description:</td><td>"
                    + product.getDescription() + "</td></tr>");
            writer.println("<tr>" + "<tr>"
                    + "<td><input name='quantity'/></td>"
                    + "<td><input type='submit' value='Buy'/>"
                    + "</td>"
                    + "</tr>");
            writer.println("<tr><td colspan='2'>"
                    + "<a href='products'>Product List</a>"
                    + "</td></tr>");
            writer.println("</table>");
            writer.println("</form></body>");
        } else {
            writer.println("No product found");
        }
```

```
    }

private void showCart(HttpServletRequest request,
        HttpServletResponse response) throws IOException {
    response.setContentType("text/html");
    PrintWriter writer = response.getWriter();
    writer.println("<html><head><title>Shopping Cart</title>"
            + "</head>");
    writer.println("<body><a href='products'>" +
            "Product List</a>");
    HttpSession session = request.getSession();
    List<ShoppingItem> cart = (List<ShoppingItem>) session
            .getAttribute(CART_ATTRIBUTE);
    if (cart != null) {
        writer.println("<table>");
        writer.println("<tr><td style='width:150px'>Quantity"
                + "</td>"
                + "<td style='width:150px'>Product</td>"
                + "<td style='width:150px'>Price</td>"
                + "<td>Amount</td></tr>");
        double total = 0.0;
        for (ShoppingItem shoppingItem : cart) {
            Product product = shoppingItem.getProduct();
            int quantity = shoppingItem.getQuantity();
            if (quantity != 0) {
                float price = product.getPrice();
                writer.println("<tr>");
                writer.println("<td>" + quantity + "</td>");
                writer.println("<td>" + product.getName()
                        + "</td>");
                writer.println("<td>"
                        + currencyFormat.format(price)
                        + "</td>");
                double subtotal = price * quantity;

                writer.println("<td>"
                        + currencyFormat.format(subtotal)
                        + "</td>");
                total += subtotal;
                writer.println("</tr>");
            }
        }
        writer.println("<tr><td colspan='4' "
                + "style='text-align:right'>"
                + "Total:"
```

```
            + currencyFormat.format(total)
            + "</td></tr>");
        writer.println("</table>");
    }
    writer.println("</table></body></html>");

    }
}
```

The **ShoppingCartServlet** servlet is mapped to these URL patterns:

- **/products**. Shows all products.
- **/viewProductDetails**. Shows a product's details.
- **/addToCart**. Adds a product to the shopping cart.
- **/viewCart**. Shows the content of the shopping cart.

All URLs except **/addToCart** invoke the **doGet** method of **ShoppingCartServlet**. **doGet** starts by checking the request's URI and generates content accordingly:

```
String uri = request.getRequestURI();
if (uri.endsWith("/products")) {
    sendProductList(response);
} else if (uri.endsWith("/viewProductDetails")) {
    sendProductDetails(request, response);
} else if (uri.endsWith("viewCart")) {
    showCart(request, response);
}
```

The following URL invokes the main page of the application.

```
http://localhost:8080/app02a/products
```

The URL will cause **doGet** to send a list of products to the browser (See Figure 2.9)

Figure 2.9: The list of products

If you click on a Details link, **doGet** will send you the details of the selected product, and you'll see something like the screen shot in Figure 2.10. Notice the input field and the Buy button? To add the product, enter a number to the input field and click on Buy.

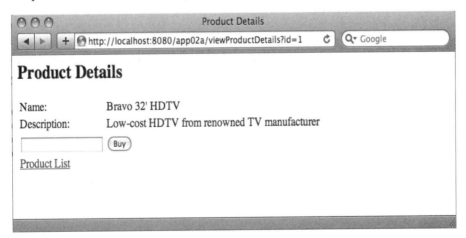

Figure 2.10: The Product Details page

Submitting the Buy form in the Product details page invokes the **doPost** method of **ShoppingCartServlet**. This is where a product is added to the user's **HttpSession**.

The **doPost** method starts by constructing a **ShoppingItem** based on the quantity entered by the user and the identifier of the selected product:

```
ShoppingItem shoppingItem = new ShoppingItem(product,
        quantity);
```

It then retrieves the current user's **HttpSession** and checks if it already contains a **List** associated with attribute name "cart".

```
HttpSession session = request.getSession();
List<ShoppingItem> cart = (List<ShoppingItem>) session
        .getAttribute(CART_ATTRIBUTE);
```

If the **List** is found, it will be used to add the **ShoppingItem**. If no **List** is found, one will be created and added to the **HttpSession**.

```
if (cart == null) {
    cart = new ArrayList<ShoppingItem>();
    session.setAttribute(CART_ATTRIBUTE, cart);
}
```

Finally, the **ShoppingItem** is added to the list.

```
cart.add(shoppingItem);
```

When the user clicks the View Cart link to view the content of the shopping cart, the **doGet** method is again invoked and the **showCart** method called. The latter retrieves the current user's **HttpSession** and calls its **getAttribute** method to get the list of shopping items:

```
HttpSession session = request.getSession();
List<ShoppingItem> cart = (List<ShoppingItem>) session
        .getAttribute(CART_ATTRIBUTE);
```

It then iterates over the **List** and sends the content of each item to the browser:

```
if (cart != null) {
    for (ShoppingItem shoppingItem : cart) {
        Product product = shoppingItem.getProduct();
        int quantity = shoppingItem.getQuantity();
        ...
```

Summary

In this chapter you've learned about session management and four session management techniques. URL rewriting and hidden fields are for 'lightweight' session tracking, suitable for cases where information does not need to span many pages. The other two techniques, cookies and **HttpSession** objects, are more flexible but not without limitations. Pay special attention when using **HttpSession** objects as each of the objects consumes server memory.

Chapter 3
JavaServer Pages

You learned in Chapter 1, "Servlets" that there are two drawbacks servlets are not capable of overcoming. First, all HTML tags written in a servlet must be enclosed in Java strings, making sending HTTP response a tedious effort. Second, all text and HTML tags are hardcoded; as such, even minor changes to the presentation layer, such as changing a background color, require recompilation.

JavaServer Pages (JSP) solves the two problems in servlets. JSP does not replace Servlet, though. Rather, it complements it. Modern Java web applications use both servlets and JSP pages. The latest version of JSP at the time of writing is 2.2.

This chapter starts with an overview of JSP and discusses in detail comments in JSP pages, implicit objects, and the three syntactic elements (directives, scripting elements, and actions). Error handling is covered towards the end of this chapter.

JSP can be written in standard syntax or XML syntax. JSP pages written in XML syntax are called JSP documents. JSP in XML syntax is very rarely used and is not covered here. In this chapter you learn JSP in standard syntax.

An Overview of JSP

A JSP page is essentially a servlet. However, working with JSP pages is easier than with servlets for two reasons. First, you do not have to compile JSP pages. Second, JSP pages are basically text files with **jsp** extension and you can use any text editor to write them.

JSP pages run on a JSP container. A servlet container is normally also a JSP container. Tomcat, for instance, is a servlet/JSP container.

The first time a JSP page is requested, a servlet/JSP container does two things:

1. Translate the JSP page into a JSP page implementation class, which is a Java class that implements the **javax.servlet.jsp.JspPage** interface or its subinterface **javax.servlet.jsp.HttpJspPage**. **JspPage** is a subinterface of **javax.servlet.Servlet** and this makes every JSP page a servlet. The class name of the generated servlet is dependent on the servlet/JSP container. You do not have to worry about this because you do not have to work with it directly. If there is a translation error, an error message will be sent to the client.
2. If the translation was successful, the servlet/JSP container compiles the servlet class. The container then loads and instantiates the Java bytecode as well as performs the lifecycle operations it normally does a servlet.

For subsequent requests for the same JSP page, the servlet/JSP container checks if the JSP page has been modified since the last time it was translated. If so, it will be retranslated, recompiled, and executed. If not, the JSP servlet already in memory is executed. This way, the first invocation of a JSP page always takes longer than subsequent requests because it involves translation and compilation. To get around this problem, you can do one of the following:

- Configure the application so that all JSP pages will be called (and, in effect, translated and compiled) when the application starts, rather than at first requests.
- Precompile the JSP pages and deploy them as servlets.

JSP comes with an API that comprises four packages:

- **javax.servlet.jsp**. Contains core classes and interfaces used by the servlet/JSP container to translate JSP pages into servlets. The **JspPage** and **HttpJspPage** interfaces are important members of this package. All JSP page implementation classes must implement either **JspPage** or **HttpJspPage**. In the HTTP environment, **HttpJspPage** is the obvious choice.

- **javax.servlet.jsp.tagext**. Contains types for developing custom tags (discussed in Chapter 6, "Writing Custom Tags.")
- **javax.el**. Provides the API for the Unified Expression Language. See Chapter 4, "The Expression Language."
- **javax.servlet.jsp.el**. Provides classes that must be supported by a servlet/JSP container to support the Expression Language in JSP.

With the exception of **javax.servlet.jsp.tagext**, you rarely have to use the JSP API directly. In fact, when writing a JSP page, you're more concerned with the Servlet API than the JSP API itself. Of course, you also need to master the JSP syntax, which will be explained throughout this chapter. One example where the JSP API is used extensively is when developing a JSP container or a JSP compiler.

You can view the JSP API here:

```
http://download.oracle.com/docs/cd/E17802_01/products/products/jsp/
2.1/docs/jsp-2_1-pfd2/index.html
```

A JSP page can contain template data and syntactic elements. An element is something with a special meaning to the JSP translator. For example, **<%** is an element because it denotes the start of a Java code block within a JSP page. **%>** is also an element because it terminates a Java code block. Everything else that is not an element is template data. Template data is sent as is to the browser. For instance, HTML tags and text in a JSP page are template data.

Listing 3.1 presents a JSP page named **welcome.jsp**. It is a simple page that sends a greeting to the client. Notice how simple the JSP page is compared to a servlet that does the same thing?

Listing 3.1: The welcome.jsp page

```
<html>
<head><title>Welcome</title></head>
<body>
Welcome
</body>
</html>
```

In Tomcat, the **welcome.jsp** page is translated into a **welcome_jsp** servlet after the page's first invocation. You can find the generated servlet in a

subdirectory under Tomcat's **work** directory The servlet extends
org.apache.jasper.runtime.HttpJspBase, an abstract class that extends
javax.servlet.http.HttpServlet and implements
javax.servlet.jsp.HttpJspPage.

Here is the generated servlet for **welcome.jsp**. Do not worry if you find
it too cryptic. You can continue without understanding it, even though it is
better if you do.

```
package org.apache.jsp;
import javax.servlet.*;
import javax.servlet.http.*;
import javax.servlet.jsp.*;

public final class welcome_jsp extends
        org.apache.jasper.runtime.HttpJspBase
        implements org.apache.jasper.runtime.JspSourceDependent {

    private static final javax.servlet.jsp.JspFactory _jspxFactory =
        javax.servlet.jsp.JspFactory.getDefaultFactory();

    private static java.util.Map<java.lang.String,java.lang.Long>
        _jspx_dependants;

    private javax.el.ExpressionFactory _el_expressionfactory;
    private org.apache.tomcat.InstanceManager _jsp_instancemanager;

    public java.util.Map<java.lang.String,java.lang.Long>
        getDependants() {
            return _jspx_dependants;
    }

    public void _jspInit() {
        _el_expressionfactory =
                _jspxFactory.getJspApplicationContext(
                getServletConfig().getServletContext())
                .getExpressionFactory();
        _jsp_instancemanager =
                org.apache.jasper.runtime.InstanceManagerFactory
                .getInstanceManager(getServletConfig());
    }

    public void _jspDestroy() {
    }
```

```
public void _jspService(final
    javax.servlet.http.HttpServletRequest request, final
    javax.servlet.http.HttpServletResponse response)
    throws java.io.IOException, javax.servlet.ServletException {

    final javax.servlet.jsp.PageContext pageContext;
    javax.servlet.http.HttpSession session = null;
    final javax.servlet.ServletContext application;
    final javax.servlet.ServletConfig config;
    javax.servlet.jsp.JspWriter out = null;
    final java.lang.Object page = this;
    javax.servlet.jsp.JspWriter _jspx_out = null;
    javax.servlet.jsp.PageContext _jspx_page_context = null;

    try {
        response.setContentType("text/html");
        pageContext = _jspxFactory.getPageContext(this, request,
            response, null, true, 8192, true);
        _jspx_page_context = pageContext;
        application = pageContext.getServletContext();
        config = pageContext.getServletConfig();
        session = pageContext.getSession();
        out = pageContext.getOut();
        _jspx_out = out;

        out.write("<html>\n");
        out.write("<head><title>Welcome</title></head>\n");
        out.write("<body>\n");
        out.write("Welcome\n");
        out.write("</body>\n");
        out.write("</html>");
    } catch (java.lang.Throwable t) {
        if (!(t instanceof
                javax.servlet.jsp.SkipPageException)){
            out = _jspx_out;
            if (out != null && out.getBufferSize() != 0)
                try {
                    out.clearBuffer();
                } catch (java.io.IOException e) {
                }
            if (_jspx_page_context != null)
                _jspx_page_context.handlePageException(t);
        }
    } finally {
        _jspxFactory.releasePageContext(_jspx_page_context);
```

```
        }
    }
}
```

As you can see in the code above, the body of the JSP page is translated into a **_jspService** method. This method is defined in **HttpJspPage** and is called from the implementation of the **service** method in **HttpJspBase**. Here is from the **HttpJspBase** class.

```
public final void service(HttpServletRequest request,
        HttpServletResponse response) throws ServletException,
        IOException {
    _jspService(request, response);
}
```

To override the **init** and **destroy** methods, you can declare methods as explained in the section "Scripting Elements" later in this chapter.

Another aspect where a JSP page differs from a servlet is the fact that the former does not need to be annotated or mapped to a URL in the deployment descriptor. Every JSP page in the application directory can be invoked by typing the path to the page in the browser. Figure 3.1 shows the directory structure of **app03a**, a JSP application accompanying this chapter.

Figure 3.1: The application directory of app03a

With only one JSP page, the structure of the **app03a** application is very simple, consisting of an empty **WEB-INF** directory and a **welcome.jsp** page.

You can invoke the **welcome.jsp** page using this URL:

```
http://localhost:8080/app03a/welcome.jsp
```

Note
You do not need to restart Tomcat after adding a new JSP page.

Listing 3.2 shows how to use Java code in JSP to produce a dynamic page. The **todaysDate.jsp** page in Listing 3.2 shows today's date.

Listing 3.2: The todaysDate.jsp page

```
<%@page import="java.util.Date"%>
<%@page import="java.text.DateFormat"%>
<html>
<head><title>Today's date</title></head>
<body>
<%
    DateFormat dateFormat =
            DateFormat.getDateInstance(DateFormat.LONG);
    String s = dateFormat.format(new Date());
    out.println("Today is " + s);
%>
</body>
</html>
```

The **todaysDate.jsp** page sends a couple of HTML tags and the string "Today is" followed by today's date to the browser.

There are two things to note. First, Java code can appear anywhere in a JSP page and is enclosed by **<%** and **%>**. Second, to import a Java type used in a JSP page, you use the **import** attribute of the **page** directive. Without importing a type, you have to write the fully-qualified name of the Java type in your code.

The **<% ... %>** block is called a scriplet and is discussed further in the section "Scripting Elements" later in this chapter. The **page** directive is explained in detail in the section "Directives" later in this chapter.

You can invoke the **todaysDate.jsp** page using this URL:

```
http://localhost:8080/app03a/todaysDate.jsp
```

Comments

Adding comments to a JSP page is good practice. There are two types of comments that can appear in a JSP page:

1. JSP comments, which are comments documenting what the page is doing.
2. HTML/XHTML comments, which are comments that will be sent to the browser.

A JSP comment starts with **<%--** and ends with **--%>**. For instance, the following is a JSP comment:

```
<%-- retrieve products to display --%>
```

A JSP comment is not sent to the browser and cannot be nested.

An HTML/XHTML comment has the following syntax:

```
<!-- [comments here] -->
```

An HTML/XHTML comment is not processed by the container and is sent to the browser as is. One use of the HTML/XHTML comment is to identify the JSP page itself:

```
<!-- this is /jsp/store/displayProducts.jspf -->
```

This is particularly useful when working with an application that has many JSP fragments. The developer can easily find out which JSP page or fragment generated a certain HTML section by viewing the HTML source in the browser.

Implicit Objects

The servlet container passes several objects to the servlets it is running. For instance, you get an **HttpServletRequest** and an **HttpServletResponse** in the servlet's **service** method and a **ServletConfig** in the **init** method. In addition, you can obtain an **HttpSession** by calling **getSession** on the **HttpServletRequest** object.

In JSP you can retrieve those objects by using implicit objects. Table 3.1 lists the implicit objects.

For example, the **request** implicit object represents the **HttpServletRequest** passed by the servlet/JSP container to the servlet's **service** method. You can use **request** as if it was a variable reference to the **HttpServletRequest**. For instance, the following code retrieves the **userName** parameter from the **HttpServletRequest** object.

```
<%
    String userName = request.getParameter("userName");
%>
```

Object	Type
request	javax.servlet.http.HttpServletRequest
response	javax.servlet.http.HttpServletResponse
out	javax.servlet.jsp.JspWriter
session	javax.servlet.http.HttpSession
application	javax.servlet.ServletContext
config	javax.servlet.ServletConfig
pageContext	javax.servlet.jsp.PageContext
page	javax.servlet.jsp.HttpJspPage
exception	java.lang.Throwable

Table 3.1: JSP Implicit Objects

pageContext refers to the **javax.servlet.jsp.PageContext** created for the page. It provides useful context information and access to various servlet-related objects via its self-explanatory methods, such as **getRequest**, **getResponse**, **getServletContext**, **getServletConfig**, and **getSession**. These methods are not very useful in scriptlets since the objects they return can be accessed more directly through the implicit objects **request**, **response**, **session**, and **application**. However, as you will see in Chapter 4, "The Expression Language" that the **PageContext** allows those objects to be accessed using the Expression Language.

Another set of interesting methods offered by **PageContext** are those for getting and setting attributes, the **getAttribute** and **setAttribute** methods. Attributes can be stored in one of four scopes: page, request, session, and application. The page scope is the narrowest scope and attributes stored here are only available in the same JSP page. The request scope refers to the current **ServletRequest**, the session scope the current **HttpSession**, and the application scope the **ServletContext**.

The **setAttribute** method in **PageContext** has the following signature:

```
public abstract void setAttribute(java.lang.String name,
      java.lang.Object value, int scope)
```

The value of *scope* can be one of the following static final **int**s in **PageContext**: **PAGE_SCOPE**, **REQUEST_SCOPE**, **SESSION_SCOPE**, and **APPLICATION_SCOPE**.

Alternatively, to store an attribute in the page scope, you can use this **setAttribute** overload:

```
public abstract void setAttribute(java.lang.String name,
        java.lang.Object value)
```

For example, the following scriptlet stores an attribute in the **ServletRequest**.

```
<%
    // product is a Java object
    pageContext.setAttribute("product", product,
            PageContext.REQUEST_SCOPE);
%>
```

The Java code above has the same effect as this:

```
<%
    request.setAttribute("product", product);
%>
```

The **out** implicit object references a **javax.servlet.jsp.JspWriter**, which is similar to the **java.io.PrintWriter** you get from calling **getWriter()** on the **HttpServletResponse**. You can call its **print** method overloads just as you would a **PrintWriter** to send messages to the browser. For instance:

```
out.println("Welcome");
```

The **implicitObjects.jsp** page in Listing 3.3 demonstrates the use of some of the implicit objects.

Listing 3.3: The implicitObjects.jsp page

```
<%@page import="java.util.Enumeration"%>
<html>
<head><title>JSP Implicit Objects</title></head>
<body>
<b>Http headers:</b><br/>
<%
    for (Enumeration<String> e = request.getHeaderNames();
            e.hasMoreElements(); ) {
        String header = e.nextElement();
        out.println(header + ": " + request.getHeader(header) +
                "<br/>");
    }
%>
```

```
<hr/>
<%
    out.println("Buffer size: " + response.getBufferSize() +
        "<br/>");
    out.println("Session id: " + session.getId() + "<br/>");
    out.println("Servlet name: " + config.getServletName() +
        "<br/>");
    out.println("Server info: " + application.getServerInfo());
%>
</body>
</html>
```

You can invoke the **implicitObjects.jsp** page with this URL:

```
http://localhost:8080/app03a/implicitObjects.jsp
```

The page produces the following text on your browser:

```
Http headers:
host: localhost:8080
user-agent: Mozilla/5.0 (Macintosh; Intel Mac OS X 10_5_8)
        AppleWebKit/534.50.2 (KHTML, like Gecko) Version/5.0.6
        Safari/533.22.3
accept:text/html,application/xhtml+xml,application/xml;q=0.9,*/*;q=
0.8
accept-language: en-us
accept-encoding: gzip, deflate
connection: keep-alive

Buffer size: 8192
Session id: 561DDD085ADD99FC03F70BDEE87AAF4D
Servlet name: jsp
Server info: Apache Tomcat/7.0.14
```

What exactly you see in your browser depend on the browser you're using and your environment.

Note that by default the JSP compiler sets the content type of a JSP page to **text/html**. If you're sending a different type, you must set the content type by calling **response.setContentType()** or by using the **page** directive (discussed in the section "Directives"). For example, the following sets the content type to text/json:

```
response.setContentType("text/json");
```

Note also that the **page** implicit object represents the current JSP page and is not normally used by the JSP page author.

Directives

Directives are the first type of JSP syntactic elements. They are instructions for the JSP translator on how a JSP page should be translated into a servlet. There are several directives defined in JSP 2.2, but only the two most important ones, **page** and **include**, are discussed in this chapter. The other directives that are covered in other chapters are **taglib**, **tag**, **attribute**, and **variable**.

The page Directive

You use the **page** directive to instruct the JSP translator on certain aspects of the current JSP page. For example, you can tell the JSP translator the size of the buffer that should be used for the **out** implicit object, what content type to use, what Java types to import, and so on.

The **page** directive has the following syntax:

```
<%@ page attribute1="value1" attribute2="value2" ... %>
```

The space between @ and **page** is optional and *attribute1*, *attribute2*, and so on are the **page** directive's attributes. Here is the list of attributes for the **page** directive.

- **import**. Specifies a Java type or Java types that will be imported and useable by the Java code in this page. For example, specifying **import="java.util.List"** imports the **List** interface. You can use the wildcard * to import the whole package, such as in **import="java.util.*"**. To import multiple types, separate two types with a comma, such as in **import="java.util.ArrayList, java.util.Calendar, java.io.PrintWriter"**. All types in the following packages are implicitly imported: **java.lang**, **javax.servlet**, **javax.servlet.http**, **javax.servlet.jsp**.
- **session**. A value of **true** indicates that this page participates in session management, and a value of **false** indicates otherwise. By default, the

value is **true**, which means the invocation of a JSP page will cause a **javax.servlet.http.HttpSession** instance to be created if one does not yet exist.

- **buffer**. Specifies the buffer size of the **out** implicit object in kilobytes. The suffix **kb** is mandatory. The default buffer size is 8kb or more, depending on the JSP container. It is also possible to assign **none** to this attribute to indicate that no buffering should be used, which will cause the output to be written directly to the corresponding **PrintWriter**.

- **autoFlush**. A value of **true**, the default value, indicates that the buffered output should be flushed automatically when the buffer is full. A value of **false** indicates that the buffer is only flushed if the **flush** method of the **response** implicit object is called. Consequently, an exception will be thrown in the event of buffer overflow.

- **isThreadSafe**. Indicates the level of thread safety implemented in the page. JSP authors are advised against using this attribute as it could result in a generated servlet containing deprecated code.

- **info**. Specifies the return value of the **getServletInfo** method of the generated servlet.

- **errorPage**. Indicates the page that will handle errors that may occur in this page.

- **isErrorPage**. Indicates if this page is an error handler.

- **contentType**. Specifies the content type of the **response** implicit object of this page. By default, the value is **text/html**.

- **pageEncoding**. Specifies the character encoding for this page. By default, the value is **ISO-8859-1**.

- **isELIgnored**. Indicates whether EL expressions are ignored. EL, which is short for expression language, is discussed in Chapter 4, "The Expression Language."

- **language**. Specifies the scripting language used in this page. By default, its value is **java** and this is the only valid value in JSP 2.2.

- **extends**. Specifies the superclass that this JSP page's implementation class must extend. This attribute is rarely used and should only be used with extra caution.

- **deferredSyntaxAllowedAsLiteral**. Specifies whether or not the character sequence #{ is allowed as a String literal in this page and translation unit. The default value is false. #{ is important because it is a special character sequence in the Expression Language (See Chapter 4, "The Expression Language.")

- **trimDirectiveWhitespaces**. Indicates whether or not template text that contains only white spaces is removed from the output. The default is false; in other words, not to trim white spaces.

The **page** directive can appear anywhere in a page. The exception is when it contains the **contentType** or the **pageEncoding** attribute, in which case it must appear before any template data and before sending any content using Java code. This is because the content type and the character encoding must be set prior to sending any content.

The **page** directive can also appear multiple times. However, an attribute that appears in multiple **page** directives must have the same value. An exception to this rule is the **import** attribute. The effect of the **import** attribute appearing in multiple **page** directives is cumulative. For example, the following page directives import both **java.util.ArrayList** and **java.io.File**.

```
<%@page import="java.util.ArrayList"%>
<%@page import="java.util.Date"%>
```

This is the same as

```
<%@page import="java.util.ArrayList, java.util.Date"%>
```

As another example, here is a **page** directive that sets the **session** attribute to **false** and allocates 16KB to the page buffer:

```
<%@page session="false" buffer="16kb"%>
```

The include Directive

You use the **include** directive to include the content of another file in the current JSP page. You can use multiple **include** directives in a JSP page. Modularizing a particular content into an include file is useful if that content is used by different pages or used by a page in different places.

The syntax of the **include** directive is as follows:

```
<%@ include file="url"%>
```

where the space between *@* and **include** is optional and *url* represents the relative path to an include file. If *url* begins with a forward slash (/), it is interpreted as an absolute path on the server. If it does not, it is interpreted as relative to the current JSP page.

The JSP translator translates the **include** directive by replacing the directive with the content of the include file. In other words, if you have written the **copyright.jspf** file in Listing 3.4.

Listing 3.4: The copyright.jspf include file

```
<hr/>
&copy;2012 BrainySoftware
<hr/>
```

And, you have the **main.jsp** page in Listing 3.5.

Listing 3.5: The main.jsp page

```
<html>
<head><title>Including a file</title></head>
<body>
This is the included content: <hr/>
<%@ include file="copyright.jspf"%>
</body>
</html>
```

Using the **include** directive in the **main.jsp** page has the same effect as writing the following JSP page.

```
<html>
<head><title>Including a file</title></head>
<body>
This is the included content: <hr/>
<hr/>
&copy;2012 BrainySoftware
<hr/>
</body>
</html>
```

For the above **include** directive to work, the **copyright.jspf** file must reside in the same directory as the including page.

By convention an include file has **jspf** extension, which stands for JSP fragment. Today JSP fragments are called JSP segments but the **jspf** extension is still retained for consistency.

Note that you can also include static HTML files.

The **include** action, discussed in the section "Actions" later in this chapter, is similar to the include directive. The subtle difference is explained in the section "Actions" and it is important you understand the difference between the two.

Scripting Elements

The second type of JSP syntactic elements, scripting elements incorporate Java code into a JSP page. There are three types of scripting elements: scriptlets, declarations, and expressions. They are discussed in the following subsections.

Scriptlets

A scriptlet is a block of Java code. A scriptlet starts with **<%** and ends with **%>**. For example, the **scriptletTest.jsp** page in Listing 3.6 uses scriptlets.

Listing 3.6: Using a scriplet (scriptletTest.jsp)

```
<%@page import="java.util.Enumeration"%>
<html>
<head><title>Scriptlet example</title></head>
<body>
<b>Http headers:</b><br/>
<%-- first scriptlet --%>
<%
    for (Enumeration<String> e = request.getHeaderNames();
            e.hasMoreElements(); ) {
        String header = e.nextElement();
        out.println(header + ": " + request.getHeader(header) +
                "<br/>");
    }
    String message = "Thank you.";
%>
<hr/>
```

```
<%-- second scriptlet --%>
<%
    out.println(message);
%>
</body>
</html>
```

There are two scriptlets in the JSP page in Listing 3.6. Note that variables defined in a scriptlet is visible to the other scriptlets below it.

It is legal for the first line of code in a scriptlet to be in the same line as the <% tag and for the %> tag to be in the same line as the last line of code. However, this would result in a less readable page.

Expressions

An expression is evaluated and its result fed to the **print** method of the **out** implicit object. An expression starts with **<%=** and ends with **%>**. For example, the text in bold in the following line is an expression:

```
Today is <%=java.util.Calendar.getInstance().getTime()%>
```

Note that there is no semicolon after an expression.

With this expression, the JSP container first evaluates **java.util.Calendar.getInstance().getTime()**, and then passes the result to **out.print()**. This is the same as writing this scriptlet:

```
Today is
<%
    out.print(java.util.Calendar.getInstance().getTime());
%>
```

Declarations

You can declare variables and methods that can be used in a JSP page. You enclose a declaration with **<%!** and **%>**. For example, the declarationTst.jsp page in Listing 3.7 shows a JSP page that declares a method named **getTodaysDate**.

Listing 3.7: Using a declaration (declarationTest.jsp)

```
<%!
    public String getTodaysDate() {
        return new java.util.Date();
    }
%>
<html>
<head><title>Declarations</title></head>
<body>
Today is <%=getTodaysDate()%>
</body>
</html>
```

A declaration can appear anywhere in a JSP page and there can be multiple declarations in the same page.

You can use declarations to override the **init** and **destroy** methods in the implementation class. To override **init**, declare a **jspInit** method. To override **destroy**, declare a **jspDestroy** method. The two methods are explained below.

- **jspInit**. This method is similar to the **init** method in **javax.servlet.Servlet**. **jspInit** is invoked when the JSP page is initialized. Unlike the **init** method, **jspInit** does not take arguments. You can still obtain the **ServletConfig** object through the **config** implicit object.
- **jspDestroy**. This method is similar to the **destroy** method in **Servlet** and is invoked when the JSP page is about to be destroyed.

Listing 3.8 presents the **lifeCycle.jsp** page that demonstrates how you can override **jspInit** and **jspDestroy**.

Listing 3.8: The lifeCycle.jsp page

```
<%!
    public void jspInit() {
        System.out.println("jspInit ...");
    }
    public void jspDestroy() {
        System.out.println("jspDestroy ...");
    }
%>
<html>
```

```
<head><title>jspInit and jspDestroy</title></head>
<body>
Overriding jspInit and jspDestroy
</body>
</html>
```

The **lifeCycle.jsp** page will be translated into the following servlet:

```
package org.apache.jsp;
import javax.servlet.*;
import javax.servlet.http.*;
import javax.servlet.jsp.*;

public final class lifeCycle_jsp extends
        org.apache.jasper.runtime.HttpJspBase
        implements org.apache.jasper.runtime.JspSourceDependent {

    public void jspInit() {
        System.out.println("jspInit ...");

    }

    public void jspDestroy() {
        System.out.println("jspDestroy ...");
    }

    private static final javax.servlet.jsp.JspFactory _jspxFactory =
            javax.servlet.jsp.JspFactory.getDefaultFactory();

    private static java.util.Map<java.lang.String,java.lang.Long>
      _jspx_dependants;

    private javax.el.ExpressionFactory _el_expressionfactory;
    private org.apache.tomcat.InstanceManager _jsp_instancemanager;

    public java.util.Map<java.lang.String,java.lang.Long>
            getDependants() {
        return _jspx_dependants;
    }

    public void _jspInit() {
        _el_expressionfactory =
                _jspxFactory.getJspApplicationContext(
                getServletConfig().getServletContext())
                .getExpressionFactory();
```

```
    _jsp_instancemanager =
            org.apache.jasper.runtime.InstanceManagerFactory
            .getInstanceManager(getServletConfig());
}

public void _jspDestroy() {
}

public void _jspService(final
        javax.servlet.http.HttpServletRequest request, final
        javax.servlet.http.HttpServletResponse response)
        throws java.io.IOException,
        javax.servlet.ServletException {

    final javax.servlet.jsp.PageContext pageContext;
    javax.servlet.http.HttpSession session = null;
    final javax.servlet.ServletContext application;
    final javax.servlet.ServletConfig config;
    javax.servlet.jsp.JspWriter out = null;
    final java.lang.Object page = this;
    javax.servlet.jsp.JspWriter _jspx_out = null;
    javax.servlet.jsp.PageContext _jspx_page_context = null;

    try {
        response.setContentType("text/html");
        pageContext = _jspxFactory.getPageContext(this, request,
            response, null, true, 8192, true);
        _jspx_page_context = pageContext;
        application = pageContext.getServletContext();
        config = pageContext.getServletConfig();
        session = pageContext.getSession();
        out = pageContext.getOut();
        _jspx_out = out;

        out.write("\n");
        out.write("<html>\n");
        out.write("<head><title>jspInit and jspDestroy" +
                "</title></head>\n");
        out.write("<body>\n");
        out.write("Overriding jspInit and jspDestroy\n");
        out.write("</body>\n");
        out.write("</html>");
    } catch (java.lang.Throwable t) {
        if (!(t instanceof
                javax.servlet.jsp.SkipPageException)){
            out = _jspx_out;
```

```
            if (out != null && out.getBufferSize() != 0)
                try {
                    out.clearBuffer();
                } catch (java.io.IOException e) {
                }
            if (_jspx_page_context != null)
                _jspx_page_context.handlePageException(t);
        }
    } finally {
        _jspxFactory.releasePageContext(_jspx_page_context);
    }
  }
}
```

Notice that the **jspInit** and **jspDestroy** methods in the generated servlet?

You can invoke **lifeCycle.jsp** by using this URL:

```
http://localhost:8080/app03a/lifeCycle.jsp
```

You will see "jspInit ..." on your console when you first invoke the JSP page, and "jspDestroy ..." when you shut down your servlet/JSP container.

Disabling Scripting Elements

With the advance of the Expression Language in JSP 2.0, the recommended practice is to use the EL to access server-side objects and not to write Java code in JSP pages. For this reason, starting JSP 2.0 scripting elements may be disabled by defining a **scripting-invalid** element within **<jsp-property-group>** in the deployment descriptor.

```
<jsp-property-group>
    <url-pattern>*.jsp</url-pattern>
    <scripting-invalid>true</scripting-invalid>
</jsp-property-group>
```

Actions

Actions are the third type of syntactic element. They are translated into Java code that performs an operation, such as accessing a Java object or invoking a method. This section discusses standard actions that must be supported by all JSP containers. In addition to standard actions, you can also create custom tags that perform certain operations. Custom tags are discussed in Chapter 6, "Writing Custom Tags."

The following are some of the standard actions. The **doBody** and **invoke** standard actions are discussed in Chapter 7, "Tag Files."

useBean

This action creates a scripting variable associated with a Java object. It was one of the earliest efforts to separate presentation and business logic. Thanks to other technologies such as custom tags and the Expression Language, **useBean** is now rarely used.

As an example, the **useBeanTest.jsp** page in Listing 3.9 creates an instance of **java.util.Date** and associates it with scripting variable **today**, which then be used in an expression.

Listing 3.9: The useBeanTest.jsp page

```
<html>
<head>
    <title>useBean</title>
</head>
<body>
<jsp:useBean id="today" class="java.util.Date"/>
<%=today%>
</body>
</html>
```

The action will be translated into this code in Tomcat.

```
java.util.Date today = null;
today = (java.util.Date) _jspx_page_context.getAttribute("today",
        javax.servlet.jsp.PageContext.REQUEST_SCOPE);
if (today == null) {
    today = new java.util.Date();
    _jspx_page_context.setAttribute("today", today,
            javax.servlet.jsp.PageContext.REQUEST_SCOPE);
}
```

Running this page prints the current date and time in your browser.

setProperty and getProperty

The **setProperty** action sets a property in a Java object and **getProperty**
prints a Java object's property. As an example, the **getSetPropertyTest.jsp**
page in Listing 3.11 sets and gets the **firstName** property of an instance of
the **Employee** class, defined in Listing 3.10.

Listing 3.10: The Employee class

```
package app03a;
public class Employee {
    private String id;
    private String firstName;
    private String lastName;

    public String getId() {
        return id;
    }
    public void setId(String id) {
        this.id = id;
    }
    public String getFirstName() {
        return firstName;
    }
    public void setFirstName(String firstName) {
        this.firstName = firstName;
    }
    public String getLastName() {
        return lastName;
    }
    public void setLastName(String lastName) {
        this.lastName = lastName;
    }
}
```

Listing 3.11: The getSetPropertyTest.jsp

```
<html>
<head>
<title>getProperty and setProperty</title>
</head>
<body>
<jsp:useBean id="employee" class="app03a.Employee"/>
<jsp:setProperty name="employee" property="firstName"
      value="Abigail"/>
```

```
First Name: <jsp:getProperty name="employee" property="firstName"/>
</body>
</html>
```

include

The **include** action is used to include another resource dynamically. You can include another JSP page, a servlet, or a static HTML page. For example, the **jspIncludeTest.jsp** page in Listing 3.12 uses the **include** action to include the **menu.jsp** page.

Listing 3.12: The jspIncludeTest.jsp page

```
<html>
<head>
<title>Include action</title>
</head>
<body>
<jsp:include page="jspf/menu.jsp">
    <jsp:param name="text" value="How are you?"/>
</jsp:include>
</body>
</html>
```

It is important that you understand the difference between the **include** directive and the **include** action. With the **include** directive, inclusion occurs at page translation time, i.e. when the JSP container translates the page into a generated servlet. With the **include** action, inclusion occurs at request time. As such, you can pass parameters using the **include** action, but not the **include** directive.

The second difference is that with the **include** directive, the file extension of the included resource does not matter. With the include action, the file extension must be jsp for it to be processed as a JSP page. Using jspf in the **include** action, for example, will make the JSP segment be treated as a static file.

forward

The **forward** action forwards the current page to a different resource. For example, the following forward action forwards the current page to the **login.jsp** page.

```
<jsp:forward page="jspf/login.jsp">
    <jsp:param name="text" value="Please login"/>
</jsp:forward>
```

Error HandlingError handling is well supported in JSP. Java code can be handled using the **try** statement, however you can also specify a page that will be displayed should any of the pages in the application encounters an uncaught exception. In such events, your users will see a well designed page that explains what happened, and not an error message that makes them frown.

You make a JSP page an error page by using the **isErrorPage** attribute of the **page** directive. The value of the attribute must be **true**. Listing 3.13 shows such an error handler.

Listing 3.13: The errorHandler.jsp page

```
<%@page isErrorPage="true"%>
<html>
<head><title>Error</title></head>
<body>
An error has occurred. <br/>
Error message:
<%
    out.println(exception.toString());
%>
</body>
</html>
```

Other pages that need protection against uncaught exceptions will have to use the **errorPage** attribute of the **page** directive, citing the path to the error handling page as the value. For example, the **buggy.jsp** page in Listing 3.14 uses the error handler in Listing 3.13.

Listing 3.14: The buggy.jsp page

```
<%@page errorPage="errorHandler.jsp"%>
```

```
Deliberately throw an exception
<%
    Integer.parseInt("Throw me");
%>
```

If you run the **buggy.jsp** page, it will throw an exception. However, you will not see an error message generated by the servlet/JSP container. Instead, the content of the **errorHandler.jsp** page is displayed.

Summary

JSP is the second technology for building web applications in Java, invented to complement Servlet technology and not to replace it. Well designed Java web applications use both servlets and JSP.

In this chapter you've learned how JSP works and how to write JSP pages. By now, you should know all there is to know about the implicit objects and be able to use the three syntactic elements that can be present in a JSP page, directives, scripting elements, and actions.

Chapter 4
The Expression Language

One of the most important features in JSP 2.0 was the Expression Language (EL), which JSP authors can use to access application data. Inspired by both the ECMAScript and the XPath expression languages, the EL is designed to make it possible and easy to author script-free JSP pages, that is, pages that do not use JSP declarations, expressions, or scriptlets. (Chapter 10, "Servlet/JSP Application Design" explains why script-free JSP pages are considered good practice.)

The EL that was adopted into JSP 2.0 first appeared in the JSP Standard Tag Library (JSTL) 1.0 specification. JSP 1.2 programmers could use the language by importing the standard libraries into their applications. JSP 2.0 and later developers can use the EL without JSTL, even though JSTL is still needed in many applications as it also contains other tags not related to the EL.

The EL in JSP 2.1 and JSP 2.2 is an attempt to unify the EL in JSP 2.0 and the expression language defined in JavaServer Faces (JSF) 1.0. JSF is a framework for rapidly building web applications in Java and was built on top of JSP 1.2. Because JSP 1.2 lacked an integrated expression language and the JSP 2.0 EL did not meet all the requirements of JSF, a variant of the EL was developed for JSF 1.0. The two language variants were later unified. This chapter is only concerned with the EL for non-JSF developers.

The Expression Language Syntax

An EL expression starts with ${ and ends with }. The construct of an EL expression is as follows:

```
${expression}
```

For example, to write the expression **x+y**, you use the following construct:

`${x+y}`

It is also common to concatenate two expressions. A sequence of expressions will be evaluated from left to right, coerced to **String**s, and concatenated. If **a+b** equals **8** and **c+d** equals **10**, the following two expressions produce **810**:

`${a+b}${c+d}`

And **${a+b}and${c+d}** results in **8and10**.

If an EL expression is used in an attribute value of a custom tag, the expression will be evaluated and the resulting string coerced to the attribute's expected type:

`<my:tag someAttribute="${`*expression*`}"/>`

The **${** sequence of characters denotes the beginning of an EL expression. If you want to send the literal **${** instead, you need to escape the first character: **\${**.

Reserved Words

The following words are reserved and must not be used as identifiers:

and	**eq**	**gt**	**true**	**instanceof**
or	**ne**	**le**	**false**	**empty**
not	**lt**	**ge**	**null**	**div**	**mod**

The [ ] and . Operators

An EL expression can return any type. If an EL expression results in an object that has a property, you can use the **[]** or **.** operators to access the property. The **[]** and **.** operators function similarly; **[]** is a more generalized form, but **.** provides a nice shortcut.

To access an object's property, you use one of the following forms.

`${object["`*propertyName*`"]}`

```
${object.propertyName}
```

However, you can only use the **[]** operator] if *propertyName* is not a valid Java variable name. For instance, the following two EL expressions can be used to access the HTTP header **host** in the implicit object header.

```
${header["host"]}
${header.host}
```

However, to access the **accept-language** header, you can only use the **[]** operator because **accept-language** is not a legal Java variable name. Using the **.** operator to access it will cause an exception to be thrown.

   If an object's property happens to return another object that in turn has a property, you can use either **[]** or **.** to access the property of the second object. For example, the **pageContext** implicit object represents the **PageContext** object of the current JSP. It has the **request** property, which represents the **HttpServletRequest**. The **HttpServletRequest** has the **servletPath** property. The following expressions are equivalent and result in the value of the **servletPath** property of the **HttpServletRequest** in **pageContext**:

```
${pageContext["request"]["servletPath"]}
${pageContext.request["servletPath"]}
${pageContext.request.servletPath}
${pageContext["request"].servletPath}
```

To access the **HttpSession**, use this syntax:

```
${pageContext.session}
```

For example, this expression prints the session identifier.

```
${pageContext.session.id}
```

The Evaluation Rule

An EL expression is evaluated from left to right. For an expression of the form *expr-a*[*expr-b*], here is how the EL expression is evaluated:

   1. Evaluate *expr-a* to get *value-a*.
   2. If *value-a* is **null**, return **null**.

3. Evaluate *expr-b* to get *value-b*.
4. If *value-b* is **null**, return **null**.
5. If the type of *value-a* is **java.util.Map**, check whether *value-b* is a key in the **Map**. If it is, return *value-a*.**get**(*value-b*). If it is not, return **null**.
6. If the type of *value-a* is **java.util.List** or if it is an array, do the following:
   a. Coerce *value-b* to **int**. If coercion fails, throw an exception.
   b. If *value-a*.**get**(*value-b*) throws an **IndexOutOfBoundsException** or if **Array.get**(*value-a*, *value-b*) throws an **ArrayIndexOutOfBoundsException**, return **null**.
   c. Otherwise, return *value-a*.**get**(*value-b*) if *value-a* is a **List**, or return **Array.get**(*value-a*, *value-b*) if *value-a* is an array.
7. If *value-a* is not a **Map**, a **List**, or an array, *value-a* must be a JavaBean. In this case, coerce *value-b* to **String**. If *value-b* is a readable property of *value-a*, call the getter of the property and return the value from the getter method. If the getter method throws an exception, the expression is invalid. Otherwise, the expression is invalid.

Accessing JavaBeans

You can use either the **.** operator or the **[]** operator to access a bean's property. Here are the constructs:

```
${beanName["propertyName"]}
${beanName.propertyName}
```

For example, to access the property **secret** on a bean named **myBean**, use the following expression:

```
${myBean.secret}
```

Object	Description
pageContext	The **javax.servlet.jsp.PageContext** for the current JSP.
initParam	A **Map** containing all context initialization parameters with the parameter names as the keys.
param	A **Map** containing all request parameters with the parameters names as the keys. The value for each key is the first parameter value of the specified name. Therefore, if there are two request parameters with the same name, only the first can be retrieved using the **param** object. For accessing all parameter values that share the same name, use the **params** object instead.
paramValues	A **Map** containing all request parameters with the parameter names as the keys. The value for each key is an array of strings containing all the values for the specified parameter name. If the parameter has only one value, it still returns an array having one element.
header	A **Map** containing the request headers with the header names as the keys. The value for each key is the first header of the specified header name. In other words, if a header has more than one value, only the first value is returned. To obtain multi-value headers, use the **headerValues** object instead.
headerValues	A **Map** containing all request headers with the header names as the keys. The value for each key is an array of strings containing all the values for the specified header name. If the header has only one value, it returns a one-element array.
cookie	A **Map** containing all **Cookie** objects in the current request object. The cookies' names are the **Map**'s keys, and each key is mapped to a **Cookie** object.
applicationScope	A **Map** that contains all attributes in the **ServletContext** object with the attribute names as the keys.
sessionScope	A **Map** that contains all the attributes in the **HttpSession** object in which the attribute names are the keys.
requestScope	A **Map** that contains all the attributes in the current **HttpServletRequest** with the attribute names as the keys.
pageScope	A **Map** that contains all attributes with the page scope. The attributes' names are the keys of the **Map**.

Table 4.1: The EL Implicit Objects

If the property is an object that in turn has a property, you can access the property of the second object too, again using the **.** or **[]** operator. Or, if the property is a **Map**, a **List**, or an array, you can use the same rule explained in the preceding section to access the **Map**'s values or the members of the **List** or the element of the array.

EL Implicit Objects

From a JSP page you can use JSP scripts to access JSP implicit objects. However, from a script-free JSP page, it is impossible to access these implicit objects. The EL allows you to access various objects by providing a set of its own implicit objects. The EL implicit objects are listed in Table 4.1.

Each of the implicit objects is given in the following subsections.

pageContext

The **pageContext** object represents the **javax.servlet.jsp.PageContext** of the current JSP page. It contains all the other JSP implicit objects, which are given in Table 4.2.

Object	Type From the EL
request	javax.servlet.http.HttpServletRequest
response	javax.servlet.http.HttpServletResponse
out	javax.servlet.jsp.JspWriter
session	javax.servlet.http.HttpSession
application	javax.servlet.ServletContext
config	javax.servlet.ServletConfig
pageContext	javax.servlet.jsp.PageContext
page	javax.servlet.jsp.HttpJspPage
exception	java.lang.Throwable

Table 4.2: JSP Implicit Objects

For example, you can obtain the current **ServletRequest** using one of the following expressions:

```
${pageContext.request}
${pageContext["request"]}
```

And, the request method can be obtained using any of the following expressions:

```
${pageContext["request"]["method"]}
${pageContext["request"].method}
${pageContext.request["method"]}
${pageContext.request.method}
```

Request parameters are accessed more frequently than other implicit objects; therefore, two implicit objects, **param** and **paramValues**, are provided. The **param** and **paramValues** implicit objects are discussed in the sections "param" and "paramValues."

initParam

The **initParam** implicit object is used to retrieve the value of a context parameter. For example, to access the context parameter named password, you use the following expression:

```
${initParam.password}
```

or

```
${initParam["password"]}
```

param

The **param** implicit object is used to retrieve a request parameter. This object represents a **Map** containing all the request parameters. For example, to retrieve the parameter called **userName**, use one of the following:

```
${param.userName}
${param["userName"]}
```

paramValues

You use the **paramValues** implicit object to retrieve the values of a request parameter. This object represents a **Map** containing all request parameters with the parameter names as the keys. The value for each key is an array of strings containing all the values for the specified parameter name. If the parameter has only one value, it still returns an array having one element. For example, to obtain the first and second values of the **selectedOptions** parameter, you use the following expressions:

```
${paramValues.selectedOptions[0]}
${paramValues.selectedOptions[1]}
```

header

The **header** implicit object represents a **Map** that contains all request headers. To retrieve a header value, use the header name as the key. For example, to retrieve the value of the **accept-language** header, use the following expression:

```
${header["accept-language"]}
```

If the header name is a valid Java variable name, such as **connection**, you can also use the . operator:

```
${header.connection}
```

headerValues

The **headerValues** implicit object represents a **Map** containing all request headers with the header names as keys. Unlike **header**, however, the **Map** returned by the **headerValues** implicit object returns an array of strings. For example, to obtain the first value of the **accept-language** header, use this expression:

```
${headerValues["accept-language"][0]}
```

cookie

You use the **cookie** implicit object to retrieve a cookie. This object represents a **Map** containing all cookies in the current **HttpServletRequest**. For example, to retrieve the value of a cookie named **jsessionid**, use the following expression:

```
${cookie.jsessionid.value}
```

To obtain the path value of the **jsessionid** cookie, use this:

```
${cookie.jsessionid.path}
```

applicationScope, sessionScope, requestScope, and pageScope

You use the **applicationScope** implicit object to obtain the value of an application-scoped variable. For example, if you have an application-scoped variable called **myVar**, you may use this expression to access the attribute:

```
${applicationScope.myVar}
```

Note that in servlet/JSP programming a scoped object is an object placed as an attribute in any of the following objects: **PageContext**, **ServletRequest**, **HttpSession**, or **ServletContext**. The **sessionScope**, **requestScope**, and **pageScope** implicit objects are similar to **applicationScope**. However, the scopes are session, request, and page, respectively.

A scoped object can also be accessed in an EL expression without the scope. In this case, the JSP container will return the first identically named object in the **PageContext**, **ServletRequest**, **HttpSession**, or **ServletContext**. Searches are conducted starting from the narrowest scope (**PageContext**) to the widest (**ServletContext**). For example, the following expression will return the object referenced by **today** in any scope.

```
${today}
```

Using Other EL Operators

In addition to the **.** and **[]** operators, the EL also provides several other operators: arithmetic operators, relational operators, logical operators, the conditional operator, and the **empty** operator. Using these operators, you can perform various operations. However, because the aim of the EL is to facilitate the authoring of script-free JSP pages, these EL operators are of limited use, except for the conditional operator.

The EL operators are given in the following subsections.

Arithmetic Operators

There are five arithmetic operators:

- Addition (+)
- Subtraction (-)
- Multiplication (*)
- Division (/ and **div**)
- Remainder/modulo (**%** and **mod**)

The division and remainder operators have two forms, to be consistent with XPath and ECMAScript.

Note that an EL expression is evaluated from the highest to the lowest precedence, and then from left to right. The following are the arithmetic operators in the decreasing lower precedence:

* / div % mod
+ -

This means that *****, **/**, **div**, **%**, and **mod** operators have the same level of precedence, and + has the same precedence as - , but lower than the first group. Therefore, the expression

```
${1+2*3}
```

results in 7 and not 6.

Relational Operators

The following is the list of relational operators:

- equality (== and **eq**)
- non-equality (!= and **ne**)
- greater than (> and **gt**)
- greater than or equal to (>= and **ge**)
- less than (< and **lt**)
- less than or equal to (<= and **le**)

For instance, the expression **${3==4}** returns **false**, and **${"b"<"d"}** returns **true**.

Logical Operators

Here is the list of logical operators:

- AND (**&&** and **and**)
- OR (**||** and **or**)
- NOT (**!** and **not**)

The Conditional Operator

The EL conditional operator has the following syntax:

```
${statement? A:B}
```

If *statement* evaluates to **true**, the output of the expression is *A*. Otherwise, the output is *B*.

For example, you can use the following EL expression to test whether the **HttpSession** contains the attribute called **loggedIn**. If the attribute is found, the string "You have logged in" is displayed. Otherwise, "You have not logged in" is displayed.

```
${(sessionScope.loggedIn==null)? "You have not logged in" :
        "You have logged in"}
```

The empty Operator

The **empty** operator is used to examine whether a value is **null** or empty. The following is an example of the use of the **empty** operator:

```
${empty X}
```

If X is **null** or if X is a zero-length string, the expression returns **true**. It also returns **true** if X is an empty **Map**, an empty array, or an empty collection. Otherwise, it returns **false**.

Using the Expression Language

As an example, the **app04a** application features a JSP page that uses the EL to print the property of a JavaBean (**Address**, in Listing 4.1) inside another JavaBean (**Employee**, in Listing 4.2), the content of a **Map**, and an HTTP header as well as the session identifier. The **EmployeeServlet** servlet in Listing 4.3 creates the required objects and put them in the **ServletRequest**. The servlet then forwards to the **employee.jsp** page using a **RequestDispatcher**.

Listing 4.1: The Address class

```
package app04a.model;
public class Address {
    private String streetName;
    private String streetNumber;
    private String city;
    private String state;
    private String zipCode;
    private String country;

    public String getStreetName() {
        return streetName;
    }
    public void setStreetName(String streetName) {
        this.streetName = streetName;
    }
    public String getStreetNumber() {
        return streetNumber;
    }
    public void setStreetNumber(String streetNumber) {
```

```
        this.streetNumber = streetNumber;
    }
    public String getCity() {
        return city;
    }
    public void setCity(String city) {
        this.city = city;
    }
    public String getState() {
        return state;
    }
    public void setState(String state) {
        this.state = state;
    }
    public String getZipCode() {
        return zipCode;
    }
    public void setZipCode(String zipCode) {
        this.zipCode = zipCode;
    }
    public String getCountry() {
        return country;
    }
    public void setCountry(String country) {
        this.country = country;
    }
}
```

Listing 4.2: The Employee class

```
package app04a.model;
public class Employee {
    private int id;
    private String name;
    private Address address;

    public int getId() {
        return id;
    }
    public void setId(int id) {
        this.id = id;
    }
    public String getName() {
        return name;
    }
    public void setName(String name) {
```

```
            this.name = name;
    }
    public Address getAddress() {
        return address;
    }
    public void setAddress(Address address) {
        this.address = address;
    }
}
```

Listing 4.3: The EmployeeServlet class

```
package app04a.servlet;
import java.io.IOException;
import java.util.HashMap;
import java.util.Map;
import javax.servlet.RequestDispatcher;
import javax.servlet.ServletException;
import javax.servlet.annotation.WebServlet;
import javax.servlet.http.HttpServlet;
import javax.servlet.http.HttpServletRequest;
import javax.servlet.http.HttpServletResponse;
import app04a.model.Address;
import app04a.model.Employee;

@WebServlet(urlPatterns = {"/employee"})
public class EmployeeServlet extends HttpServlet {
    private static final int serialVersionUID = -5392874;
    @Override
    public void doGet(HttpServletRequest request,
            HttpServletResponse response)
            throws ServletException, IOException {
        Address address = new Address();
        address.setStreetName("Rue D'Anjou");
        address.setStreetNumber("5090B");
        address.setCity("Brossard");
        address.setState("Quebec");
        address.setZipCode("A1A B2B");
        address.setCountry("Canada");

        Employee employee = new Employee();
        employee.setId(1099);
        employee.setName("Charles Unjeye");
        employee.setAddress(address);
        request.setAttribute("employee", employee);
```

```
        Map<String, String> capitals = new HashMap<String,
                String>();
        capitals.put("China", "Beijing");
        capitals.put("Austria", "Vienna");
        capitals.put("Australia", "Canberra");
        capitals.put("Canada", "Ottawa");
        request.setAttribute("capitals", capitals);

        RequestDispatcher rd =
                request.getRequestDispatcher("/employee.jsp");
        rd.forward(request, response);
    }
}
```

Listing 4.4: The employee.jsp page

```
<html>
<head>
<title>Employee</title>
</head>
<body>
accept-language: ${header['accept-language']}
<br/>
session id: ${pageContext.session.id}
<br/>
employee: ${requestScope.employee.name}, ${employee.address.city}
<br/>
capital: ${capitals["Canada"]}
</body>
</html>
```

Note that in **app04a** the use of a servlet to contain Java code and a JSP page to display JavaBean properties and other values is in compliance with the recommended design of modern web applications, discussed further in Chapter 10, "Application Design."

Pay special attention to the EL expressions in the JSP page. The **employee** request-scoped object can be accessed with or without the implicit object **requestScope**.

```
employee: ${requestScope.employee.name}, ${employee.address.city}
```

You can test the application by invoking the **EmployeeServlet** with this URL:

```
http://localhost:8080/app04a/employee
```

Configuring the EL in JSP 2.0 and Later Versions

With the EL, JavaBeans, and custom tags, it is now possible to write script-free JSP pages. JSP 2.0 and later versions even provide a switch to disable scripting in all JSP pages. Software architects can now enforce the writing of script-free JSP pages.

On the other hand, in some circumstances you'll probably want to disable the EL in your applications. For example, you'll want to do so if you are using a JSP 2.0-compliant container but are not ready yet to upgrade to JSP 2.0. In this case, you can disable the evaluation of EL expressions.

This section discusses how to enforce script-free JSP pages and how to disable the EL in JSP 2.0 and later.

Achieving Script-Free JSP Pages

To disable scripting elements in JSP pages, use the **jsp-property-group** element with two subelements: **url-pattern** and **scripting-invalid**. The **url-pattern** element defines the URL pattern to which scripting disablement will apply. Here is how you disable scripting in all JSP pages in an application:

```
<jsp-config>
    <jsp-property-group>
        <url-pattern>*.jsp</url-pattern>
        <scripting-invalid>true</scripting-invalid>
    </jsp-property-group>
</jsp-config>
```

Note
There can be only one **jsp-config** element in the deployment descriptor. If you have specified a **jsp-property-group** for deactivating the EL, you must write your **jsp-property-group** for disabling scripting under the same **jsp-config** element.

Deactivating EL Evaluation

In some circumstances, such as when you need to deploy JSP 1.2 applications in a JSP 2.0 or later container, you may want to deactivate EL evaluation in a JSP page. When you do so, an occurrence of the EL construct will not be evaluated as an EL expression. There are two ways to deactivate EL evaluation in a JSP.

First, you can set the **isELIgnored** attribute of the **page** directive to **true**, such as in the following:

```
<%@ page isELIgnored="true" %>
```

The default value of the **isELIgnored** attribute is **false**. Using the **isELIgnored** attribute is recommended if you want to deactivate EL evaluation in one or a few JSP pages.

Second, you can use the **jsp-property-group** element in the deployment descriptor. The **jsp-property-group** element is a subelement of the **jsp-config** element. You use **jsp-property-group** to apply certain settings to a set of JSP pages in the application.

To use the **jsp-property-group** element to deactivate EL evaluation, you must have two subelements: **url-pattern** and **el-ignored**. The **url-pattern** element specifies the URL pattern to which EL deactivation will apply. The **el-ignored** element must be set to **true**.

As an example, here is how to deactivate EL evaluation in a JSP page named **noEl.jsp**.

```
<jsp-config>
    <jsp-property-group>
        <url-pattern>/noEl.jsp</url-pattern>
        <el-ignored>true</el-ignored>
    </jsp-property-group>
</jsp-config>
```

You can also deactivate the EL evaluation in all the JSP pages in an application by assigning ***.jsp** to the **url-pattern** element, as in the following:

```
<jsp-config>
    <jsp-property-group>
```

```
        <url-pattern>*.jsp</url-pattern>
        <el-ignored>true</el-ignored>
    </jsp-property-group>
</jsp-config>
```

EL evaluation in a JSP page will be deactivated if either the **isELIgnored** attribute of its **page** directive is set to **true** or its URL matches the pattern in the **jsp-property-group** element whose **el-ignored** subelement is set to **true**. For example, if you set the **page** directive's **isELIgnored** attribute of a JSP page to **false** but its URL matches the pattern of JSP pages whose EL evaluation must be deactivated in the deployment descriptor, EL evaluation of that page will be deactivated.

In addition, if you use the deployment descriptor that is compliant to Servlet 2.3 or earlier, the EL evaluation is already disabled by default, even though you are using a JSP 2.0 or later container.

Summary

The EL is one of the most important features in JSP 2.0 and later. It can help you write shorter and more effective JSP pages, as well as helping you author script-free pages. In this chapter you have seen how to use the EL to access JavaBeans and implicit objects. Additionally, you have seen how to use EL operators. In the last section of this chapter, you learned how to use EL-related application settings related in a JSP 2.0 and later container.

Chapter 5
JSTL

The JavaServer Pages Standard Tag Library (JSTL) is a collection of custom tag libraries for solving common problems such as iterating over a map or collection, conditional testing, XML processing, and even database access and data manipulation.

This chapter discusses the most important tags in JSTL, especially those for accessing scoped objects, iterating over a collection, and formatting numbers and dates. If you are interested to know more, a complete discussion of all JSTL tags can be found in the JSTL Specification document.

Downloading JSTL

JSTL is currently at version 1.2 and defined by the JSR-52 expert group under the Java Community Process (www.jcp.org). The implementation is available for download from java.net:

```
http://jstl.java.net
```

There are two pieces of software you need to download, the JSTL API and the JSTL implementation. The JSTL API contains the **javax.servlet.jsp.jstl** package, which consists of types defined in the JSTL specification. The JSTL implementation contains the implementation classes. You must copy both jar files to the **WEB-INF/lib** directory of every application utilizing JSTL.

JSTL Libraries

JSTL is referred to as the standard tag library; however, it exposes its actions through multiple tag libraries. The tags in JSTL 1.2 can be categorized into five areas, which are summarized in Table 5.1.

Area	Subfunction	URI	Prefix
Core	Variable Support	http://java.sun.com/jsp/jstl/core	c
	Flow Control		
	URL Management		
	Miscellaneous		
XML	Core	http://java.sun.com/jsp/jstl/xml	x
	Flow Control		
	Transformation		
I18n	Locale	http://java.sun.com/jsp/jstl/fmt	fmt
	Message formatting		
	Number and date formatting		
Database	SQL	http://java.sun.com/jsp/jstl/sql	sql
Functions	Collection length	http://java.sun.com/jsp/jstl/functions	fn
	String manipulation		

Table 5.1: JSTL Tag Libraries

To use a JSTL library in a JSP page, use the **taglib** directive with the following format:

```
<%@ taglib uri="uri" prefix="prefix" %>
```

For instance, to use the Core library, declare this at the beginning of the JSP page:

```
<%@ taglib uri="http://java.sun.com/jsp/jstl/core" prefix="c" %>
```

The prefix can be anything. However, using the convention makes your code look more familiar to the other developers in your team and others who later join the project. It is therefore recommended to use the prescribed prefixes.

Note
Each of the tags discussed in this chapter is presented in its own section and the attributes for each tag are listed in a table. An asterisk (*) following an attribute name indicates that the attribute is required. A plus sign (+) indicates the value of the **rtexprvalue** element for that attribute is **true**, which means the attribute can be assigned a static string or a dynamic value (a Java expression, an Expression Language expression, or a value set by a **<jsp:attribute>**). A value of **false** for **rtexprvalue** means that the attribute can only be assigned a static string only.

Note
The body content of a JSTL tag can be empty, JSP, or tagdependent.

General-Purpose Actions

The following section discusses three general-purpose actions in the Core library used for manipulating scoped variables: **out**, **set**, **remove**.

The out Tag

The **out** tag evaluates an expression and outputs the result to the current **JspWriter**. The syntax for **out** has two forms, with and without a body content:

```
<c:out value="value" [escapeXml="{true|false}"]
        [default="defaultValue"]/>

<c:out value="value" [escapeXml="{true|false}"]>
    default value
</c:out>
```

Note
In a tag's syntax, [ ] indicates optional attributes. The underlined value, if any, indicates the default value.

The body content for **out** is JSP. The list of the tag's attributes is given in Table 5.2.

Attribute	Type	Description
value*+	Object	The expression to be evaluated.
escapeXml+	boolean	Indicates whether the characters <, >, &, ', and " in the result will be converted to the corresponding character entity codes, i.e. < to <, etc.
default+	Object	The default value

Table 5.2: The out tag's attributes

For example, the following **out** tag prints the value of the scoped variable **x**:

```
<c:out value="${x}"/>
```

By default, **out** encodes the special characters <, >, ', ", and **&** to their corresponding character entity codes **<**, **>**, **'**, **"**, and **&**, respectively.

Prior to JSP 2.0, the **out** tag was the easiest way to print the value of a scoped object. In JSP 2.0 or later, unless you need to XML-escape a value, you can safely use an EL expression:

```
${x}
```

Warning

If a string containing one or more special characters is not XML escaped, its value may not be rendered correctly in the browser. On top of that, unescaped special characters will make your web site susceptible to cross-site scripting attacks, i.e. someone can post a JavaScript function/expression that will be automatically executed.

The **default** attribute in **out** lets you assign a default value that will be displayed if the EL expression assigned to its **value** attribute returns **null**. The **default** attribute may be assigned a dynamic value. If this dynamic value returns **null**, the **out** tag will display an empty string.

For example, in the following **out** tag, if the variable **myVar** is not found in the **HttpSession**, the value of the application-scoped variable **myVar** is displayed. If the latter is also not found, an empty string is sent to the output.

```
<c:out value="${sessionScope.myVar}"
        default="${applicationScope.myVar}"/>
```

The set Tag

You can use the **set** tag to do the following.

1. Create a string and a scoped variable that references the string.
2. Create a scoped variable that references an existing scoped object.
3. Set the property of a scoped object.

If **set** is used to create a scoped variable, the variable can be used throughout the same JSP page after the occurrence of the tag.

The **set** tag's syntax has four forms. The first form is used to create a scoped variable in which the **value** attribute specifies the string to be created or an existing scoped object.

```
<c:set value="value"  var="varName"
        [scope="{page|request|session|application}"]/>
```

where the **scope** attribute specifies the scope of the scoped variable.

For instance, the following **set** tag creates the string "The wisest fool" and assigns it to the newly created page-scoped variable **foo**.

```
<c:set var="foo" value="The wisest fool"/>
```

The following **set** tag creates a scoped variable named **job** that references the request-scoped object **position**. The variable **job** has a **page** scope.

```
<c:set var="job" value="${requestScope.position}" scope="page"/>
```

Note
The last example might be a bit confusing because it created a page-scoped variable that references a request-scoped object. This should not be so if you bear in mind that the scoped object itself is not really "inside" the **HttpServletRequest**. Instead, a reference (named **position**) exists that references the object. With the **set** tag in the last example, you were simply creating another scoped variable (**job**) that referenced the same object.

The second form is similar to the first form, except that the string to be created or the scoped object to be referenced is passed as the body content.

```
<c:set var="varName" [scope="{page|request|session|application}"]>
    body content
</c:set>
```

The second form allows you to have JSP code in the body content.

The third form sets the value of a scoped object's property. The **target** attribute specifies the scoped object and the **property** attribute the scoped object's property. The value to assign to the property is specified by the **value** attribute.

```
<c:set target="target" property="propertyName" value="value"/>
```

For example, the following **set** tag assigns the string "Tokyo" to the **city** property of the scoped object **address**.

```
<c:set target="${address}" property="city" value="Tokyo"/>
```

Note that you must use an EL expression in the **target** attribute to reference the scoped object.

The fourth form is similar to the third form, but the value to assign is passed as body content.

```
<c:set target="target" property="propertyName">
    body content
</c:set>
```

Attribute	Type	Description
value+	Object	The string to be created, or the scoped object to reference, or the new property value.
var	String	The scoped variable to be created.
scope	String	The scope of the newly created scoped variable.
target+	Object	The scoped object whose property will be assigned a new value; this must be a JavaBeans instance or a **java.util.Map** object.
property+	String	The name of the property to be assigned a new value.

Table 5.3: The set tag's attributes

For example, the following **set** tag assigns the string "Beijing" to the **city** property of the scoped object **address**.

```
<c:set target="${address}" property="city">Beijing</c:set>
```

The list of the **set** tag's attributes is given in Table 5.3.

The remove Tag

You use the **remove** tag to remove a scoped variable. The syntax is as follows:

```
<c:remove var="varName"
          [scope="{page|request|session|application}"]/>
```

Note that the object referenced by the scoped variable is not removed. Therefore, if another scoped variable is also referencing the same object, you can still access the object through the other scoped variable.

The list of the **remove** tag's attributes is given in Table 5.4.

Attribute	Type	Description
var	String	The name of the scoped variable to remove.
scope	String	The scope of the scoped variable to be removed

Table 5.4: The remove tag's attributes

As an example, the following **remove** tag removes the page-scoped variable **job**.

```
<c:remove var="job" scope="page"/>
```

Conditional Actions

Conditional actions are used to deal with situations in which the output of a page depends on the value of certain input, which in Java are solved using **if, if ... else**, and **switch** statements.

There are four tags that perform conditional actions in JSTL: **if, choose, when**, and **otherwise**. Each will be discussed in a section below.

The if Tag

The **if** tag tests a condition and processes its body content if the condition evaluates to **true**. The test result is stored in a **Boolean** object, and a scoped variable is created to reference the **Boolean** object. You specify the name of the scoped variable using the **var** attribute and the scope in the **scope** attribute.

The syntax of **if** has two forms. The first form has no body content:

```
<c:if test="testCondition" var="varName"
        [scope="{page|request|session|application}"]/>
```

In this case, normally the scoped object specified by **var** will be tested by some other tag at a later stage in the same JSP.

The second form is used with a body content:

```
<c:if test="testCondition [var="varName"]
        [scope="{page|request|session|application}"]>
    body content
</c:if>
```

The body content is JSP and will be processed if the test condition evaluates to **true**. The list of the **if** tag's attributes is given in Table 5.5.

Attribute	Type	Description
test+	Boolean	The test condition that determines whether any existing body content should be processed
var	String	The name of the scoped variable that references the value of the test condition; the type of **var** is **Boolean**
scope	String	The scope of the scoped variable specified by **var**.

Table 5.5: The if tag's attributes

For example, the following **if** tag displays "You logged in successfully" if there exists a request parameter named **user** and its value is **ken** and there exists a request parameter named **password** and its value is **blackcomb**:

```
<c:if test="${param.user=='ken' && param.password=='blackcomb'}">
    You logged in successfully.
</c:if>
```

To simulate an **else**, use two **if** tags with conditions that are opposite. For instance, the following snippet displays "You logged in successfully" if the **user** and **password** parameters are **ken** and **blackcomb**, respectively. Otherwise, it displays "Login failed".

```
<c:if test="${param.user=='ken' && param.password=='blackcomb'}">
    You logged in successfully.
</c:if>
<c:if test="${!(param.user=='ken' && param.password=='blackcomb')}">
    Login failed.
</c:if>
```

The following **if** tag tests whether the **user** and **password** parameters are **ken** and **blackcomb**, respectively, and stores the result in the page-scoped variable **loggedIn**. You then use an EL expression to display "You logged in successfully" if the **loggedIn** variable is **true** or "Login failed" if the **loggedIn** variable is **false**.

```
<c:if var="loggedIn"
        test="${param.user=='ken' && param.password=='blackcomb'}"/>
    ...
${(loggedIn)? "You logged in successfully" : "Login failed"}
```

The choose, when and otherwise Tags

The **choose** and **when** tags act similarly to the **switch** and **case** keywords in Java, that is, they are used to provide the context for mutually exclusive conditional execution. The **choose** tag must have one or more **when** tags nested inside it, and each **when** tag represents a case that can be evaluated and processed. The **otherwise** tag is used for a default conditional block that will be processed if none of the **when** tags' test conditions evaluates to **true**. If present, **otherwise** must appear after the last **when**.

choose and **otherwise** do not have attributes. **when** must have the **test** attribute specifying the test condition that determines whether the body content should be processed.

As an example, the following code tests the value of a parameter called **status**. If the value of **status** is **full**, it displays "You are a full member". If the value is **student**, it displays "You are a student member". If the parameter **status** does not exist or if its value is neither **full** nor **student**, the code displays nothing.

```
<c:choose>
    <c:when test="${param.status=='full'}">
        You are a full member
    </c:when>
    <c:when test="${param.status=='student'}">
        You are a student member
    </c:when>
</c:choose>
```

The following example is similar to the preceding one, but it uses the **otherwise** tag to display "Please register" if the **status** parameter does not exist or if its value is not **full** or **student**:

```
<c:choose>
    <c:when test="${param.status=='full'}">
        You are a full member
    </c:when>
    <c:when test="${param.status=='student'}">
        You are a student member
    </c:when>
    <c:otherwise>
        Please register
    </c:otherwise>
</c:choose>
```

Iterator Actions

Iterator actions are useful when you need to iterate a number of times or over a collection of objects. JSTL provides two tags that perform iterator actions, **forEach** and **forTokens**, both of which are discussed in the following sections.

The forEach Tag

forEach iterates a body content a number of times or iterates over a collection of objects. Objects that can be iterated over include all implementations of **java.util.Collection** and **java.util.Map**, and arrays of objects or primitive types. You can also iterate over a **java.util.Iterator** and **java.util.Enumeration**, but you should not use **Iterator** or **Enumeration** in more than one action because neither **Iterator** nor **Enumeration** will be reset.

Attribute	Type	Description
var	String	The name of the scoped variable that references the current item of the iteration.
items+	Any of the supported type.	Collections of objects to iterate over.
varStatus	String	The name of the scoped variable that holds the status of the iteration. The value is of type **javax.servlet.jsp.jstl.core.LoopTagStatus**.
begin+	int	If **items** is specified, iteration begins at the item located at the specified index, in which the first item of the collection has an index of 0. If **items** is not specified, iteration begins with the index set at the value specified. If specified, the value of **begin** must be equal to or greater than zero.
end+	int	If **items** is specified, iteration ends at the item located at the specified index (inclusive). If **items** is not specified, iteration ends when index reaches the value specified.
step+	int	Iteration will process only every **step** items of the collection, starting with the first one. If present, the value of step must be equal to or greater than 1.

Table 5.6: The forEach Tag's attributes

The syntax for **forEach** has two forms. The first form is for repeating the body content a fixed number of times:

```
<c:forEach [var="varName"] begin="begin" end="end" step="step">
    body content
</c:forEach>
```

The second form is used to iterate over a collection of objects:

```
<c:forEach items="collection" [var="varName"]
        [varStatus="varStatusName"] [begin="begin"] [end="end"]
        [step="step"]>
```

```
    body content
</c:forEach>
```

The body content is JSP. The **forEach** tag's attributes are given in Table 5.6.

For example, the following **forEach** tag displays "1, 2, 3, 4, 5".

```
<c:forEach var="x" begin="1" end="5">
    <c:out value="${x}"/>,
</c:forEach>
```

And, the following **forEach** tag iterates over the **phones** property of an **address** scoped variable.

```
<c:forEach var="phone" items="${address.phones}">
    ${phone}"<br/>
</c:forEach>
```

For each iteration, the **forEach** tag creates a scoped variable whose name is specified by the **var** attribute. In this case, the scoped variable is named **phone**. The EL expression within the **forEach** tag is used to display the value of **phone**. The scoped variable is only available from within the beginning and closing **forEach** tags, and will be removed right before the closing **forEach** tag.

The **forEach** tag has a **varStatus** variable of type **javax.servlet.jsp.jstl.core.LoopTagStatus**. The **LoopTagStatus** interface has the **count** property that returns the "count" of the current round of iteration. The value of **status.count** is 1 for the first iteration, 2 for the second iteration, and so on. By testing the remainder of **status.count%2**, you know whether the tag is processing an even-numbered or odd-numbered element.

As an example, consider the **BooksServlet** servlet and **books.jsp** page in the **app05a** application. The **BooksServlet** class, presented in Listing 5.1, creates three **Book** objects in its **doGet** method and puts the **Book**s in a **List** that is then stored as a **ServletRequest** attribute. The **Book** class is given in Listing 5.2. At the end of the **doGet** method, the servlet forwards to the **books.jsp** page that iterates over the book collection using the **forEach** tag.

Listing 5.1: The BooksServlet class

```
package app05a.servlet;
import java.io.IOException;
import java.util.ArrayList;
import java.util.List;
import javax.servlet.RequestDispatcher;
import javax.servlet.ServletException;
import javax.servlet.annotation.WebServlet;
import javax.servlet.http.HttpServlet;
import javax.servlet.http.HttpServletRequest;
import javax.servlet.http.HttpServletResponse;
import app05a.model.Book;

@WebServlet(urlPatterns = {"/books"})
public class BooksServlet extends HttpServlet {
    private static final int serialVersionUID = -234237;
    @Override
    public void doGet(HttpServletRequest request,
            HttpServletResponse response) throws ServletException,
            IOException {

        List<Book> books = new ArrayList<Book>();
        Book book1 = new Book("978-0980839616",
                "Java 7: A Beginner's Tutorial", 45.00);
        Book book2 = new Book("978-0980331608",
                "Struts 2 Design and Programming: A Tutorial",
                49.95);
        Book book3 = new Book("978-0975212820",
                "Dimensional Data Warehousing with MySQL: A "
                + "Tutorial", 39.95);
        books.add(book1);
        books.add(book2);
        books.add(book3);
        request.setAttribute("books", books);
        RequestDispatcher rd =
                request.getRequestDispatcher("/books.jsp");
        rd.forward(request, response);
    }
}
```

Listing 5.2: The Book class

```
package app05a.model;
public class Book {
    private String isbn;
```

```
    private String title;
    private double price;

    public Book(String isbn, String title, double price) {
        this.isbn = isbn;
        this.title = title;
        this.price = price;
    }

    public String getIsbn() {
        return isbn;
    }
    public void setIsbn(String isbn) {
        this.isbn = isbn;
    }
    public String getTitle() {
        return title;
    }
    public void setTitle(String title) {
        this.title = title;
    }
    public double getPrice() {
        return price;
    }
    public void setPrice(double price) {
        this.price = price;
    }
}
```

Listing 5.3: The books.jsp page

```jsp
<%@ taglib uri="http://java.sun.com/jsp/jstl/core" prefix="c" %>
<html>
<head>
<title>Book List</title>
<style>
table, tr, td {
    border: 1px solid brown;
}
</style>
</head>
<body>
Books in Simple Table
<table>
    <tr>
        <td>ISBN</td>
```

```
        <td>Title</td>
    </tr>
    <c:forEach items="${requestScope.books}" var="book">
    <tr>
        <td>${book.isbn}</td>
        <td>${book.title}</td>
    </tr>
    </c:forEach>
</table>
<br/>
Books in Styled Table
<table>
    <tr style="background:#ababff">
        <td>ISBN</td>
        <td>Title</td>
    </tr>
    <c:forEach items="${requestScope.books}" var="book"
            varStatus="status">
        <c:if test="${status.count%2 == 0}">
            <tr style="background:#eeeeff">
        </c:if>
        <c:if test="${status.count%2 != 0}">
            <tr style="background:#dedeff">
        </c:if>
        <td>${book.isbn}</td>
        <td>${book.title}</td>
    </tr>
    </c:forEach>
</table>

<br/>
ISBNs only:
    <c:forEach items="${requestScope.books}" var="book"
            varStatus="status">
        ${book.isbn}<c:if test="${!status.last}">,</c:if>
    </c:forEach>
</body>
</html>
```

Note that the **books.jsp** page displays the books three times, the first one using **forEach** without the **varStatus** attribute.

```
<table>
    <tr>
        <td>ISBN</td>
```

```
        <td>Title</td>
    </tr>
    <c:forEach items="${requestScope.books}" var="book">
    <tr>
        <td>${book.isbn}</td>
        <td>${book.title}</td>
    </tr>
    </c:forEach>
</table>
```

The second time the books are displayed using **forEach** with the **varStatus** attribute in order to give the table rows different colors depending whether a row is an even-numbered row or an odd-numbered row.

```
<table>
    <tr style="background:#ababff">
        <td>ISBN</td>
        <td>Title</td>
    </tr>
    <c:forEach items="${requestScope.books}" var="book"
            varStatus="status">
        <c:if test="${status.count%2 == 0}">
            <tr style="background:#eeeeff">
        </c:if>
        <c:if test="${status.count%2 != 0}">
            <tr style="background:#dedeff">
        </c:if>
        <td>${book.isbn}</td>
        <td>${book.title}</td>
    </tr>
    </c:forEach>
</table>
```

The third **forEach** is used to display the ISBNs in comma-delimited format. The use of **status.last** makes sure that a comma is not rendered after the last element.

```
    <c:forEach items="${requestScope.books}" var="book"
            varStatus="status">
        ${book.isbn}<c:if test="${!status.last}">,</c:if>
    </c:forEach>
```

You can test the example by using this URL:

```
http://localhost:8080/app05/books
```

The output should be similar to the screen shot in Figure 5.1. (Pardon my horrible choice of colors.)

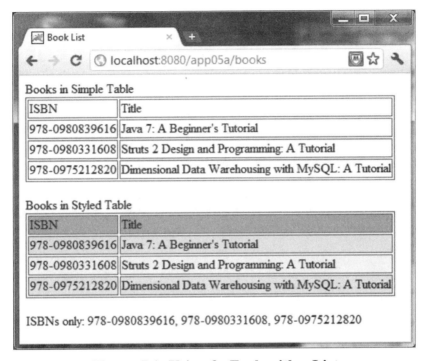

Figure 5.1: Using forEach with a List

You can also use **forEach** to iterate over a map. You refer to a map key and a map value using the **key** and **value** properties, respectively. The pseudocode for iterating over a map is as follows.

```
<c:forEach var="mapItem" items="map">
    ${mapItem.key} : ${mapItem.value}
</c:forEach>
```

The next example illustrates the use of **forEach** with a **Map**. The **BigCitiesServlet** servlet in Listing 5.4 instantiates two **Maps** and populates them with key/value pairs. Each element in the first **Map** is a **String/String** pair and each element in the second **Map** a **String/String[]** pair.

Listing 5.4: The BigCitiesServlet class

```
package app05a.servlet;
```

```
import java.io.IOException;
import java.util.Collections;
import java.util.HashMap;
import java.util.List;
import java.util.Map;
import javax.servlet.RequestDispatcher;
import javax.servlet.ServletException;
import javax.servlet.annotation.WebServlet;
import javax.servlet.http.HttpServlet;
import javax.servlet.http.HttpServletRequest;
import javax.servlet.http.HttpServletResponse;

@WebServlet(urlPatterns = {"/bigCities"})
public class BigCitiesServlet extends HttpServlet {
    private static final int serialVersionUID = 112233;
    @Override
    public void doGet(HttpServletRequest request,
      HttpServletResponse response) throws ServletException,
      IOException {

        Map<String, String> capitals =
                new HashMap<String, String>();
        capitals.put("Indonesia", "Jakarta");
        capitals.put("Malaysia", "Kuala Lumpur");
        capitals.put("Thailand", "Bangkok");
        request.setAttribute("capitals", capitals);


        Map<String, String[]> bigCities =
                new HashMap<String, String[]>();
        bigCities.put("Australia", new String[] {"Sydney",
                "Melbourne", "Perth"});
        bigCities.put("New Zealand", new String[] {"Auckland",
                "Christchurch", "Wellington"});
        bigCities.put("Indonesia", new String[] {"Jakarta",
                "Surabaya", "Medan"});

        request.setAttribute("capitals", capitals);
        request.setAttribute("bigCities", bigCities);
        RequestDispatcher rd =
                request.getRequestDispatcher("/bigCities.jsp");
        rd.forward(request, response);
    }
}
```

At the end of the **doGet** method, the servlet forwards to the **bigCities.jsp** page, which uses **forEach** to iterate over the **Map**s. The **bigCities.jsp** is given in Listing 5.5.

Listing 5.5: The bigCities.jsp page

```
<%@ taglib uri="http://java.sun.com/jsp/jstl/core" prefix="c" %>
<html>
<head>
<title>Big Cities</title>
<style>
table, tr, td {
    border: 1px solid #aaee77;
    padding: 3px;
}
</style>
</head>
<body>
Capitals
<table>
    <tr style="background:#448755;color:white;font-weight:bold">
        <td>Country</td>
        <td>Capital</td>
    </tr>
    <c:forEach items="${requestScope.capitals}" var="mapItem">
    <tr>
        <td>${mapItem.key}</td>
        <td>${mapItem.value}</td>
    </tr>
    </c:forEach>
</table>
<br/>
Big Cities
<table>
    <tr style="background:#448755;color:white;font-weight:bold">
        <td>Country</td>
        <td>Cities</td>
    </tr>
    <c:forEach items="${requestScope.bigCities}" var="mapItem">
    <tr>
        <td>${mapItem.key}</td>
        <td>
            <c:forEach items="${mapItem.value}" var="city"
                    varStatus="status">
                ${city}<c:if test="${!status.last}">,</c:if>
```

```
            </c:forEach>
        </td>
    </tr>
    </c:forEach>
</table>
</body>
</html>
```

Of special importance is the second **forEach** that nests another **forEach**:

```
<c:forEach items="${requestScope.bigCities}" var="mapItem">
        <c:forEach items="${mapItem.value}" var="city"
                    varStatus="status">
            ${city}<c:if test="${!status.last}">,</c:if>
        </c:forEach>
    </c:forEach>
```

Here the second **forEach** iterates over the **Map**'s element value, which is a **String** array.

You can test the example by directing your browser here:

```
http://localhost:8080/app05a/bigCities
```

Your browser should display several capitals and big cities in HTML tables like the ones in Figure 5.2.

Figure 5.2: forEach with Map

The forTokens Tag

You use the **forTokens** tag to iterate over tokens that are separated by the specified delimiters. The syntax for this action is as follows:

```
<c:forTokens items="stringOfTokens" delims="delimiters"
        [var="varName"] [varStatus="varStatusName"]
        [begin="begin"] [end="end"] [step="step"]
>
    body content
</c:forTokens>
```

The body content is JSP. The list of the **forTokens** tag's attributes is given in Table 5.7.

Attribute	Type	Description
var	String	The name of the scoped variable that references the current item of the iteration.
items+	String	The string of tokens to iterate over.
varStatus	String	The name of the scoped variable that holds the status of the iteration. The value is of type **javax.servlet.jsp.jstl.core.LoopTagStatus**.
begin+	int	The start index of the iteration, where index is zero-based. If specified, **begin** must be 0 or greater.
end+	int	The end index of the iteration, where index is zero-based.
step+	int	Iteration will process only every **step** tokens of the string, starting with the first one. If specified, **step** must be 1 or greater.
delims+	String	The set of delimiters.

Table 5.7: The forTokens tag's attributes

Here is an example of **forTokens**:

```
<c:forTokens var="item" items="Argentina,Brazil,Chile" delims=",">
    <c:out value="${item}"/><br/>
</c:forTokens>
```

When pasted in a JSP, the preceding **forTokens** will result in the following:

```
Argentina
Brazil
```

```
Chile
```

Formatting Actions

JSTL provides tags for formatting and parsing numbers and dates. The tags are **formatNumber**, **formatDate**, **timeZone**, **setTimeZone**, **parseNumber**, and **parseDate**. These tags are discussed in the sections to follow.

The formatNumber Tag

You use **formatNumber** to format numbers. This tag gives you the flexibility of using its various attributes to get a format that suits your need. The syntax of **formatNumber** has two forms. The first is used without a body content:

```
<fmt:formatNumber value="numericValue"
        [type="{number|currency|percent}"]
        [pattern="customPattern"]
        [currencyCode="currencyCode"]
        [currencySymbol="currencySymbol"]
        [groupingUsed="{true|false}"]
        [maxIntegerDigits="maxIntegerDigits"]
        [minIntegerDigits="minIntegerDigits"]
        [maxFractionDigits="maxFractionDigits"]
        [minFractionDigits="minFractionDigits"]
        [var="varName"]
        [scope="{page|request|session|application}"]
/>
```

The second form is used with a body content:

```
<fmt:formatNumber [type="{number|currency|percent}"]
        [pattern="customPattern"]
        [currencyCode="currencyCode"]
        [currencySymbol="currencySymbol"]
        [groupingUsed="{true|false}"]
        [maxIntegerDigits="maxIntegerDigits"]
        [minIntegerDigits="minIntegerDigits"]
        [maxFractionDigits="maxFractionDigits"]
        [minFractionDigits="minFractionDigits"]
```

```
    [var="varName"]
    [scope="{page|request|session|application}"]>
  numeric value to be formatted
</fmt:formatNumber>
```

The body content is JSP. The **formatNumber** tag's attributes are given in Table 5.8.

Attribute	Type	Description
value+	String or Number	Numeric value to be formatted.
type+	String	Indicates whether the value is to be formatted as number, currency, or percentage. The value of this attribute is one of the following: **number**, **currency**, **percent**.
pattern+	String	Custom formatting pattern.
currencyCode+	String	ISO 4217 code. See Table 5.9.
currencySymbol+	String	Currency symbol.
groupingUsed+	Boolean	Indicates whether the output will contain grouping separators.
maxIntegerDigits+	int	The maximum number of digits in the integer portion of the output.
minIntegerDigits+	int	The minimum number of digits in the integer portion of the output.
maxFractionDigits+	int	The maximum number of digits in the fractional portion of the output.
minFractionDigits+	int	The minimum number of digits in the fractional portion of the output.
var	String	The name of the scoped variable to store the output as a String.
scope	String	The scope of **var**. If the **scope** attribute is present, the **var** attribute must be specified.

Table 5.8: The formatNumber tag's attributes

One of the uses of **formatNumber** is to format numbers as currencies. For this, you can use the **currencyCode** attribute to specify an ISO 4217 currency code. Some of the codes are given in Table 5.9.

Currency	ISO 4217 Code	Major Unit Name	Minor Unit Name
Canadian Dollar	CAD	dollar	cent
Chinese Yuan	CNY	yuan	jiao
Euro	EUR	euro	euro-cent
Japanese Yen	JPY	yen	sen
Sterling	GBP	pound	pence
US Dollar	USD	dollar	cent

Table 5.9: ISO 4217 Currency Codes

The examples of how to use **formatNumber** are given in Table 5.10.

Action	Result
<fmt:formatNumber value="12" type="number"/>	12
<fmt:formatNumber value="12" type="number" minIntegerDigits="3"/>	012
<fmt:formatNumber value="12" type="number" minFractionDigits="2"/>	12.00
<fmt:formatNumber value="123456.78" pattern=".000"/>	123456.780
<fmt:formatNumber value="123456.78" pattern="#,#00.0#"/>	123,456.78
<fmt:formatNumber value="12" type="currency"/>	$12.00
<fmt:formatNumber value="12" type="currency" currencyCode="GBP"/>	GBP 12.00
<fmt:formatNumber value="0.12" type="percent"/>	12%
<fmt:formatNumber value="0.125" type="percent" minFractionDigits="2"/>	12.50%

Table 5.10: Using the formatNumber tag

Note that when formatting currencies, if the **currencyCode** attribute is not specified, the browser's locale is used.

The formatDate Tag

You use the **formatDate** tag to format dates. The syntax is as follows:

```
<fmt:formatDate value="date"
        [type="{time|date|both}"]
        [dateStyle="{default|short|medium|long|full}"]
        [timeStyle="{default|short|medium|long|full}"]
        [pattern="customPattern"]
```

```
        [timeZone="timeZone"]
        [var="varName"]
        [scope="{page|request|session|application}"]
/>
```

The body content is JSP. The **formatDate** tag's attributes are given in Table 5.11.

Attribute	Type	Description
value+	java.util.Date	Date and/or time to be formatted
type+	String	Indicates whether the time, the date, or both the time and the date components are to be formatted
dateStyle+	String	Predefined formatting style for dates that follows the semantics defined in **java.text.DateFormat**.
timeStyle+	String	Predefined formatting style for times that follows the semantics defined in **java.text.DateFormat**.
pattern+	String	The custom pattern for formatting
timezone+	String or **java.util.TimeZone**	The time in which to represent the time
var	String	The name of the scoped variable to store the result as a string
scope	String	Scope of **var**.

Table 5.11: The formatDate tag's attributes

For possible values of the **timeZone** attribute, see the section, "The timeZone Tag".

The following code uses the **formatDate** tag to format the **java.util.Date** object referenced by the scoped variable **now**.

```
Default: <fmt:formatDate value="${now}"/>
Short: <fmt:formatDate value="${now}" dateStyle="short"/>
Medium: <fmt:formatDate value="${now}" dateStyle="medium"/>
Long: <fmt:formatDate value="${now}" dateStyle="long"/>
Full: <fmt:formatDate value="${now}" dateStyle="full"/>
```

The following **formatDate** tags are used to format times.

```
Default: <fmt:formatDate type="time" value="${now}"/>
```

```
Short: <fmt:formatDate type="time" value="${now}"
       timeStyle="short"/>
Medium: <fmt:formatDate type="time" value="${now}"
       timeStyle="medium"/>
Long: <fmt:formatDate type="time" value="${now}" timeStyle="long"/>
Full: <fmt:formatDate type="time" value="${now}" timeStyle="full"/>
```

The following **formatDate** tags format both dates and times.

```
Default: <fmt:formatDate type="both" value="${now}"/>
Short date short time: <fmt:formatDate type="both"
  value="${now}" dateStyle="short" timeStyle="short"/>
Long date long time format: <fmt:formatDate type="both"
  value="${now}" dateStyle="long" timeStyle="long"/>
```

The following **formatDate** tags are used to format times with time zones.

```
Time zone CT: <fmt:formatDate type="time" value="${now}"
       timeZone="CT"/><br/>
Time zone HST: <fmt:formatDate type="time" value="${now}"
       timeZone="HST"/><br/>
```

The following **formatDate** tags are used to format dates and times using custom patterns.

```
<fmt:formatDate type="both" value="${now}" pattern="dd.MM.yy"/>
<fmt:formatDate type="both" value="${now}" pattern="dd.MM.yyyy"/>
```

The timeZone Tag

The **timeZone** tag is used to specify the time zone in which time information is to be formatted or parsed in its body content. The syntax is as follows:

```
<fmt:timeZone value="timeZone">
    body content
</fmt:timeZone>
```

The body content is JSP. The attribute value can be passed a dynamic value of type **String** or **java.util.TimeZone**. The values for US and Canada time zones are given in Table 5.12.

If the **value** attribute is **null** or empty, the GMT time zone is used.

The following example uses the **timeZone** tag to format dates with time zones.

```
<fmt:timeZone value="GMT+1:00">
    <fmt:formatDate value="${now}" type="both"
            dateStyle="full" timeStyle="full"/>
</fmt:timeZone>
<fmt:timeZone value="HST">
    <fmt:formatDate value="${now}" type="both"
            dateStyle="full" timeStyle="full"/>
</fmt:timeZone>
<fmt:timeZone value="CST">
    <fmt:formatDate value="${now}" type="both"
            dateStyle="full" timeStyle="full"/>
</fmt:timeZone>
```

Abbreviation	Full Name	Time Zone
NST	Newfoundland Standard Time	UTC-3:30 hours
NDT	Newfoundland Daylight Time	UTC-2:30 hours
AST	Atlantic Standard Time	UTC-4 hours
ADT	Atlantic Daylight Time	UTC-3 hours
EST	Eastern Standard Time	UTC-5 hours
EDT	Eastern Daylight Saving Time	UTC-4 hours
ET	Eastern Time, as EST or EDT	*
CST	Central Standard Time	UTC-6 hours
CDT	Central Daylight Saving Time	UTC-5 hours
CT	Central Time, as either CST or CDT	*
MST	Mountain Standard Time	UTC-7 hours
MDT	Mountain Daylight Saving Time	UTC-6 hours
MT	Mountain Time, as either MST or MDT	*
PST	Pacific Standard Time	UTC-8 hours
PDT	Pacific Daylight Saving Time	UTC-7 hours
PT	Pacific Time, as either PST or PDT	*
AKST	Alaska Standard Time	UTC-9 hours
AKDT	Alaska Standard Daylight Saving Time	UTC-8 hours
HST	Hawaiian Standard Time	UTC-10 hours

Table 5.12: US and Canada Time Zones

The setTimeZone Tag

You use the **setTimeZone** tag to store the specified time zone in a scoped variable or the time configuration variable. The syntax of **setTimeZone** is as follows:

```
<fmt:setTimeZone value="timeZone" [var="varName"]
        [scope="{page|request|session|application}"]
/>
```

Table 5.13 presents the **setTimeZone** tag's attributes.

Attribute	Type	Description
value+	**String** or **java.util.TimeZone**	The time zone
var	String	The name of the scoped variable to hold the time zone of type **java.util.TimeZone**
scope	String	The scope of **var** or the time zone configuration variable

Table 5.13: The setTimeZone tag's attributes

The parseNumber Tag

You use **parseNumber** to parse a string representation of a number, a currency, or a percentage in a locale-sensitive format into a number. The syntax has two forms. The first form is used without body content:

```
<fmt:parseNumber value="numericValue"
        [type="{number|currency|percent}"]
        [pattern="customPattern"]
        [parseLocale="parseLocale"]
        [integerOnly="{true|false}"]
        [var="varName"]
        [scope="{page|request|session|application}"]
/>
```

The second form is used with body content:

```
<fmt:parseNumber [type="{number|currency|percent}"]
        [pattern="customPattern"]
        [parseLocale="parseLocale"]
        [integerOnly="{true|false}"]
```

```
       [var="varName"]
       [scope="{page|request|session|application}"]>
    numeric value to be parsed
</fmt:parseNumber>
```

The body content is JSP. The **parseNumber** tag's attributes are given in Table 5.14.

As an example, the following **parseNumber** tag parses the value referenced by the scoped variable **quantity** and stores the result in the **formattedNumber** scoped variable.

```
<fmt:parseNumber var="formattedNumber" type="number"
        value="${quantity}"/>
```

Attribute	Type	Description
value+	**String**	String to be parsed
type+	**String**	Indicates whether the string to be parsed is to be parsed as a number, currency, or percentage
pattern+	**String**	Custom formatting pattern that determines how the string in the **value** attribute is to be parsed
parseLocale+	**String** or **java.util.Locale**	Locale whose default formatting pattern is to be used during the parse operation, or to which the pattern specified via the pattern attribute is applied
integerOnly+	**Boolean**	Indicates whether only the integer portion of the given value should be parsed
var	**String**	The name of the scoped variable to hold the result
scope	**String**	The scope of **var**

Table 5.14: The parseNumber tag's attributes

The parseDate Tag

parseDate parses the string representation of a date and time in locale-sensitive format. The syntax has two forms. The first form is used without a body content:

```
<fmt:parseDate value="dateString"
```

```
        [type="{time|date|both}"]
        [dateStyle="{default|short|medium|long|full}"]
        [timeStyle="{default|short|medium|long|full}"]
        [pattern="customPattern"]
        [timeZone="timeZone"]
        [parseLocale="parseLocale"]
        [var="varName"]
        [scope="{page|request|session|application}"]
/>
```

The second form is used with a body content:

```
<fmt:parseDate [type="{time|date|both}"]
        [dateStyle="{default|short|medium|long|full}"]
        [timeStyle="{default|short|medium|long|full}"]
        [pattern="customPattern"]
        [timeZone="timeZone"]
        [parseLocale="parseLocale"]
        [var="varName"]
        [scope="{page|request|session|application}"]>
    date value to be parsed
</fmt:parseDate>
```

The body content is JSP. Table 5.15 lists the **parseDate** tag's attributes.

Attribute	Type	Description
value+	**String**	String to be parsed
type+	**String**	Indicates whether the string to be parsed contains a date, a time, or both
dateStyle+	**String**	The formatting style of the date
timeStyle+	**String**	The formatting style of the time
pattern+	**String**	Custom formatting pattern that determines how the string is to be parsed
timeZone+	**String** or **java.util.TimeZone**	Time zone in which to interpret any time information in the date string
parseLocale+	**String** or **java.util.Locale**	Locale whose default formatting pattern is to be used during the parse operation, or to which the pattern specified via the pattern attribute is applied
var	**String**	The name of the scoped variable to hold the result
scope	**String**	The scope of **var**

Table 5.15: The parseDate tag's attributes

As an example, the following **parseDate** tag parses a date referenced by the scoped variable **myDate** and stores the resulting **java.util.Date** in a page-scoped variable **formattedDate**.

```
<c:set var="myDate" value="12/12/2005"/>
<fmt:parseDate var="formattedDate" type="date"
        dateStyle="short" value="${myDate}"/>
```

Functions

In addition to custom actions, JSTL 1.1 and 1.2 define a set of standard functions you can use in EL expressions. These functions are grouped in the function tag library. To use the functions, you must use the following **taglib** directive on top of your JSP.

```
<%@ taglib uri="http://java.sun.com/jsp/jstl/functions"
        prefix="fn" %>
```

To invoke a function, you use an EL in this format.

```
${fn:functionName}
```

where *functionName* is the name of the function.

Most of the functions are for string manipulation. For instance, the **length** function works for both strings and collections, returning the number of items in a collection or array or the number of characters in a string.

All these functions are described in the sections to follow.

The contains Function

The **contains** function tests whether a string contains the specified substring. The return value is **true** if the string contains the substring, and **false** otherwise. Its syntax is as follows:

```
contains(string, substring).
```

For example, both of these EL expressions return **true**:

```
<c:set var="myString" value="Hello World"/>
```

```
${fn:contains(myString, "Hello")}
```

```
${fn:contains("Stella Cadente", "Cadente")}
```

The containsIgnoreCase Function

The **containsIgnoreCase** function is similar to the **contains** function, but testing is performed in a case-insensitive way. The syntax is as follows:

```
containsIgnoreCase(string, substring)
```

For instance, the following EL expression returns **true**:

```
${fn:containsIgnoreCase("Stella Cadente", "CADENTE")}
```

The endsWith Function

The **endsWith** function tests whether a string ends with the specified suffix. The return value is a **Boolean**. Its syntax is as follows:

```
endsWith(string, suffix)
```

For example, the following EL expression returns **true**:

```
${fn:endsWith("Hello World", "World")}
```

The escapeXml Function

This function is useful for encoding a **String**. The conversion is the same as the **out** tag with its **escapeXml** attribute set to **true**. The syntax of **escapeXml** is as follows:

```
escapeXml(string)
```

For example, the EL expression

```
${fn:escapeXml("Use <br/> to change lines")}
```

is rendered as the following:

```
Use &lt;br/&gt; to change lines
```

The indexOf Function

The **indexOf** function returns the index within a string of the first occurrence of the specified substring. If the substring is not found, it returns -1. Its syntax is as follows:

```
indexOf(string, substring)
```

For instance, the following EL expression returns 7:

```
${fn:indexOf("Stella Cadente", "Cadente")}
```

The join Function

The **join** function joins all elements of a **String** array into a string, separated by the specified separator. The syntax is as follows:

```
join(array, separator)
```

If the array is **null**, an empty string is returned.

For example, if **myArray** is a **String** array having the two elements "my" and "world", the EL expression

```
${fn:join(myArray,",")}
```

returns "my,world".

The length Function

The **length** function returns the number of items in a collection, or the number of characters in a string. Its syntax is as follows:

```
length{input}
```

As an example, the following EL expression returns 14:

```
${fn:length("Stella Cadente", "Cadente")}
```

The replace Function

The **replace** function replaces all occurrences of *beforeString* with *afterString* in a string and returns the result. Its syntax is as follows:

```
replace(string, beforeSubstring, afterSubstring)
```

For example, the EL expression

```
${fn:replace("Stella Cadente", "e", "E")}
```

returns "StElla CadEntE".

The split Function

The **split** function splits a string into an array of substrings. It does the opposite of the join function. For example, the following code splits the string "my,world" and stores the result in the scoped variable **split**. It then formats split into an HTML table using the **forEach** tag.

```
<c:set var="split" value='${fn:split("my,world",",")}'/>
<table>
<c:forEach var="substring" items="${split}">
    <tr><td>${substring}</td></tr>
</c:forEach>
</table>
```

The result is this:

```
<table>
    <tr><td>my</td></tr>
    <tr><td>world</td></tr>
</table>
```

The startsWith Function

The **startsWith** function tests whether a string starts with the specified prefix. The syntax is as follows:

```
startsWith(string, prefix)
```

For instance, the following EL expression returns **true**:

```
${fn:startsWith("Stella Cadente", "St")}
```

The substring Function

The **substring** function returns a substring from the specified zero-based begin index (inclusive) to the specified zero-based end index. The syntax is as follows:

```
substring(string, beginIndex, endIndex)
```

For example, the following EL expression returns "Stel".

```
${fn:substring("Stella Cadente", 0, 4)}
```

The substringAfter Function

The **substringAfter** function returns the portion of a string after the first occurrence of the specified substring. Its syntax is as follows:

```
substringAfter(string, substring)
```

For example, the EL expression

```
${fn:substringAfter("Stella Cadente", "e")}
```

returns "lla Cadente".

The substringBefore Function

The **substringBefore** function returns the portion of a string before the first occurrence of the specified substring. Its syntax is as follows:

```
substringBefore(string, substring)
```

For instance, the following EL expression returns "St".

```
${fn:substringBefore("Stella Cadente", "e")}
```

The toLowerCase Function

The **toLowerCase** function converts a string into its lowercase version. Its syntax is as follows:

```
toLowerCase(string)
```

For example, the following EL expression returns "stella cadente".

```
${fn:toLowerCase("Stella Cadente")}
```

The toUpperCase Function

The **toUpperCase** function converts a string into its uppercase version. Its syntax is as follows:

```
toUpperCase(string)
```

For instance, the following EL expression returns "STELLA CADENTE".

```
${fn:toUpperCase("Stella Cadente")}
```

The trim Function

The **trim** function removes the leading and trailing whitespaces of a string. Its syntax is as follows:

```
trim(string)
```

For example, the following EL expression returns "Stella Cadente".

```
${fn:trim("                Stella Cadente   ")}
```

Summary

You can use JSTL for common tasks (such as iteration, collection, and conditionals), for processing XML documents, formatting text, accessing databases and manipulating data, etc. This chapter discussed the more important tags such as the tags for manipulating scoped objects (**out**, **set**, **remove**), for performing conditional tests (**if**, **choose**, **when**, **otherwise**), for iterating over a collection or token (**forEach**, **forTokens**), for parsing and formatting dates and numbers (**parseNumber**, **formatNumber**, **parseDate**, **formatDate**, etc), and JSTL 1.2 functions that can be used from EL expressions.

Chapter 6
Writing Custom Tags

In Chapter 5, "JSTL," you learned how to use custom tags in JSTL. The libraries in JSTL provide tags for solving common problems, but if your problems are not so common, you will have to write your own custom tags by extending a member of the **javax.servlet.jsp.tagext** package. This chapter teaches you how.

Custom Tag Overview

Using JSP standard actions to access and manipulate JavaBeans was the first attempt to allow separation of presentation (HTML) and business logic implementation (Java code). However, standard actions were not powerful enough that using them alone developers would often still have to resort to Java code in JSP pages. For example, standard actions cannot be used to iterate over a collection the way the JSTL **forEach** tag can.

In recognition of the imperfection of JavaBeans as a solution to separation of presentation and business logic, JSP 1.1 defined custom tags. Custom tags offer benefits that are not present in JavaBeans. Among others, custom tags have access to JSP implicit objects and can have attributes.

While using custom tags enables you to write script-free JSP pages, custom tags in JSP 1.1 and 1.2, called the classic custom tags, were notoriously hard to write. JSP 2.0 added two new features that made writing them easier. The first feature was a new interface called **SimpleTag**, which is discussed in this chapter. The second feature was a mechanism to write custom tags as tag files. Tag files are explained in Chapter 7, "Tag Files."

The implementation for a custom tag is called a tag handler, and simple tag handlers refer to tag handlers that implement **SimpleTag**. In this chapter, you'll explore how custom tags work and how to write tag handlers. Only simple tag handlers will be discussed as there is no reason to write classic tag handlers anymore.

In addition to being easier to write than classic tag handlers, simple tag handlers, unlike classic tag handlers, may not be cached by the JSP container. However, this does not mean simple tag handlers are slower than their predecessors. The JSP specification authors wrote in section JSP.7.1.5 of the specification, "Initial performance metrics show that caching a tag handler instance does not necessarily lead to greater performance, and to accommodate such caching makes writing portable tag handlers difficult and makes the tag handler prone to error."

Simple Tag Handlers

The designers of JSP 2.0 realized how complex it was to write custom tags and tag handlers in JSP 1.1 and JSP 1.2. As such, in JSP 2.0 they added a new interface to the **javax.servlet.jsp.tagext** package: **SimpleTag**. Tag handlers implementing **SimpleTag** are called simple tag handlers, and tag handlers implementing **Tag**, **IterationTag**, or **BodyTag** are called classic tag handlers.

Simple tag handlers have a simpler lifecycle and are easier to write than classic tag handlers. The **SimpleTag** interface has one method in regard to tag invocation that will be called only once: **doTag**. Business logic, iteration, and body manipulation are to be written here. A body in a simple tag handler is represented by an instance of the **JspFragment** class. **JspFragment** is discussed in the subsection, "JspFragment" towards the end of this section.

The lifecycle of a simple tag handler is as follows:

1. The JSP container creates an instance of a simple tag handler by calling its no-argument constructor. Therefore, a simple tag handler must have a no-argument constructor.

2. The JSP container calls the **setJspContext** method, passing a **JspContext** object: The most important method of **JspContext** is **getOut**, which returns a **JspWriter** for sending response to the client. The signature of the **setJspContext** method is as follows.

```
public void setJspContext(JspContext jspContext)
```
In most cases, you will need to assign the passed in **JspContext** to a class variable for later use.

3. If the custom tag representing the tag handler is nested within another tag, the JSP container calls the **setParent** method. This method has the following signature:

```
public void setParent(JspTag parent)
```

4. The JSP container calls the setter for each attribute defined for this tag.

5. If a body exists, the JSP container calls the **setJspBody** method of the **SimpleTag** interface, passing the body as a **JspFragment**. The JSP container will not call this method if the tag does not have a body.

6. The JSP container calls the **doTag** method. All variables are synchronized when the **doTag** method returns.

The **javax.servlet.jsp.tagext** package also includes a support class for **SimpleTag**: **SimpleTagSupport**. **SimpleTagSupport** provides default implementations for all methods in **SimpleTag** and serves as a convenient class that you can extend to write a simple tag handler. The **getJspContext** method in the **SimpleTagSupport** class returns the **JspContext** instance passed by the JSP container when it calls the **setJspContext** method of the **SimpleTag** interface.

SimpleTag Example

This section presents the **app06a** application, an example of a simple tag handler. There are two steps required in creating a custom tag, writing a tag handler and registering the tag. Both steps are explained below.

Note that you need the Servlet API and JSP API packages in your build path to compile a tag handler. If you're using Tomcat, you can find the jar files containing the APIs in Tomcat's **lib** directory (the **servlet-api.jar** fie and the **jsp-api.jar** file).

The application directory structure for **app06a** is given in Figure 6.1. The custom tag consists of a tag handler (located under **WEB-INF/classes**) and a descriptor (the **mytags.tld** file under **WEB-INF**). Figure 6.1 also includes a JSP file for testing the custom tag.

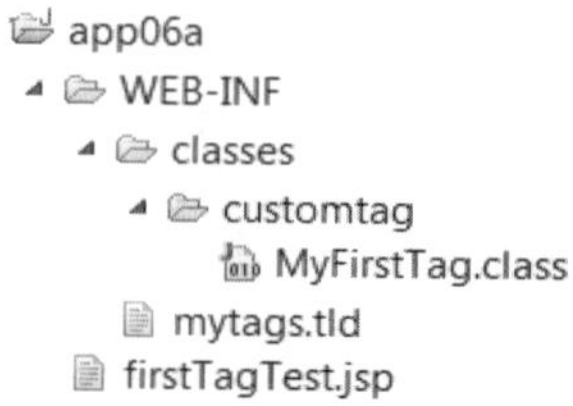

```
app06a
  ▲ WEB-INF
      ▲ classes
          ▲ customtag
                MyFirstTag.class
          mytags.tld
      firstTagTest.jsp
```

Figure 6.1: The app06a application directory structure

Writing the Tag Handler

Listing 6.1 shows the **MyFirstTag** class, an implementation of **SimpleTag**.

Listing 6.1: The MyFirstTag class

```java
package customtag;
import java.io.IOException;
import javax.servlet.jsp.JspContext;
import javax.servlet.jsp.JspException;
import javax.servlet.jsp.tagext.JspFragment;
import javax.servlet.jsp.tagext.JspTag;
import javax.servlet.jsp.tagext.SimpleTag;

public class MyFirstTag implements SimpleTag {
    JspContext jspContext;

    public void doTag() throws IOException, JspException {
        System.out.println("doTag");
        jspContext.getOut().print("This is my first tag.");
    }

    public void setParent(JspTag parent) {
        System.out.println("setParent");
    }

    public JspTag getParent() {
```

```
        System.out.println("getParent");
        return null;
    }

    public void setJspContext(JspContext jspContext) {
        System.out.println("setJspContext");
        this.jspContext = jspContext;
    }

    public void setJspBody(JspFragment body) {
        System.out.println("setJspBody");
    }
}
```

The **MySimpleTag** class has a **jspContext** variable of type **JspContext**. The **setJspContext** method assigns the **JspContext** it receives from the JSP container to this variable. The **doTag** method uses the **JspContext** to obtain a **JspWriter**. You call the **print** method on the **JspWriter** to output the **String** "This is my first tag".

Registering the Tag

Before a tag handler can be used in a JSP page, it must be registered in a tag library descriptor, an XML file with tld extension. The tag library descriptor for this example is called **mytags.tld** and is given in Listing 6.2. This file must be saved in the **WEB-INF** directory.

Listing 6.2: The tag library descriptor (mytags.tld file)

```
<?xml version="1.0" encoding="UTF-8"?>
<taglib xmlns="http://java.sun.com/xml/ns/j2ee"
    xmlns:xsi="http://www.w3.org/2001/XMLSchema-instance"
    xsi:schemaLocation="http://java.sun.com/xml/ns/j2ee
➥web-jsptaglibrary_2_1.xsd"
    version="2.1">

    <description>
        Simple tag examples
    </description>
    <tlib-version>1.0</tlib-version>
    <short-name>My First Taglib Example</short-name>
    <tag>
```

```
        <name>firstTag</name>
        <tag-class>customtag.MyFirstTag</tag-class>
        <body-content>empty</body-content>
    </tag>
</taglib>
```

The main element in the tag library descriptor is the **tag** element, which describes the tag. It contains a **name** element and a **tag-class** element. **name** specifies the name that will be used to refer to this tag. **tag-class** specifies the fully-qualified name of the tag handler. A tag library descriptor may contain multiple **tag** elements.

In addition, you may have other elements in a tag library descriptor. The **description** element is used to provide a description of the tags described in this descriptor. The **tlib-version** element specifies the version of the custom tags and the **short-name** element provides a short name for the tags.

Using the Tag

To use a custom tag, you use the **taglib** directive. The **uri** attribute of the **taglib** directive may reference a relative path or an absolute path. In this example, a relative path is used. However, if you're using a tag library that is packaged in a jar file, you'll use an absolute path. The section "Distributing Custom Tags" later in this chapter shows you how to package a custom tag library for easy distribution.

To test the **firstTag** custom tag, use the **firstTagTest.jsp** page in Listing 6.3.

Listing 6.3: The firstTagTest.jsp

```
<%@ taglib uri="/WEB-INF/mytags.tld" prefix="easy"%>
<html>
<head>
    <title>Testing my first tag</title>
</head>
<body>
Hello!!!!
<br/>
<easy:firstTag></easy:firstTag>
</body>
</html>
```

You can invoke the **firstTagTest.jsp** page with this URL:

```
http://localhost:8080/app06a/firstTagTest.jsp
```

When you invoke the **firstTagTest.jsp** page, the JSP container calls the tag handler's **setJspContext** method. Since the tag in **firstTagTest.jsp** does not have a body, the JSP container doesn't call the **setJspBody** method before calling the **doTag** method. In your console, you can see the following output:

```
setJspContext

doTag
```

Note that the JSP container does not call the tag handler's **setParent** method either because the simple tag is not nested within another tag.

Handling Attributes

Tag handlers that implement **SimpleTag** or extend **SimpleTagSupport** can have attributes. Listing 6.4 presents a tag handler called **DataFormaterTag** that formats comma-delimited items into an HTML table. You pass two attributes to this tag, **header** and **items**. The **header** attribute value will become the header of the table. For example, if you pass "Cities" as the value for the **header** attribute and "London,Montreal" as the value for the **items** attribute, you'll get the following output:

```
<table style="border:1px solid green">
<tr><td><b>Cities</b></td></tr>
<tr><td>London</td></tr>
<tr><td>Montreal</td></tr>
</table>
```

Listing 6.4: The DataFormatterTag class

```
package customtag;
import java.io.IOException;
import java.util.StringTokenizer;
import javax.servlet.jsp.JspContext;
import javax.servlet.jsp.JspException;
import javax.servlet.jsp.JspWriter;
import javax.servlet.jsp.tagext.SimpleTagSupport;
```

```
public class DataFormatterTag extends SimpleTagSupport {
    private String header;
    private String items;

    public void setHeader(String header) {
        this.header = header;
    }

    public void setItems(String items) {
        this.items = items;
    }

    public void doTag() throws IOException, JspException {
        JspContext jspContext = getJspContext();
        JspWriter out = jspContext.getOut();

        out.print("<table style='border:1px solid green'>\n"
                + "<tr><td><span style='font-weight:bold'>"
                + header + "</span></td></tr>\n");
        StringTokenizer tokenizer = new StringTokenizer(items,
                ",");
        while (tokenizer.hasMoreTokens()) {
            String token = tokenizer.nextToken();
            out.print("<tr><td>" + token + "</td></tr>\n");
        }
        out.print("</table>");
    }
}
```

The **DataFormatterTag** class provides two setters to receive attributes: **setHeader** and **setItems**. The **doTag** method does the rest.

The **doTag** method first obtains the **JspContext** passed by the JSP container by calling the **getJspContext** method:

```
JspContext jspContext = getJspContext();
```

Then, it calls the **getOut** method on the **JspContext** instance to obtain a **JspWriter** it can use to write response to the client:

```
JspWriter out = jspContext.getOut();
```

Next, the **doTag** method uses a **StringTokenizer** to parse the **items** attribute and turn each item to a table row:

```
out.print("<table style='border:1px solid green'>\n"
        + "<tr><td><span style='font-weight:bold'>"
        + header + "</span></td></tr>\n");
StringTokenizer tokenizer = new StringTokenizer(items, ",");
while (tokenizer.hasMoreTokens()) {
    String token = tokenizer.nextToken();
    out.print("<tr><td>" + token + "</td></tr>\n");
}
out.print("</table>");
```

To use the **DataFormatterTag** tag handler, you must register it using the **tag** element in Listing 6.5. Simply add it to the **mytags.tld** file used in the previous example.

Listing 6.5: Registering dataFormatter tag

```
<tag>
    <name>dataFormatter</name>
    <tag-class>customtag.DataFormatterTag</tag-class>
    <body-content>empty</body-content>
    <attribute>
        <name>header</name>
        <required>true</required>
    </attribute>
    <attribute>
        <name>items</name>
        <required>true</required>
    </attribute>
</tag>
```

You can then use the **dataFormatterTagTest.jsp** page in Listing 6.6 to test the tag handler.

Listing 6.6: The dataFormatterTagTest.jsp Page

```
<%@ taglib uri="/WEB-INF/mytags.tld" prefix="easy"%>
<html>
<head>
    <title>Testing DataFormatterTag</title>
</head>
<body>
<easy:dataFormatter header="States"
    items="Alabama,Alaska,Georgia,Florida"
/>
```

```
<br/>
<easy:dataFormatter header="Countries">
    <jsp:attribute name="items">
        US,UK,Canada,Korea
    </jsp:attribute>
</easy:dataFormatter>
</body>
</html>
```

Note that the JSP page in Listing 6.6 uses the **dataFormatter** tag twice, passing attributes in two different ways, in a tag attribute and by using the **attribute** standard action. You can invoke **dataFormatterTagTest.jsp** using this URL:

```
http://localhost:8080/app06a/dataFormatterTagTest.jsp
```

Figure 6.2 shows the result of invoking **dataFormatterTagTest.jsp**.

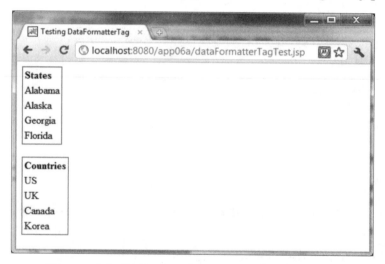

Figure 6.2: Using attributes with SimpleTag

Manipulating the Tag Body

With **SimpleTag**, you can manipulate the tag body via the **JspFragment** passed by the JSP container. The **JspFragment** class represents a portion of JSP code that can be invoked zero or more time. The definition of the JSP fragment must not contain scriptlets or scriptlet expressions. It can only contain template text and JSP action elements.

The **JspFragment** class has two methods: **getJspContext** and **invoke**. The signatures of the methods are as follows:

```
public abstract JspContext getJspContext()

public abstract void invoke(java.io.Writer writer)
        throws JspException, java.io.IOException
```

The **getJspContext** method returns the **JspContext** associated with this **JspFragment**. You call the **invoke** method to execute the fragment (the tag body) and directs all output to the given **Writer**. If you pass null to the **invoke** method, the output will be directed to the **JspWriter** returned by the **getOut** method of the **JspContext** associated with this fragment.

Consider the **SelectElementTag** class in Listing 6.7. You use this tag handler to send an HTML select element with the following format:

```
<select>
<option value="value-1">text-1</option>
<option value="value-2">text-2</option>
...
<option value="value-n">text-n</option>
</select>
```

In this case, the values are country names in the **String** array **countries**.

Listing 6.7: SelectElementTag

```
package customtag;
import java.io.IOException;
import javax.servlet.jsp.JspContext;
import javax.servlet.jsp.JspException;
import javax.servlet.jsp.JspWriter;
import javax.servlet.jsp.tagext.SimpleTagSupport;

public class SelectElementTag extends SimpleTagSupport {
    private String[] countries = {"Australia", "Brazil", "China" };

    public void doTag() throws IOException, JspException {
        JspContext jspContext = getJspContext();
        JspWriter out = jspContext.getOut();
        out.print("<select>\n");
```

```
        for (int i=0; i<3; i++) {
            getJspContext().setAttribute("value", countries[i]);
            getJspContext().setAttribute("text", countries[i]);
            getJspBody().invoke(null);
        }
        out.print("</select>\n");
    }
}
```

Listing 6.8 shows the **tag** element used to register **SelectElementTag** and maps it to the tag called **select**. Again, add this element to the **mytags.tld** file used in the previous examples.

Listing 6.8: Registering SelectElementTag

```
<tag>
    <name>select</name>
    <tag-class>customtag.SelectElementTag</tag-class>
    <body-content>scriptless</body-content>
</tag>
```

Listing 6.9 presents a JSP page (**selectElementTagTest.jsp**) that uses **SelectElementTag**.

Listing 6.9: The selectElementTagTest.jsp Page

```
<%@ taglib uri="/WEB-INF/mytags.tld" prefix="easy"%>
<html>
<head>
    <title>Testing SelectElementFormatterTag</title>
</head>
<body>
<easy:select>
    <option value="${value}">${text}</option>
</easy:select>
</body>
</html>
```

Note that the **select** tag is used by passing a body in the following format:

```
<option value="${value}">${text}</option>
```

The **value** and **text** attributes get their values from each invocation of the **JspFragment** in the **doTag** method of the **SelectElementTag** tag handler:

```
    for (int i=0; i<3; i++) {
        getJspContext().setAttribute("value", countries[i]);
```

```
      getJspContext().setAttribute("text", countries[i]);
      getJspBody().invoke(null);
   }
```

You can invoke **selectElementTagTest.jsp** using this URL:

```
http://localhost:8080/app06a/selectElementTagTest.jsp
```

Figure 6.3 shows the result.

Figure 6.3: Using JspFragment

If you view the source in your web browser, you'll see the following:

```
<select>
  <option value="Australia">Australia</option>
  <option value="Brazil">Brazil</option>
  <option value="China">China</option>
</select>
```

Writing EL Functions

Chapter 4, "The Expression Language" discussed the JSP expression language (EL) and mentioned that you can write functions that you can invoke by using an EL expression. Writing EL functions is discussed in this chapter rather than in Chapter 4 because it involves the use of a tag library descriptor.

Basically, you can write an EL function by following these two steps:

1. Create a public class containing static methods. Each static method represents a function. This class does not have to implement an interface or extend a class. Deploy this class as you would any other

class. This class must be saved to the **WEB-INF/classes** directory or a directory under it.
2. Register the function in a tag library descriptor using the **function** element.

The **function** element must be placed directly under the **taglib** element and can have the following sub-elements:

- **description**. An optional tag-specific information.
- **display-name**. A short name to be displayed by XML tools.
- **icon**. An optional icon element that can be used by XML tools.
- **name**. A unique name for this function.
- **function-class**. The fully-qualified name of the Java class that implements the function.
- **function-signature**. The signature of the static Java method representing the function.
- **example**. An optional informal description of an example that uses this function.
- **function-extension**. Zero or more extensions that provide extra information about this function, used by XML tools.

To use a function, you employ the **taglib** directive with its **uri** attribute pointing to the tag library descriptor and a prefix indicating the prefix to be used. You then call the function by using the following syntax in your JSP page:

```
${prefix:functionName(parameterList)}
```

As an example, consider the **app06b** application accompanying this book. Listing 6.10 presents the **MyFunctions** class that encapsulates the static method **reverseString**.

Listing 6.10: The reverseString method in the MyFunctions class

```
package function;
public class StringFunctions {
    public static String reverseString(String s) {
        return new StringBuffer(s).reverse().toString();
    }
}
```

Listing 6.11 shows the **functiontags.tld** descriptor that contains a **function** element that describes the **reverseString** function. This TLD must be saved in the WEB-INF directory of the application that is using it.

Listing 6.11: The functiontags.tld file

```
<?xml version="1.0" encoding="UTF-8"?>
<taglib xmlns="http://java.sun.com/xml/ns/j2ee"
    xmlns:xsi="http://www.w3.org/2001/XMLSchema-instance"
    xsi:schemaLocation="http://java.sun.com/xml/ns/j2ee
➡web-jsptaglibrary_2_1.xsd"
    version="2.1">

    <description>
        Function tag examples
    </description>
    <tlib-version>1.0</tlib-version>
    <function>
        <description>Reverses a String</description>
        <name>reverseString</name>
        <function-class>function.StringFunction</function-class>
        <function-signature>
            java.lang.String reverseString(java.lang.String)
        </function-signature>
    </function>
</taglib>
```

Listing 6.12 shows the **reverseStringFunctionTest.jsp** page for testing the EL function.

Listing 6.12: Using the EL Function

```
<%@ taglib uri="/WEB-INF/functiontags.tld" prefix="f"%>
<html>
<head>
    <title>Testing reverseString function</title>
</head>
<body>
${f:reverseString("Hello World")}
</body>
</html>
```

You can invoke **useELFunctionTest.jsp** using the following URL:

```
http://localhost:8080/app06b/reverseStringFunctionTest.jsp
```

Upon invoking the JSP page, you'll see "Hello World" in reverse.

Distributing Custom Tags

You can package your custom tag handlers and tag library descriptor in a jar file so that you can distribute it for others to use, just like JSTL. In this case, you need to include all the tag handlers and the tld file that describes them. In addition, you need to specify an absolute URI in a uri element in the descriptor.

For example, application **app06c** accompanying this book packages the tag and the descriptor in **app06b** into a **mytags.jar** file. The content of the jar file is shown in Figure 6.4.

```
mytags.jar
    function
        StringFunction.class
    META-INF
        functiontags.tld
```

Figure 6.4: The mytags.jar file

Listing 6.13 presents the **functiontags.tld** file. Note that a **uri** element has been added to the descriptor. The value of the element is **http://example.com/taglib/function**.

Listing 6.13: The functiontags.tld file of the packaged custom tag

```
<?xml version="1.0" encoding="UTF-8"?>
<taglib xmlns="http://java.sun.com/xml/ns/j2ee"
    xmlns:xsi="http://www.w3.org/2001/XMLSchema-instance"
    xsi:schemaLocation="http://java.sun.com/xml/ns/j2ee
        web-jsptaglibrary_2_1.xsd"
    version="2.1">
    <description>
        Function tag examples
    </description>
    <tlib-version>1.0</tlib-version>

    <uri>http://example.com/taglib/function</uri>
```

```
<function>
    <description>Reverses a String</description>
    <name>reverseString</name>
    <function-class>function.StringFunction</function-class>
    <function-signature>
        java.lang.String reverseString(java.lang.String)
    </function-signature>
</function>
</taglib>
```

To use the library in an application, you must copy the jar file to the **WEB-INF/lib** directory of the application. On top of that, any JSP page that uses the custom tag must specify the same URI as the one defined in the tag library descriptor.

The **reverseStringFunction.jsp** page in Listing 6.14 shows a JSP page that uses the custom tag.

Listing 6.14: The reverseStringFunction.jsp file in app06c

```
<%@ taglib uri="http://example.com/taglib/function" prefix="f"%>
<html>
<head>
    <title>Testing reverseString function</title>
</head>
<body>
${f:reverseString("Welcome")}
</body>
</html>
```

You can test the example by directing your browser to this URL.

```
http://localhost:8080/app06c/reverseStringFunction.jsp
```

Summary

You have seen in this chapter that custom tags are a better solution than JavaBeans to the issue of separation of presentation and business logic. To write a custom tag, you need to create a tag handler and register the tag in a tag library descriptor.

As of JSP 2.2, there are two types of tag handlers, classic tag handlers and simple tag handlers. The former implement the **Tag**, **IterationTag**, or **BodyTag** interface or extend one of the two support classes, **TagSupport** and **BodyTagSupport**. Simple tag handlers, on the other hand, implement the **SimpleTag** interface or extend **SimpleTagSupport**. Simple tag handlers are easier to write and have a simpler lifecycle than classic tag handlers. Simple tag handlers are the recommended type and this chapter presented a couple of simple tag examples. You can also distribute your custom tag library in a jar file for others to use.

Chapter 7
Tag Files

You have seen in Chapter 6, "Writing Custom Tags" that custom tags enable you to write script-free JSP pages, thus promoting separation of labor, which means the page designer and the Java coder can work simultaneously. However, you've also learned that writing custom tags is a tedious chore, involving writing and compiling tag handlers and defining the tags in the tag library descriptor.

Starting from JSP 2.0, you can write tag files, which are custom actions without tag handlers and tag library descriptors. With tag files no compilation is necessary and no tag library descriptor is required.

This chapter discusses tag files in detail. It starts with an introduction to tag files and then covers several aspects of writing custom tags using tag files only. The **doBody** and **invoke** standard actions are also discussed in the sections towards the end of the chapter.

Introduction to Tag Files

Tag files simplify the process of writing custom tags in two ways. First, tag files don't need to be compiled as they are compiled the first time they are invoked. In addition, with tag files tag extensions can be written using JSP syntax alone. This means, someone who does not know Java can also write tag extensions!

Secondly, no tag library descriptor is needed. The **tag** element in the tag library descriptor describes the name to be used in a JSP page to reference the custom action. Using tag files, the name of a custom action is the same as the tag file representing the action, thus eliminating the need for the tag library descriptor.

JSP containers may choose to compile tag files into Java tag handlers or interpret the tag files. For example, Tomcat translates tag files into simple tag handlers that implement the **javax.servlet.jsp.tagext.SimpleTag** interface.

A tag file looks like a JSP page. It can have directives, scripts, EL expressions, standard actions, and custom tags. A tag file has a **tag** or **tagx** extension and can also include other files that contain a common resource. An include file for a tag file has **tagf** extension.

In order to work, tag files must be placed in the **WEB-INF/tags** directory of an application directory or a subdirectory under it. Just like tag handlers, tag files can be packaged into jar files.

A number of implicit objects are available from inside a tag file. You can access these objects from a script or an EL expression. Table 7.1 lists the implicit objects available in tag files. These implicit objects are similar to JSP implicit objects, discussed in Chapter 3, "JavaServer Pages."

Object	Type
request	javax.servlet.http.HttpServletRequest
response	javax.servlet.http.HttpServletResponse
out	javax.servlet.jsp.JspWriter
session	javax.servlet.http.HttpSession
application	javax.servlet.ServletContext
config	javax.servlet.ServletConfig
jspContext	javax.servlet.jsp.JspContext

Table 7.1: Implicit Objects available in tag files

Your First Tag File

This section shows how easy it is to write a tag file and use it. The example consists of one tag file and one JSP page that uses the tag file. The directory structure of the application is depicted in Figure 7.1.

```
⌂ app07a
  ▲ ⌂ WEB-INF
      ▲ ⌂ tags
            ▤ firstTag.tag
      ▤ firstTagTest.jsp
```

Figure 7.1: The Directory Structure

The tag file is called **firstTag.tag** and is printed in Listing 7.1.

Listing 7.1: The firstTag.tag File

```
<%@ tag import="java.util.Date" import="java.text.DateFormat"%>
<%
    DateFormat dateFormat =
            DateFormat.getDateInstance(DateFormat.LONG);
    Date now = new Date(System.currentTimeMillis());
    out.println(dateFormat.format(now));
%>
```

As you can see in Listing 7.1, a tag file looks like a JSP page. The **firstTag.tag** file contains a **tag** directive with two **import** attributes and a scriptlet. The output of this tag file is the current date in long format. To use this tag file as a tag extension, all you need to do is save it in the **WEB-INF/tags** directory of your application. The tag file name is important because it indicates the tag name. The tag name for the **firstTag.tag** file is **firstTag**.

Listing 7.2 presents a **firstTagTest.jsp** page that uses the **firstTag.tag** file.

Listing 7.2: The firstTagTest.jsp Page

```
<%@ taglib prefix="easy" tagdir="/WEB-INF/tags" %>
Today is <easy:firstTag/>
```

You can invoke the **firstTagTest.jsp** page using this URL:

```
http://localhost:8080/app07a/firstTagTest.jsp
```

Tag File Directives

Just like JSP pages, tag files can use directives to control how the JSP container will compile or interpret the tag files. Tag file directives have the same syntax as JSP directives:

```
<%@ directive (attribute="value")* %>
```

The asterisk (*) means that what is enclosed in the brackets can be repeated zero or more times. The syntax can be re-written in a more informal way as follows:

```
<%@ directive attribute1="value1" attribute2="value2" ... %>
```

Attributes must be enclosed with single quotes or double quotes, and white spaces after the opening **<%@** and before the closing **%>** are optional but can improve readability.

All JSP directives except **page** are available in tag files. Instead of **page**, you have the **tag** directive at your disposal. Also, in tag files, there are two more directives you can use, **attribute** and **variable**. Table 7.2 lists all the directives that can appear in a tag file.

Directive	Description
tag	This directive is similar to the **page** directive for JSP pages.
include	Use this directive to include other resources from the tag file
taglib	Use this directive to use a custom tag library from inside the tag file
attribute	Use this directive to declare an attribute in a tag file.
variable	Use this directive to define a variable that you can expose to the calling JSP page.

Table 7.2: Tag File Directives

Each of the directives is given in a separate section below.

The tag Directive

The **tag** directive is similar to the **page** directive you use in JSP pages. Here is the syntax of the **tag** directive:

```
<%@ tag (attribute="value")* %>
```

The syntax can be expressed in the following more informal form:

```
<%@ tag attribute1="value1" attribute2="value2" ... %>
```

The attributes for the **tag** directive are given in Table 7.3. All attributes are optional.

Attribute	Description
display-name	A short name to be displayed by an XML tool. The default value is the tag file name, without **tag** extension.
body-content	The information about the body content of this tag. The value can be **empty**, **tagdependent**, or **scriptless** (default).
dynamic-attributes	Indicates the support for dynamic attributes. The value identifies a scoped attribute in which to place a **Map** containing the names and values of the dynamic attributes passed during this invocation.
small-icon	A context-relative path, or a path relative to the tag source file, of a small image file to be used by XML tools. You don't normally use this attribute.
large-icon	A context-relative path, or a path relative to the tag source file, of an image containing a large icon to be used by XML tools. You don't normally use this attribute either.
description	A string describing this tag.
example	An informal description of an example of a use of this action.
language	The scripting language used in the tag file. The value for this attribute for the current version of JSP must be "java"
import	Used to import a Java type. The same as the **import** attribute in the page directive.
pageEncoding	Describes the character encoding for this tag file. The value is of the form "CHARSET", which must be the IANA name for a character encoding. This attribute is the same as the **pageEncoding** attribute of the **page** directive.
isELIgnored	Indicates whether EL expressions are ignored or evaluated. The default value for this attribute is "false", which means EL expressions are evaluated. This attribute is the same as the **isELIgnored** attribute of the **page** directive.

Table 7.3: Attribute of tag

Except for the **import** attribute, all other attributes can only appear once within a **tag** directive or in multiple **tag** directives in the same tag file. For example, the following **tag** file is invalid because the **body-content** attributes appear more than once in multiple **tag** directives:

```
<%@ tag display-name="first tag file" body-content="scriptless" %>
<%@ tag body-content="empty" %>
```

The following is a valid **tag** directive even though the **import** attribute appears twice. This is because **import** can appear as many times as desired.

```
<%@ tag import="java.util.ArrayList" import="java.util.Iterator" %>
```

The following is also valid:

```
<%@ tag body-content="empty" import="java.util.Enumeration" %>
<%@ tag import="java.sql.*" %>
```

The include Directive

The **include** directive for a tag file is the same as the **include** directive for a JSP page. You use this directive to include the contents of other files in the current tag file. It is useful when you have a common resource that will be used by more than one tag files. The included resource can be static (e.g. an HTML file) or dynamic (e.g. another tag file).

As an example, the **includeDemoTag.tag** page in Listing 7.3 shows a tag file that includes a static resource (**included.html**) and a dynamic resource (**included.tagf**).

Listing 7.3: The includeDemoTag.tag file

```
This tag file shows the use of the include directive.
The first include directive demonstrates how you can include
a static resource called included.html.
<br/>
Here is the content of included.html:
<%@ include file="included.html" %>
<br/>
<br/>
The second include directive includes another dynamic resource:
included.tagf.
<br/>
<%@ include file="included.tagf" %>
```

The **included.html** and **included.tagf** files are given in Listings 7.4 and 7.5, respectively. Both are to be saved in the same directory as the tag file.

Note that the recommended extension for a segment for a tag file is **tagf**.

Listing 7.4: The included.html file

```
<table>
<tr>
    <td><b>Menu</b></td>
</tr>
<tr>
    <td>CDs</td>
</tr>
<tr>
    <td>DVDs</td>
</tr>
<tr>
    <td>Others</td>
</tr>
</table>
```

Listing 7.5: The included.tagf file

```
<%
    out.print("Hello from included.tagf");
%>
```

To test the **includeDemoTag.tag** file, use the **includeDemoTagTest.jsp** page in Listing 7.6.

Listing 7.6: The includeDemoTagTest.jsp page

```
<%@ taglib prefix="easy" tagdir="/WEB-INF/tags" %>
<easy:includeDemoTag/>
```

You can invoke the **includeDemoTagTest.jsp** page using the following URL:

```
http://localhost:8080/app07a/includeDemoTagTest.jsp
```

The result is shown in Figure 7.2.

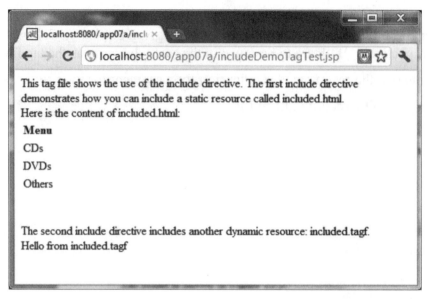

Figure 7.2: Including other resources from a tag file.

For more information on the **include** directive, see Chapter 3, "JavaServer Pages."

The taglib Directive

You can use custom tags from your tag file using the **taglib** directive. The **taglib** directive has the following syntax:

```
<%@ taglib uri="tagLibraryURI" prefix="tagPrefix" %>
```

The **uri** attribute specifies an absolute or relative URI that uniquely identifies the tag library descriptor associated with this prefix.

The **prefix** attribute defines a string that will become the prefix to distinguish a custom action.

With the **taglib** directive, you can use a custom tag of the following format for a custom tag that does not have a content body:

```
<prefix:tagName/>
```

Or, you can use this format for a custom tag that has a content body:

```
<prefix:tagName>body</prefix:tagName>
```

The **taglib** directive in a tag file is the same as the **taglib** directive in a JSP page.

As an example, consider the **taglibDemo.tag** file in Listing 7.7.

Listing 7.7: The taglibDemo.tag file

```
<%@ taglib prefix="simple" tagdir="/WEB-INF/tags" %>
The server's date: <simple:firstTag/>
```

It uses the **firstTag.tag** file in Listing 7.1 to display the server's date. The **taglibDemo.tag** file is used by the **taglibDemoTest.jsp** page in Listing 7.8.

Listing 7.8: The taglibDemoTest.jsp page

```
<%@ taglib prefix="easy" tagdir="/WEB-INF/tags" %>
<easy:taglibDemo/>
```

You can invoke this JSP page using the following URL:

```
http://localhost:8080/app07a/taglibDemoTest.jsp
```

The attribute Directive

The **attribute** directive supports the use of attributes in a tag file. It is equivalent to the **attribute** element in the tag library descriptor. Here is the syntax of the **attribute** directive:

```
<%@ attribute (attribute="value")* %>
```

The syntax can be expressed in the following more informal form:

```
<%@ attribute attribute1="value1" attribute2="value2" ... %>
```

The attributes for the **attribute** directive is given in Table 7.4. The only required attribute is the **name** attribute.

As an example, consider the **encode.tag** file in Listing 7.9 that can be used to HTML-encode a string. This **encode** tag defines an attribute, **input**, which is of type **java.lang.String**.

Attribute	Description
name	The name for the attribute that this tag file accepts. The value for the name attribute must be unique throughout the current tag file.
required	Indicates whether this attribute is required. The value can be true or false (default)
fragment	Indicates whether this attribute is a fragment to be evaluated by the tag handler or a normal attribute to be evaluated by the container prior to being passed to the tag handler. The value is either true or false (default). The value is true if this attribute is to be evaluated by the tag handler.
rtexprvalue	Specifies whether the attribute value may be dynamically calculated at runtime by a scriplet expression. The value is either true (default) or false.
type	The type of the attribute value. The default is **java.lang.String**.
description	The description of this attribute.

Table 7.4: Attributes of attribute

Listing 7.9: The encode.tag file

```
<%@ attribute name="input" required="true" %>
<%!
    private String encodeHtmlTag(String tag) {
        if (tag==null) {
            return null;
        }
        int length = tag.length();
        StringBuilder encodedTag = new StringBuilder(2 * length);
        for (int i=0; i<length; i++) {
            char c = tag.charAt(i);
            if (c=='<') {
                encodedTag.append("&lt;");
            } else if (c=='>') {
                encodedTag.append("&gt;");
            } else if (c=='&') {
                encodedTag.append("&amp;");
            } else if (c=='"') {
                encodedTag.append("&quot;");
            } else if (c==' ') {
                encodedTag.append(" ");
            } else {
                encodedTag.append(c);
            }
        }
        return encodedTag.toString();
```

```
    }
%>
<%=encodeHtmlTag(input)%>
```

To test the **encode.tag** file, use the **encodeTagTest.jsp** page in Listing 7.10.

Listing 7.10: The encodeTagTest.jsp page

```
<%@ taglib prefix="easy" tagdir="/WEB-INF/tags" %>
<easy:encode input="<br/> means changing line"/>
```

You can invoke the **encodeTagTest.jsp** page using the following URL:

```
http://localhost:8080/app07a/encodeTagTest.jsp
```

The result is shown in Figure 7.3.

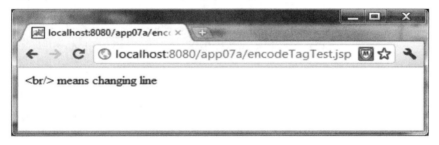

Figure 7.3: Using attributes in a tag file.

The variable Directive

It is sometimes useful to expose values in a tag file to the calling JSP page. This is possible through the use of the **variable** directive in the tag file. In a tag file, the **variable** directive is analogous to the **variable** element in the tag library descriptor and defines the details of a variable in the tag handler that is accessible from the calling JSP page. Because a tag file can have multiple **variable** directives, it is possible to provide multiple values to the calling JSP page. Compare **variable** with the **attribute** directive that you use to pass a value from a JSP page to a tag file.

The syntax of the **variable** directive is as follows:

```
<%@ variable (attribute="value")* %>
```

The syntax can be expressed in the following more informal form:

```
<%@ variable attribute1="value1" attribute2="value2" ... %>
```

The attributes for the **variable** directive are given in Table 7.5.

Attribute	Description
name-given	The variable name that will be available to the scripting language or EL expressions in the calling JSP page. If the **name-from-attribute** is used, the **name-given** attribute must not be present, and vice-versa. The value for **name-given** must not be the same as any of the attributes in this tag file.
name-from-attribute	This attribute is similar to the **name-given** attribute. However, the value for this attribute is the name of an attribute whose value at the start of the tag invocation will give the name of the variable. A translation error will result if both or neither of the **name-given** and **name-from-attribute** attributes is specified.
alias	A locally scoped attribute to hold the value of this variable.
variable-class	The type of this variable. The default is **java.lang.String**.
declare	Indicates whether the variable is declared in the calling page or tag file after this tag invocation. The default is true.
scope	The scope of the scripting variable defined. The possible values are **AT_BEGIN**, **AT_END**, and **NESTED** (default).
description	The description of this variable.

Table 7.5: Attributes of variable

You probably ask why you need the **variable** directive at all if you can just print the processing result to the **JspWriter** of the calling JSP page. This is because simply sending a **String** to the **JspWriter** deprives the calling JSP page of flexibility on how to use the result. As an example, the **firstTag.tag** file in Listing 7.1 outputs the server's current date in long format. If you want to also provide the server's current date in short format, then you'll have to write another tag file. Having two tag files that perform similar functionality adds unnecessary maintenance headache. Alternatively, you can expose two variables in the tag file, **longDate** and **shortDate**.

The tag file in Listing 7.11 provides the server's current date in two formats: long and short. It has two variables called **longDate** and **shortDate**.

Listing 7.11: The varDemo.tag

```
<%@ tag import="java.util.Date" import="java.text.DateFormat"%>
<%@ variable name-given="longDate" %>
<%@ variable name-given="shortDate" %>
<%
    Date now = new Date(System.currentTimeMillis());
    DateFormat longFormat =
            DateFormat.getDateInstance(DateFormat.LONG);
    DateFormat shortFormat =
            DateFormat.getDateInstance(DateFormat.SHORT);
    jspContext.setAttribute("longDate", longFormat.format(now));
    jspContext.setAttribute("shortDate", shortFormat.format(now));
%>
<jsp:doBody/>
```

Notice that you set a variable using the **setAttribute** method on the **JspContext** of the tag. The **jspContext** implicit object represents this object. (See the section, "Implicit Objects" later in this chapter). The **set** tag in the JSP Standard Tag Library (JSTL) encapsulates this functionality. If you are familiar with JSTL, you can use this tag instead of the **setAttribute** method. JSTL was discussed in length in Chapter 5, "JSTL."

Also note that you must use the **doBody** standard action to invoke the tag body. For more information, see the sections **doBody** and **invoke** later in this chapter.

To test the **varDemo.tag** file, use the **varDemoTest.jsp** page in Listing 7.12.

Listing 7.12: The varDemoTest.jsp page

```
<%@ taglib prefix="tags" tagdir="/WEB-INF/tags" %>
Today's date:
<br/>
<tags:varDemo>
In long format: ${longDate}
<br/>
In short format: ${shortDate}
</tags:varDemo>
```

You can invoke the **varDemoTest.jsp** page using the following URL:

`http://localhost:8080/app07a/varDemoTest.jsp`

Figure 7.4 shows the result.

Figure 7.4: The result of varDemoTest.jsp

There are many cases in which you would want to use variables. As another example, suppose you want to write a custom action that fetches the details of a product from the database given a product identifier. To solve this problem, you can use an attribute to pass the product identifier. For each piece of information, you provide a variable to store that information. Therefore, you'd end up with the following variables: **name**, **price**, **description**, **imageUrl**, etc.

doBody

The **doBody** standard action can only be used from inside a tag file. You use it to invoke the body of a tag. You've seen **doBody** in action in the tag file in Listing 7.11. In this section you'll learn about **doBody** in more detail.

The **doBody** action can have attributes. You use these attributes if you want to direct the output of the tag invocation to a variable. If used without an attribute, the **doBody** standard action writes the output to the **JspWriter** of the calling JSP page.

The **doBody** standard action's attributes are given in Table 7.6. All attributes are optional.

Attribute	Description
var	The name of a scoped attribute to store the output of the tag body invocation. The value is stored as a **java.lang.String**. Only one of the **var** or **varReader** attribute may be present.
varReader	The name of a scoped attribute to store the output of the tag body invocation. The value is stored as a **java.io.Reader**. Only one of the **var** or **varReader** attribute may be present.
scope	The scope for the resulting variable.

Table 7.6: Attributes of doBody

The following example shows how to use **doBody** to invoke a tag body and store the output in a session-scoped variable called **referer**. Suppose you have a web site for selling toys and you advertised your web site heavily in many search engines. Of course, you would want to know which search engine redirects the most traffic that results in a sale. To find out, you could record the **referer** header of the main page of your web application. You use a tag file to store the value of the **referer** header as a session attribute. Later, if the user decides to purchase a product, you can obtain the session attribute value and insert it into a database table.

The example consists of an HTML file (**searchEngine.html**), two JSP pages (**main.jsp** and **viewReferer.jsp**), and one tag file (**doBodyDemo.tag**). The **main.jsp** page is the main page for the web site. It uses the **doBodyDemo** custom tag to store the **referer** header. To view the **referer** header value, you use the **viewReferer.jsp** page. If you invoke the **main.jsp** page by directly typing its URL, the **referer** header will be null. Therefore, you have to use the **searchEngine.html** file to go to the main.jsp page.

The **doBodyDemo.tag** file is given in Listing 7.13.

Listing 7.13: The doBodyDemo.tag

```
<jsp:doBody var="referer" scope="session"/>
```

That's right. The **doBodyDemo.tag** file consists only of one line: a **doBody** standard action. What it does is invoke the body of the tag and store the output in a session attribute called **referer**.

The **main.jsp** page is presented in Listing 7.14.

Listing 7.14: The main.jsp page

```
<%@ taglib prefix="tags" tagdir="/WEB-INF/tags" %>
Your referer header: ${header.referer}
<br/>
<tags:doBodyDemo>
    ${header.referer}
</tags:doBodyDemo>
<a href="viewReferer.jsp">View</a> the referer as a Session
        attribute.
```

The **main.jsp** page prints the value of the **referer** header, using text and an EL expression:

```
Your referer header: ${header.referer}
<br/>
```

It then uses the **doBodyDemo** tag, passing the **referer** header as the body.

```
<tags:doBodyDemo>
    ${header.referer}
</tags:doBodyDemo>
```

Next it prints a link to the **viewReferer.jsp** page for your convenience:

```
<a href="viewReferer.jsp">View</a> the referer as a Session
        attribute.
```

The **viewReferer.jsp** page is shown in Listing 7.15.

Listing 7.15: The viewReferer.jsp page

```
The referer header of the previous page is ${sessionScope.referer}
```

The **viewReferer.jsp** page prints the value of a session attribute called **referer** using an EL expression.

Last, the **searchEngine.html** is given in Listing 7.16:

Listing 7.16: The searchEnginer.html file

```
Please click <a href="main.jsp">here</a>
```

To test the example, first invoke the **searchEngine.html** file using the following URL:

```
http://localhost:8080/app07a/searchEngine.html
```

You'll see the **searchEngine.html** page in Figure 7.5.

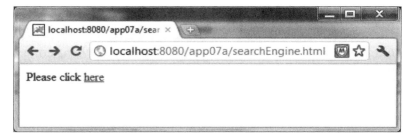

Figure 7.5: The searchEngine.html page

Now, click the link to go to the **main.jsp** page. The **referer** header of the **main.jsp** page will be the URL of the **searchEngine.html**. Figure 7.6 shows the content of the **main.jsp** page.

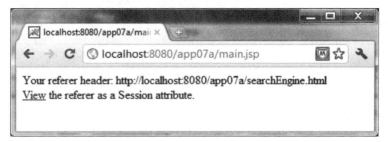

Figure 7.6: The main.jsp page

The **main.jsp** page invoke the **doBodyDemo** custom action that stores the **referer** session attribute. Now, click the **view** link in the **main.jsp** page to see the session attribute value. You'll see something similar to Figure 7.7.

Figure 7.7: The viewReferer.jsp page

invoke

The **invoke** standard action is similar to **doBody** and can be used in a tag file to invoke a fragment attribute. Recall that an attribute can have a **fragment** attribute whose value is either **true** or **false**. If the **fragment** attribute value is **true**, the attribute is a fragment attribute, which you can invoke as many times as you want from a tag file. **invoke** can have attributes too. The attributes for **invoke** are presented in Table 7.7. Note that only the **fragment** attribute is required.

Attribute	Description
fragment	The name used to identify this fragment during this tag invocation.
var	The name of a scoped attribute to store the output of the tag body invocation. The value is stored as a **java.lang.String**. Only one of the **var** or **varReader** attribute can be present.
varReader	The name of a scoped attribute to store the output of the tag body invocation. The value is stored as a **java.io.Reader**. Only one of the **var** or **varReader** attribute can be present.
scope	The scope for the resulting variable.

Table 7.7: Attributes of invoke

As an example, consider the **invokeDemo.tag** file in Listing 7.17.

Listing 7.17: The invokeDemo.tag file

```
<%@ attribute name="productDetails" fragment="true" %>
<%@ variable name-given="productName" %>
<%@ variable name-given="description" %>
<%@ variable name-given="price" %>
<%
    jspContext.setAttribute("productName", "Pelesonic DVD Player");
    jspContext.setAttribute("description",
        "Dolby Digital output through coaxial digital-audio jack," +
        " 500 lines horizontal resolution-image digest viewing");
    jspContext.setAttribute("price", "65");
%>
<jsp:invoke fragment="productDetails"/>
```

The **invokeDemo.tag** file uses the **attribute** directive and its **fragment** attribute is set to **true**. It also defines three variables and sets the value for

those variables. The last line of the tag file invoke the fragment
productDetails. Because there is no **var** or **varReader** attribute in the
invoke standard action, the result of tag invocation will be directed to the
JspWriter of the calling JSP page.

To test the tag file, use the **invokeTest.jsp** page in Listing 7.18.

Listing 7.18: The invokeTest.jsp page

```
<%@ taglib prefix="easy" tagdir="/WEB-INF/tags" %>
<html>
<head>
<title>Product Details</title>
</head>
<body>
<easy:invokeDemo>
    <jsp:attribute name="productDetails">
        <table width="220" border="1">
        <tr>
            <td><b>Product Name</b></td>
            <td>${productName}</td>
        </tr>
        <tr>
            <td><b>Description</b></td>
            <td>${description}</td>
        </tr>
        <tr>
            <td><b>Price</b></td>
            <td>${price}</td>
        </tr>
        </table>
    </jsp:attribute>
</easy:invokeDemo>
</body>
</html>
```

You can use the following URL to call the invokeTest.jsp page.

```
http://localhost:8080/app07a/invokeTest.jsp
```

The result is shown in Figure 7.8.

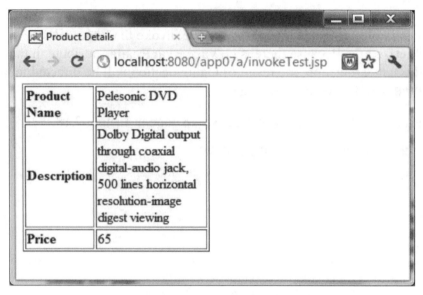

Figure 7.8: Using the fragment attribute

Summary

In this chapter you have learned about tag files and how they make writing tag extensions much simpler. With tag files, you don't need the tag library descriptor and you don't even need to compile the tag handler. You have also seen how to use the **invoke** and **doBody** standard actions.

Chapter 8
Listeners

The Servlet API comes with a set of event classes and listener interfaces for event-driven programming in servlet/JSP applications. All event classes are derived from **java.util.Event** and listeners are available in three different levels, the **ServletContext** level, the **HttpSession** level, and the **ServletRequest** level.

This chapter demonstrates how to write listeners and use them in servlet/JSP applications. One of the listener interfaces, **javax.servlet.AsyncListener**, is a new addition to Servlet 3.0 and discussed in Chapter 14, "Asynchronous Operations."

Listener Interfaces and Registration

The listener interfaces for creating listeners are part of the **javax.servlet** and **javax.servlet.http** packages. They are listed below.

- **javax.servlet.ServletContextListener**. A listener to respond to servlet context lifecycle events. One of its method is called right after the servlet context is created and another method right before the servlet context is shut down.
- **javax.servlet.ServletContextAttributeListener**. A listener that can act upon a servlet context attribute being added, removed, or replaced.
- **javax.servlet.http.HttpSessionListener**. A listener to respond to the creation, timing-out, and invalidation of an **HttpSession**.
- **javax.servlet.http.HttpSessionAttributeListener**. A listener that gets called when a session attribute is added, removed, or replaced.
- **javax.servlet.http.HttpSessionActivationListener**. A listener that gets called when an **HttpSession** has been activated or passivated.

- **javax.servlet.http.HttpSessionBindingListener**. A class whose instances are to be stored as **HttpSession** attributes may implement this interface. An instance of a class implementing **HttpSessionBindingListener** will get a notification when it is added to or removed from the **HttpSession**.
- **javax.servlet.ServletRequestListener**. A listener to respond to the creation and removal of a **ServletRequest**.
- **javax.servlet.ServletRequestAttributeListener**. A listener whose methods get called when an attribute has been added, removed, or replaced from a **ServletRequest**.
- **javax.servlet.AsyncListener**. A listener used for asynchronous operations. It will be explained in detail in Chapter 14, "Asynchronous Operations."

To create a listener, simply create a Java class that implements the relevant interface. In Servlet 3.0 there are two ways to register a listener so that it will be recognized by the servlet container. The first one is to use the **WebListener** annotation type like this:

```
@WebListener
public class ListenerClass implements ListenerInterface {

}
```

The second way to register a listener is by using a **listener** element in the deployment descriptor.

```
</listener>
    <listener-class>fully-qualified listener class</listener-class>
</listener>
```

You can have as many listeners as you want in your application. Note that calls to a listener method are performed synchronously.

Servlet Context Listeners

There are two listener interfaces at the **ServletContext** level, **ServletContextListener** and **ServletContextAttributeListener**. Both are explained in the sections below.

ServletContextListener

A **ServletContextListener** responds to the initialization and destruction of the **ServletContext**. When the **ServletContext** is initialized, the servlet container calls the **contextInitialized** method on all registered **ServletContextListener**s. Its signature is as follows.

```
void contextInitialized(ServletContextEvent event)
```

When the **ServletContext** is about to be decommissioned and destroyed, the servlet container calls the **contextDestroyed** method on all registered **ServletContextListener**s. Here is the signature of **contextDestroyed**.

```
void contextDestroyed(ServletContextEvent event)
```

Both **contextInitialized** and **contextDestroyed** receive a **ServletContextEvent** from the servlet container. A descendant of **java.util.EventObject**, the **javax.servlet.ServletContextEvent** class defines a **getServletContext** method that returns the **ServletContext**:

```
ServletContext getServletContext()
```

This method is important as this is the only easy way to access the **ServletContext**. Many **ServletContextListener**s are there to store an attribute in the **ServletContext**.

As an example, consider the **app08a** application that accompanies this book. The **AppListener** class in Listing 8.1 is a **ServletContextListener** that places a **Map** containing country codes and names as a **ServletContext** attribute right after the **ServletContext** is initialized.

Listing 8.1: The AppListener class

```
package app08a.listener;
import java.util.HashMap;
import java.util.Map;
import javax.servlet.ServletContext;
import javax.servlet.ServletContextEvent;
import javax.servlet.ServletContextListener;
import javax.servlet.annotation.WebListener;

@WebListener
public class AppListener implements ServletContextListener {
```

```
@Override
public void contextDestroyed(ServletContextEvent sce) {
}

@Override
public void contextInitialized(ServletContextEvent sce) {
    ServletContext servletContext = sce.getServletContext();

    Map<String, String> countries =
            new HashMap<String, String>();
    countries.put("ca", "Canada");
    countries.put("us", "United States");
    servletContext.setAttribute("countries", countries);
}
}
```

Pay attention to the implementation of the **contextInitialized** method in the class in Listing 8.1. It starts by calling the **getServletContext** method on the **ServletContextEvent** passed by the servlet container. It then creates a Map an populates it with two countries and puts the **Map** as a **ServletContext** attribute. In real world applications, data stored in a **ServletContext** may come from a database.

To test the listener, use the **countries.jsp** page in Listing 8.2.

Listing 8.2: The countries.jsp page

```
<%@ taglib uri="http://java.sun.com/jsp/jstl/core" prefix="c" %>
<html>
<head>
<title>Country List</title>
</head>
<body>
We operate in these countries:
<ul>
    <c:forEach items="${countries}" var="country">
        <li>${country.value}</li>
    </c:forEach>
</ul>
</body>
</html>
```

The **countries.jsp** page uses the JSTL **forEach** tag to iterate over the **countries** map. Note that you need the JSTL libraries in your **WEB-INF/lib** directory of the **app08a** application for this example to work.

After you copy the JSTL libraries to the **lib** directory, restart your servlet container and direct your browser to this URL:

```
http://localhost:8080/app08a/countries
```

You should see a screen similar to Figure 8.1.

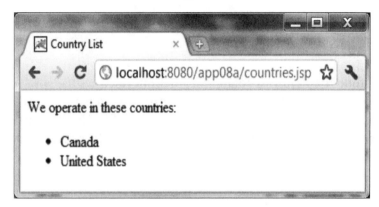

Figure 8.1: Using ServletContextListener to load initial values

ServletContextAttributeListener

An implementation of **ServletContextAttributeListener** receives notification whenever an attribute is added to, removed from, or replaced in the **ServletContext**. Here are the three methods defined in this listener interface.

```
void attributeAdded(ServletContextAttributeEvent event)

void attributeRemoved(ServletContextAttributeEvent event)

void attributeReplaced(ServletContextAttributeEvent event)
```

The **attributeAdded** method is called by the servlet container when an attribute is added to the **ServletContext**. The **attributeRemoved** method gets invoked when an attribute is removed from the **ServletContext** and the **attributeReplaced** method gets called when a **ServletContext** attribute is replaced by a new one. All the listener methods received an instance of **ServletContextAttributeEvent** from which you can retrieve the attribute name and value.

The **ServletContextAttributeEvent** class is derived from **ServletContextAttribute** and adds these two methods to retrieve the attribute name and value, respectively.

```
java.lang.String getName()

java.lang.Object getValue()
```

Session Listeners

There are four **HttpSession**-related listener interfaces, **HttpSessionListener**, **HttpSessionActivationListener**, **HttpSessionAttributeListener**, and **HttpSessionBindingListener**. All these interfaces are members of the **javax.servlet.http** package and are explained in the sections below.

HttpSessionListener

The servlet container calls all registered **HttpSessionListener**s when an **HttpSession** is created or destroyed. The two methods defined in **HttpSessionListener** are **sessionCreated** and **sessionDestroyed**.

```
void sessionCreated(HttpSessionEvent event)

void sessionDestroyed(HttpSessionEvent event)
```

Both methods receive an instance of **HttpSessionEvent**, which is a descendant of **java.util.Event**. You can call the **getSession** method on the **HttpSessionEvent** to obtain the **HttpSession** created or destroyed. The signature of the **getSession** method is as follows:

```
HttpSession getSession()
```

As an example, look at the **SessionListener** class in **app08a**, which is printed in Listing 8.3. This listener provides the number of **HttpSessions** in the application. An **AtomicInteger** is used as a counter and stored as a **ServletContext** attribute. When an **HttpSession** is created, this counter is incremented. When an **HttpSession** is invalidated, this counter is decremented. As such, it provides an accurate snapshot of the number of users having a valid session at the time the counter is read. An **AtomicInteger** is used instead of an Integer to guarantee the atomicity of the incrementing and decrementing operations.

Listing 8.3: The SessionListener class

```java
package app08a.listener;
import java.util.concurrent.atomic.AtomicInteger;
import javax.servlet.ServletContext;
import javax.servlet.ServletContextEvent;
import javax.servlet.ServletContextListener;
import javax.servlet.annotation.WebListener;
import javax.servlet.http.HttpSession;
import javax.servlet.http.HttpSessionEvent;
import javax.servlet.http.HttpSessionListener;

@WebListener
public class SessionListener implements HttpSessionListener,
        ServletContextListener {

    @Override
    public void contextInitialized(ServletContextEvent sce) {
        ServletContext servletContext = sce.getServletContext();
        servletContext.setAttribute("userCounter",
                new AtomicInteger());
    }

    @Override
    public void contextDestroyed(ServletContextEvent sce) {
    }

    @Override
    public void sessionCreated(HttpSessionEvent se) {
        HttpSession session = se.getSession();
        ServletContext servletContext = session.getServletContext();
        AtomicInteger userCounter = (AtomicInteger) servletContext
                .getAttribute("userCounter");
        int userCount = userCounter.incrementAndGet();
        System.out.println("userCount incremented to :" +
                userCount);
    }
```

```
    @Override
    public void sessionDestroyed(HttpSessionEvent se) {
        HttpSession session = se.getSession();
        ServletContext servletContext = session.getServletContext();
        AtomicInteger userCounter = (AtomicInteger) servletContext
                .getAttribute("userCounter");
        int userCount = userCounter.decrementAndGet();
        System.out.println("---------- userCount decremented to :"
                + userCount);
    }
}
```

As you can see in Listing 8.3, the **SessionListener** class implements the **ServletContextListener** interface and the **HttpSessionListener** interface. Therefore, you need to implement methods from both interfaces.

The **contextInitialized** method is inherited from the **ServletContextListener** interface and it creates and stores an **AtomicInteger** in the **ServletContext**. Since the initial value of an **AtomicInteger** is zero, it indicates that at the time the application is started there is zero user. The name of the **ServletContext** attribute is **userCounter**.

```
    public void contextInitialized(ServletContextEvent sce) {
        ServletContext servletContext = sce.getServletContext();
        servletContext.setAttribute("userCounter",
                new AtomicInteger());
    }
```

The **sessionCreated** method is invoked every time an **HttpSession** is created. What this method does is retrieve the **HttpSession** created and obtains the **userCounter** attribute from the **ServletContext**. It then calls the **incrementAndGet** method on the **userCounter AtomicInteger**. The value is printed to make it easy for you to see how the listener works.

```
    public void sessionCreated(HttpSessionEvent se) {
        HttpSession session = se.getSession();
        ServletContext servletContext = session.getServletContext();
        AtomicInteger userCounter = (AtomicInteger) servletContext
                .getAttribute("userCounter");
        int userCount = userCounter.incrementAndGet();
        System.out.println("userCount incremented to :" +
                userCount);
    }
```

The **sessionDestroyed** method is called right before an **HttpSession** is about to be destroyed. The method implementation is similar to that of **sessionCreated**, except that it decrements the value of **userCounter** instead of incrementing is.

```
public void sessionDestroyed(HttpSessionEvent se) {
    HttpSession session = se.getSession();
    ServletContext servletContext = session.getServletContext();
    AtomicInteger userCounter = (AtomicInteger) servletContext
            .getAttribute("userCounter");
    int userCount = userCounter.decrementAndGet();
    System.out.println("---------- userCount decremented to :"
            + userCount);
}
```

To test the listener, request the **countries.jsp** page again using different browsers and watch what's printed on your console. Here is the URL to invoke countries.jsp:

```
http://localhost:8080/app08a/countries.jsp
```

The first invocation will cause this printed in your console:

```
userCount incremented to :1
```

Another request from the same browser won't change the value of **userCounter** as it will be associated with the same **HttpSession**. However, invoking the page using a different browser will increase the value of **userCounter**.

Now, if you have time wait until the **HttpSession**s expire and take note of what is printed on the console again.

HttpSessionAttributeListener

An **HttpSessionAttributeListener** is like a **ServletContextAttributeListener**, except that it gets invoked when an attribute is added to, removed from, or replaced in an **HttpSession**. The following are methods defined in the **HttpSessionAttributeListener** interface.

```
void attributeAdded(HttpSessionBindingEvent event)
```

```
void attributeRemoved( HttpSessionBindingEvent event)

void attributeReplaced( HttpSessionBindingEvent event)
```

The **attributeAdded** method is called by the servlet container when an attribute is added to the **HttpSession**. The **attributeRemoved** method gets invoked when an attribute is removed from the **HttpSession** and the **attributeReplaced** method gets called when a **HttpSession** attribute is replaced by a new one. All the listener methods received an instance of **HttpSessionBindingEvent** from which you can retrieve the corresponding **HttpSession** and the attribute name and value.

```
java.lang.String getName()

java.lang.Object getValue()
```

Since **HttpSessionBindingEvent** is a subclass of **HttpSessionEvent**, you can also obtain the affected **HttpSession** in your **HttpSessionAttributeListener** class.

HttpSessionActivationListener

In a distributed environment where multiple servlet containers are configured to scale, the servlet containers may migrate or serialize session attributes in order to conserve memory. Typically, relatively rarely accessed object may be serialized into secondary storage when memory is low. When doing so, the servlet containers notify session attributes whose classes implement the **HttpSessionActivationListener** interface.

There are two methods defined in this interface, **sessionDidActivate** and **sessionWillPassivate**:

```
void sessionDidActivate(HttpSessionEvent event)

void sessionWillPassivate(HttpSessionEvent event)
```

The **sessionDidActivate** method is invoked after the **HttpSession** containing this object has just been activated. The **HttpSessionEvent** the servlet container passes to the method lets you obtain the **HttpSession** that was activated.

The **sessionWillPassivate** method is called when the **HttpSession** containing this listener is about to be passivated. Like **sessionDidActivate**, the servlet container passes an **HttpSessionEvent** to the method so that the session attribute may act on the **HttpSession**.

HttpSessionBindingListener

An **HttpSessionBindingListener** gets notification when it is bound and unbound to an **HttpSession**. A class whose instances are to be stored as session attributes may implement this interface if knowing when it's bound to or unbound from an **HttpSession** is of interest. For example, an object whose class implements this interface might update itself when it is stored as an **HttpSession** attribute. Or, an implementation of **HttpSessionBindingListener** might release resources it is holding once it's unbound from the **HttpSession**.

As an example, the **Product** class in Listing 8.4 implements **HttpSessionBindingListener**.

Listing 8.4: A class implementing HttpSessionBindingListener

```java
package app08a.model;
import javax.servlet.http.HttpSessionBindingEvent;
import javax.servlet.http.HttpSessionBindingListener;

public class Product implements HttpSessionBindingListener {
    private String id;
    private String name;
    private double price;

    public String getId() {
        return id;
    }
    public void setId(String id) {
        this.id = id;
    }
    public String getName() {
        return name;
    }
    public void setName(String name) {
        this.name = name;
    }
    public double getPrice() {
        return price;
    }
```

```
    }
    public void setPrice(double price) {
        this.price = price;
    }

    @Override
    public void valueBound(HttpSessionBindingEvent event) {
        String attributeName = event.getName();
        System.out.println(attributeName + " valueBound");
    }

    @Override
    public void valueUnbound(HttpSessionBindingEvent event) {
        String attributeName = event.getName();
        System.out.println(attributeName + " valueUnbound");
    }
}
```

The listener does not do more than printing to the console when it's bound to an **HttpSession** and when it's unbound.

ServletRequest Listeners

There are three listener interfaces at the **ServletRequest** level, **ServletRequestListener**, **ServletRequestAttributeListener**, and **AsyncListener**. The first two listeners are discussed in this section and **AsyncListener** is covered in Chapter 14, "Asynchronous Operations."

ServletRequestListener

A **ServletRequestListener** responds to the creation and destruction of a **ServletRequest**. In a servlet container that pools and reuses **ServletRequest**s, the creation of a **ServletRequest** is taken to be the time it is retrieved from the pool and its destruction the time it is returned to the pool.

The **ServletRequestListener** interface defines two methods, **requestInitialized** and **requestDestroyed**. Their signatures are as follows.

```
void requestInitialized(ServletRequestEvent event)
```

```
void requestDestroyed(ServletRequestEvent event)
```

The **requestInitialized** method is invoked when a **ServletRequest** has been created (or taken from the pool) and the **requestDestroyed** method when a **ServletRequest** is about to be destroyed (or returned to the pool). Both methods receive a **ServletRequestEvent**, from which you can retrieve the corresponding **ServletRequest** instance by calling the **getServletRequest** method.

```
ServletRequest getServletRequest()
```

In addition, the **ServletRequestEvent** interface also defines the **getServletContext** method that returns the **ServletContext**. The method signature is as follows.

```
ServletContext getServletContext()
```

As an example, consider the **PerfStatListener** class in **app08a**. The listener measures the difference between the time the **ServletRequest** is destroyed and the time it was created, thus effectively the time taken to execute a request.

The **PerfStatListener** class in Listing 8.5 takes advantage of the **ServletRequestListener** interface to measure how long it takes an HTTP request to complete. It relies on the fact that the servlet container calls the **requestInitialized** method on a **ServletRequestListener** at the beginning of a request and calls the **requestDestroyed** method after it processes it. By reading the current time at the starts of the two events and compare the two, you can get the approximate of how long it took an HTTP request to complete.

Listing 8.5: The PerfStatListener

```
package app08a.listener;
import javax.servlet.ServletRequest;
import javax.servlet.ServletRequestEvent;
import javax.servlet.ServletRequestListener;
import javax.servlet.annotation.WebListener;
import javax.servlet.http.HttpServletRequest;

@WebListener
public class PerfStatListener implements ServletRequestListener {
```

```
@Override
public void requestInitialized(ServletRequestEvent sre) {
    ServletRequest servletRequest = sre.getServletRequest();
    servletRequest.setAttribute("start", System.nanoTime());
}

@Override
public void requestDestroyed(ServletRequestEvent sre) {
    ServletRequest servletRequest = sre.getServletRequest();
    Long start = (Long) servletRequest.getAttribute("start");
    Long end = System.nanoTime();
    HttpServletRequest httpServletRequest =
            (HttpServletRequest) servletRequest;
    String uri = httpServletRequest.getRequestURI();
    System.out.println("time taken to execute " + uri +
            ":"  + ((end - start) / 1000) + "microseconds");
}
}
```

The **requestInitialized** method in Listing 8.5 calls **System.nanoTime()** and puts the return value (that will be boxed as **Long**) as a **ServletRequest** attribute.

```
public void requestInitialized(ServletRequestEvent sre) {
    ServletRequest servletRequest = sre.getServletRequest();
    servletRequest.setAttribute("start", System.nanoTime());
}
```

The **nanoTime** method returns a **long** indicating some arbitrary time. The return value is not related to any notion of system or wall-clock time, but two return values taken in the same JVM are perfect for measuring the time that elapsed between the first **nanoTime** call and the second.

As you may have guessed, the **requestDestroyed** method calls the **nanoTime** method the second time and compares its value with the first.

```
public void requestDestroyed(ServletRequestEvent sre) {
    ServletRequest servletRequest = sre.getServletRequest();
    Long start = (Long) servletRequest.getAttribute("start");
    Long end = System.nanoTime();
    HttpServletRequest httpServletRequest =
            (HttpServletRequest) servletRequest;
    String uri = httpServletRequest.getRequestURI();
    System.out.println("time taken to execute " + uri +
            ":"  + ((end - start) / 1000) + "microseconds");
```

}

To test the **PerfStatListener**, invoke the **countries.jsp** page in **app08a** again.

ServletRequestAttributeListener

A **ServletRequestAttributeListener** gets called when an attribute has been added to, removed from, or replaced in a **ServletRequest**. There are three methods defined in the **ServletRequestAttributeListener** interface, **attributeAdded**, **attributeReplaced**, and **attributeRemoved**. The signatures of the methods are as follows.

```
void attributeAdded(ServletRequestAttributeEvent event)

void attributeRemoved(ServletRequestAttributeEvent event)

void attributeReplaced(ServletRequestAttributeEvent event)
```

All the methods receive an instance of **ServletRequestAttributeEvent**, which is a child class of **ServletRequestEvent**. The **ServletRequestAttributeEvent** class exposes the related attribute through the **getName** and **getValue** methods:

```
java.lang.String getName()

java.lang.Object getValue()
```

Summary

In this chapter you've learned the various listener types that can be found in the Servlet API. Those listeners may fall into one of three scopes: application, session, and request. Putting listeners to work is also straightforward, involving a simple registration process. You can register a listener by annotating the implementation class using **@WebListener** or by using the **listener** element in the deployment descriptor.

One of the listener interfaces, **javax.servlet.AsyncListener**, is a new addition to Servlet 3.0 and discussed in Chapter 14, "Asynchronous Operations."

Chapter 9
Filters

A filter is an object that intercepts a request and processes the **ServletRequest** or the **ServletResponse** passed to the resource being requested. Filters can be used for logging, encryption and decryption, session checking, image transformation, and so on. Filters can be configured to intercept a resource or multiple resources.

Filter configuration can be done through annotations or the deployment descriptor. If multiple filters are applied to the same resource or the same set of resources, the invocation order is sometimes important and in this case you need the deployment descriptor.

This chapter explains how to write and register filters. Several examples are also given.

The Filter API

The following section explains the interfaces that are used in a filter, including **Filter**, **FilterConfig**, and **FilterChain**.

A filter class must implement the **javax.servlet.Filter** interface. This interface exposes three lifecycle methods for a filter: **init**, **doFilter**, and **destroy**.

The **init** method is called by the servlet container when the filter is being put into service, i.e. when the application is started. In other words, the **init** method does not wait until a resource associated with the filter is invoked. This method is only called once and should contain initialization code for the filter. The signature of the init method is as follows.

```
void init(FilterConfig filterConfig)
```

Note that the servlet container passes a **FilterConfig** to the **init** method. The **FilterConfig** interface is explained below.

The **doFilter** method of a **Filter** instance is called by the servlet container every time a resource associated with the filter is invoked. This method receives a **ServletRequest**, a **ServletResponse**, and a **FilterChain**.

Here is the signature of **doFilter**:

```
void doFilter(ServletRequest request, ServletResponse response,
        FilterChain filterChain)
```

As you can see here, an implementation of **doFilter** has access to the **ServletRequest** and the **ServletResponse**. As such, it is possible to add an attribute to the **ServletRequest** or a header to the **ServletResponse**. You can even decorate the **ServletRequest** or the **ServletResponse** to change their behavior, as explained in Chapter 13, "Decorating Requests and Responses."

The last line of code in a **doFilter** method implementation should be a call to the **doChain** method on the **FilterChain** passed as the third argument to **doFilter**:

```
filterChain.doFilter(request, response)
```

A resource may be associated with multiple filters (or in a more technical term, a chain of filters), and **FilterChain.doFilter()** basically causes the next filter in the chain to be invoked. Calling **FilterChain.doFilter()** on the last filter in the chain causes the resource itself to be invoked.

If you do not call **FilterChain.doFilter()** at the end of your **Filter.doFilter()** implementation, processing will stop there and the request will not be invoked.

Note that the **doFilter** method is the only method in the **FilterChain** interface. This method is slightly different from the **doFilter** method in **Filter**. In **FilterChain**, **doFilter** only take two arguments instead of three.

The last lifecycle method in **Filter** is **destroy**. Here is its signature.

```
void destroy()
```

This method is called by the servlet container before the filter is taken out of service, which normally happens when the application is stopped.

Unless a filter class is declared in multiple **filter** element in the deployment descriptor, the servlet container will only create a single instance of each type of filter. Since a servlet/JSP application is normally a multi-user application, a filter instance may be accessed by multiple threads at the same time and you need to handle multi-threading issue carefully. For an example of how to handle thread safety, see the Download Counter filter example later in this chapter.

Filter Configuration

After you finish writing a filter class, you still have to configure the filter. Filter configuration has these objectives:

- Determine what resources the filter will intercept.
- Setup initial values to be passed to the filter's **init** method.
- Give the filter a name. Giving a filter a name in most cases does not have much significance but can sometimes be helpful. For example, you might want to log the time a filter starts, and if you have multiple filters in the same application, it is often useful to see the order in which the filters are invoked.

The **FilterConfig** interface allows you to access the **ServletContext** through its **getServletContext** method.

```
ServletContxt getServletContext()
```

If a filter has a name, the **getFilterName** method in **FilterConfig** returns the name. Here is the signature of **getFilterName**.

```
java.lang.String getFilterName()
```

However, you are most often interested in getting initial parameters, which are initialization values that the developer or deployer passes to the filter. There are two methods you can use to handle initial parameters, the first of which is **getParameterNames**:

```
java.util.Enumeration<java.lang.String> getInitParameterNames()
```

This method returns an **Enumeration** of filter parameter names. If no parameter exists for the filter, this method returns an empty **Enumeration**.

The second method for handling initial parameters is **getParameter**:

```
java.lang.String getInitParameter(java.lang.String parameterName)
```

There are two ways to configure a filter. You can configure a filter using the **WebFilter** annotation type or by registering it in the deployment descriptor. Using **@WebFilter** is easy as you just need to annotate the filter class and you do not need the deployment descriptor. However, changing the configuration settings requires that the filter class be recompiled. On the other hand, configuring a filter in the deployment descriptor means changing configuration values is a matter of editing a text file.

To use **@WebFilter**, you need to be familiar with its attributes. Table 9.1 lists attributes that may appear in the **WebFilter** annotation type. All attributes are optional.

Attribute	Description
asyncSupported	Specifies whether or not the filter supports the asynchronous operation mode
description	The description of the filter
dispatcherTypes	The dispatcher types to which the filter applies
displayName	The display name of the filter
filterName	The name of the filter
initParams	The initial parameters
largeIcon	The name of the large icon for the filter
servletNames	The names of the servlets to which the filter applies
smallIcon	The name of the small icon for the filter
urlPatterns	The URL patterns to which the filter applies
value	The URL patterns to which the filter applies

Table 9.1: WebFilter attributes

For instance, the following **@WebFilter** annotation specifies that the filter name is **DataCompressionFilter** and it applies to all resources.

```
@WebFilter(filterName="DataCompressionFilter", urlPatterns={"/*"})
```

This is equivalent to declaring these **filter** and **filter-mapping** elements in the deployment descriptor.

```
<filter>
    <filter-name>DataCompressionFilter</filter-name>
    <filter-class>
        the fully-qualified name of the filter class
    </filter-class>
</filter>
<filter-mapping>
    <filter-name>DataCompresionFilter</filter-name>
    <url-pattern>/*</url-pattern>
</filter-mapping>
```

As another example, the following filter is passed two initial parameters:

```
@WebFilter(filterName = "Security Filter", urlPatterns = { "/*" },
        initParams = {
            @WebInitParam(name = "frequency", value = "1909"),
            @WebInitParam(name = "resolution", value = "1024")
        }
)
```

Using the **filter** and **filter-mapping** elements in the deployment descriptor, the configuration settings would be as follows.

```
<filter>
    <filter-name>Security Filter</filter-name>
    <filter-class>filterClass</filter-class>
    <init-param>
        <param-name>frequency</param-name>
        <param-value>1909</param-value>
     </init-param>
    <init-param>
        <param-name>resolution</param-name>
        <param-value>1024</param-value>
    </init-param>
</filter>
<filter-mapping>
    <filter-name>DataCompresionFilter</filter-name>
    <url-pattern>/*</url-pattern>
</filter-mapping>
```

The deployment descriptor is discussed in detail in Chapter 16, "Deployment."

Example 1: Logging Filter

As the first example, consider a simple filter in the **app09a** application that is used to log request URIs in a text file. The name of the text file is configurable through an initial parameter. In addition, each entry in the log can be prefixed with a preset string that is also passed as an initial parameter. You can derive valuable information from the log, such as which resource in your application is the most popular or at what time of the day your web site is most busy.

The filter class is called **LoggingFilter** and is printed in Listing 9.1. By convention, a filter class name ends with **Filter**.

Listing 9.1: The LoggingFilter class

```
package filter;
import java.io.File;
import java.io.FileNotFoundException;
import java.io.IOException;
import java.io.PrintWriter;
import java.util.Date;

import javax.servlet.Filter;
import javax.servlet.FilterChain;
import javax.servlet.FilterConfig;
import javax.servlet.ServletException;
import javax.servlet.ServletRequest;
import javax.servlet.ServletResponse;
import javax.servlet.annotation.WebFilter;
import javax.servlet.annotation.WebInitParam;
import javax.servlet.http.HttpServletRequest;

@WebFilter(filterName = "LoggingFilter", urlPatterns = { "/*" },
        initParams = {
                @WebInitParam(name = "logFileName",
                        value = "log.txt"),
                @WebInitParam(name = "prefix", value = "URI: ") })
public class LoggingFilter implements Filter {

    private PrintWriter logger;
    private String prefix;

    @Override
    public void init(FilterConfig filterConfig)
```

```
            throws ServletException {
    prefix = filterConfig.getInitParameter("prefix");
    String logFileName = filterConfig
            .getInitParameter("logFileName");
    String appPath = filterConfig.getServletContext()
            .getRealPath("/");
    // without path info in logFileName, the log file will be
    // created in $TOMCAT_HOME/bin

    System.out.println("logFileName:" + logFileName);
    try {
        logger = new PrintWriter(new File(appPath,
                logFileName));
    } catch (FileNotFoundException e) {
        e.printStackTrace();
        throw new ServletException(e.getMessage());
    }
}

@Override
public void destroy() {
    System.out.println("destroying filter");
    if (logger != null) {
        logger.close();
    }
}

@Override
public void doFilter(ServletRequest request,
        ServletResponse response, FilterChain filterChain)
        throws IOException, ServletException {
    System.out.println("LoggingFilter.doFilter");
    HttpServletRequest httpServletRequest =
            (HttpServletRequest) request;
    logger.println(new Date() + " " + prefix
            + httpServletRequest.getRequestURI());
    logger.flush();
    filterChain.doFilter(request, response);
}
}
```

Let's look at the filter class closely.

First and foremost, the filter class implements the **Filter** interface and declares two variables, a **PrintWriter** called **logger** and a **String** named **prefix**:

```
private PrintWriter logger;
private String prefix;
```

The **PrintWriter** will be used for writing to a text file. The **prefix** String will be used as the prefix for each log entry.

The filter class is annotated with **@WebFilter**, passing two initial parameters (**logFileName** and **prefix**) to the filter:

```
@WebFilter(filterName = "LoggingFilter", urlPatterns = { "/*" },
     initParams = {
             @WebInitParam(name = "logFileName",
                     value = "log.txt"),
             @WebInitParam(name = "prefix", value = "URI: ")
     }
)
```

The **init** method calls the **getInitParameter** method on the passed-in **FilterConfig** to retrieve the **prefix** and **logFileName** initial parameters. The value of the **prefix** parameter is assigned to the class-level variable **prefix** and **logFileName** is used to create a **PrintWriter**.

```
prefix = filterConfig.getInitParameter("prefix");
String logFileName = filterConfig
        .getInitParameter("logFileName");
```

Since servlet/JSP applications are started by the servlet/JSP container, the current working directory is the location in which java was invoked. In Tomcat this is the **bin** directory of the Tomcat installation. To create a log file in the application directory, you need the absolute path to it. You can retrieve it using the **ServletContext.getRealPath** method. Combining the application path and the **logFileName** initial parameter, you have this:

```
String appPath = filterConfig.getServletContext()
        .getRealPath("/");
// without path info in logFileName, the log file will be
// created in $TOMCAT_HOME/bin

try {
    logger = new PrintWriter(new File(appPath,
            logFileName));
```

```
    } catch (FileNotFoundException e) {
        e.printStackTrace();
        throw new ServletException(e.getMessage());
    }
```

A log file will be created when the **init** method is executed. If a file with the same name already exists in the application directory, the file will be overwritten by the new file.

When the application is shut down, the **PrintWriter** must be closed. Therefore, in the filter's **destroy** method, you write

```
    if (logger != null) {
        logger.close();
    }
```

The **doFilter** method logs all requests by downcasting the **ServletRequest** to **HttpServletRequest** and calling its **getRequestURI** method. The result of **getRequestURI** is then fed to the **println** method of the **PrintWriter**.

```
    HttpServletRequest httpServletRequest =
            (HttpServletRequest) request;
    logger.println(new Date() + " " + prefix
            + httpServletRequest.getRequestURI());
```

Each entry is given a timestamp and a prefix to make it easy to figure out when an entry is made. The **doFilter** method then flushes the **PrintWriter** and calls **FilterChain.doFilter** to invoke the resource.

```
    logger.flush();
    filterChain.doFilter(request, response);
```

When you run Tomcat, the filter will be put in service without waiting for the first request. You should see printed on your console the value of the **logFileName** parameter.

To test this filter, invoke the **test.jsp** page in the **app09a** application using this URL:

```
http://localhost:8080/app09a/test.jsp
```

Verify that the filter is working correctly by examining the content of the log file.

Example 2: Image Protector Filter

The Image Protector Filter in this example prevents an image from being downloaded by typing the image URL in the browser's Address box. An image in the application will only show if the link to the image is clicked on a page. The filter works by checking the value of the **referer** HTTP header. A null value means the current request has no referrer, in other words the resource is being requested directly by typing its URL. A resource with a non-null referer header will have the page of origin as its referrer. Note that the header name is spelled with one r between the second e and the third e.

The filter class, **ImageProtectorFilter**, is given in Listing 9.2. From the **WebFilter** annotation you know that the filter is applied to all resources having png, jpg, or gif extension.

Listing 9.2: The ImageProtectorFilter class

```
package filter;
import java.io.IOException;
import javax.servlet.Filter;
import javax.servlet.FilterChain;
import javax.servlet.FilterConfig;
import javax.servlet.ServletException;
import javax.servlet.ServletRequest;
import javax.servlet.ServletResponse;
import javax.servlet.annotation.WebFilter;
import javax.servlet.http.HttpServletRequest;

@WebFilter(filterName = "ImageProtetorFilter", urlPatterns = {
        "*.png", "*.jpg", "*.gif" })
public class ImageProtectorFilter implements Filter {

    @Override
    public void init(FilterConfig filterConfig)
            throws ServletException {
    }

    @Override
    public void destroy() {
    }

    @Override
    public void doFilter(ServletRequest request,
```

```
            ServletResponse response, FilterChain filterChain)
            throws IOException, ServletException {
        System.out.println("ImageProtectorFilter");
        HttpServletRequest httpServletRequest =
                (HttpServletRequest) request;
        String referrer = httpServletRequest.getHeader("referer");
        System.out.println("referrer:" + referrer);
        if (referrer != null) {
            filterChain.doFilter(request, response);
        } else {
            throw new ServletException("Image not available");
        }
    }
}
```

The **init** and **destroy** methods are empty. The **doFilter** method reads the value of the **referer** header and either invokes the resource or throws an exception:

```
String referrer = httpServletRequest.getHeader("referer");
System.out.println("referrer:" + referrer);
if (referrer != null) {
    filterChain.doFilter(request, response);
} else {
    throw new ServletException("Image not available");
}
```

To test the filter, try opening the **logo.png** image by typing this URL in your browser's Address box:

```
http://localhost:8080/app09a/image/logo.png
```

You'll get an "Image not available" error message.

Now, invoke the image.jsp page:

```
http://localhost:8080/app09a/image.jsp
```

You should see the image. The reason why this works is because the **image.jsp** page contains this link that instructs the browser to download the image:

```
<img src='image/logo.png'/>
```

When the browser asked for the image for the link, it also sent the URL of the page (in this case, http://localhost:8080/app09a/image.jsp) to the server as the value of the **referer** header.

Example 3: Download Counter Filter

The Download Counter filter in this example features a filter for counting how many times a resource has been downloaded. This is particularly useful if you want to know how popular your documents or your videos are. The numbers are stored in a properties file and not in a database for simplicity's sake. The resource URI is used as the property key in the properties file.

Because we're storing values in a properties file and a filter can be accessed by multiple threads at the same time, there is a thread-safety issue that needs to be resolved. A user can request a resource and the filter will need to read the corresponding property value, increment it by one, and store back the new value. What if a second user requests the same resource before the first thread finishes its business? Well, the count will be inaccurate. Synchronizing the code that reads and writes values does not sound like an ideal solution as scalability may suffer.

This example shows how to resolve this thread-safety problem by using a **Queue** and an **Executor**. If you're not familiar with these two Java types, please refer to Chapter 18, "Working wth Threads and Thread Safety" or my other book, *"Java: A Beginner's Tutorial (Third Edition)."*

In short, all incoming requests place a task in a queue in a single-threaded **Executor**. Placing a task is fast because it's an asynchronous operation so that you don't have to wait for the task to be complete. The **Executor** will take one item at a time from the queue and increment the correct property. Since the **Executor** uses only one thread, we have eliminated any chance of multiple threads accessing the property file.

The **DownloadCounterFilter** class is given in Listing 9.3.

Listing 9.3: DownloadCounterFilter

```
package filter;
import java.io.File;
import java.io.FileReader;
```

```java
import java.io.FileWriter;
import java.io.IOException;
import java.util.Properties;
import java.util.concurrent.ExecutorService;
import java.util.concurrent.Executors;

import javax.servlet.Filter;
import javax.servlet.FilterChain;
import javax.servlet.FilterConfig;
import javax.servlet.ServletException;
import javax.servlet.ServletRequest;
import javax.servlet.ServletResponse;
import javax.servlet.annotation.WebFilter;
import javax.servlet.http.HttpServletRequest;

@WebFilter(filterName = "DownloadCounterFilter",
        urlPatterns = { "/*" })
public class DownloadCounterFilter implements Filter {

    ExecutorService executorService = Executors
            .newSingleThreadExecutor();
    Properties downloadLog;
    File logFile;

    @Override
    public void init(FilterConfig filterConfig)
            throws ServletException {
        System.out.println("DownloadCounterFilter");
        String appPath = filterConfig.getServletContext()
                .getRealPath("/");
        logFile = new File(appPath, "downloadLog.txt");
        if (!logFile.exists()) {
            try {
                logFile.createNewFile();
            } catch (IOException e) {
                e.printStackTrace();
            }
        }
        downloadLog = new Properties();
        try {
            downloadLog.load(new FileReader(logFile));
        } catch (IOException e) {
            e.printStackTrace();
        }
    }
```

```
@Override
public void destroy() {
    executorService.shutdown();
}

@Override
public void doFilter(ServletRequest request,
        ServletResponse response, FilterChain filterChain)
        throws IOException, ServletException {
    HttpServletRequest httpServletRequest = (HttpServletRequest)
  request;

    final String uri = httpServletRequest.getRequestURI();
    executorService.execute(new Runnable() {
        @Override
        public void run() {
            String property = downloadLog.getProperty(uri);
            if (property == null) {
                downloadLog.setProperty(uri, "1");
            } else {
                int count = 0;
                try {
                    count = Integer.parseInt(property);
                } catch (NumberFormatException e) {
                    // silent
                }
                count++;
                downloadLog.setProperty(uri,
                        Integer.toString(count));
            }
            try {
                downloadLog
                        .store(new FileWriter(logFile), "");
            } catch (IOException e) {
            }
        }
    });
    filterChain.doFilter(request, response);
}
}
```

The filter's **init** method creates a **downloadLog.txt** file in the application directory if one does not yet exist.

```
String appPath = filterConfig.getServletContext()
```

```
        .getRealPath("/");
logFile = new File(appPath, "downloadLog.txt");
if (!logFile.exists()) {
    try {
        logFile.createNewFile();
    } catch (IOException e) {
        e.printStackTrace();
    }
}
```

It then creates a **Properties** object and loads the file:

```
downloadLog = new Properties();
try {
    downloadLog.load(new FileReader(logFile));
} catch (IOException e) {
    e.printStackTrace();
}
```

Note that the filter class has an **ExecutorService** (a subclass of **Executor**) as a class-level object reference.

```
ExecutorService executorService = Executors
        .newSingleThreadExecutor();
```

The filter shuts down the **ExecutorService** when the filter is about to be destroyed.

```
public void destroy() {
    executorService.shutdown();
}
```

The **doFilter** method does the bulk of the job. It takes the URI of each request, calls the **execute** method of the **ExecutorService**, and calls **FilterChain.doFilter()**. The task that is passed to the **execute** method is easy to understand. It basically uses the URI as a property key and fetches the property value from the **Properties** object, increments it by one, and flushes the value back to the underlying log file.

```
@Override
public void run() {
    String property = downloadLog.getProperty(uri);
    if (property == null) {
        downloadLog.setProperty(uri, "1");
```

```
            } else {
                int count = 0;
                try {
                    count = Integer.parseInt(property);
                } catch (NumberFormatException e) {
                    // silent
                }
                count++;
                downloadLog.setProperty(uri,
                        Integer.toString(count));
            }
            try {
                downloadLog
                        .store(new FileWriter(logFile), "");
            } catch (IOException e) {
            }
        }
```

The filter works on any resource, but you can easily limit it to, say, PDF or AVI files only if you wish.

Filter Order

If you have multiple filters applied to the same resource and the order of invocation is important, you have to use the deployment descriptor to manage which filter should be invoked first. For example, if **Filter1** must be invoked before **Filter2**, the declaration of **Filter1** should appear before the declaration of **Filter2** in the deployment descriptor.

```
<filter>
    <filter-name>Filter1</filter-name>
    <filter-class>
        the fully-qualified name of the filter class
    </filter-class>
</filter>
<filter>
    <filter-name>Filter2</filter-name>
    <filter-class>
        the fully-qualified name of the filter class
    </filter-class>
</filter>
```

It is not possible to manage filter invocation order without the deployment descriptor. See Chapter 16, "Deployment," for more information about the deployment descriptor.

Summary

In this chapter you've learned about the Filter API that includes the **Filter** interface, the **FilterConfig** interface, and the **FilterChain** interface. You also have learned how to write a filter by implementing the **Filter** interface and annotate the class using **@WebFilter** and registering it in the deployment descriptor.

There is only one instance for each type of filter. Therefore, thread safety may be an issue if you need to keep and change state in your filter class. The last filter example shows how to deal with this issue.

Chapter 10
Application Design

There are two models used in Java web application design, conveniently called Model 1 and Model 2. Model 1 is page-centric and suitable for very small applications only. Model 2 is the recommended architecture for all but the simplest Java web applications.

This chapter discusses Model 2 in minute detail and provides five Model 2 sample applications. The first example features a basic Model 2 application with a servlet as controller. The second example is also a simple Model 2 application, however it uses a filter as controller. The third example introduces the validator component for validating user input. The fourth example shows how you can use the Data Access Object pattern to facilitate database access and data manipulation in a Model 2 application. Finally, the fifth example presents a Model 2 application with support for dependency injection.

Model 1 Overview

When you first learn JSP, your sample applications would normally enable navigation from one page to another by providing a clickable link to the latter. While this navigation method is straightforward, in medium-sized or large applications with significant numbers of pages this approach can cause a maintenance headache. Changing the name of a JSP page, for instance, could force you to rename the links to the page in many other pages. As such, Model 1 is not recommended unless your application will only have two or three pages.

Model 2 Overview

Model 2 is based on the Model-View-Controller (MVC) design pattern, the central concept behind the Smalltalk-80 user interface. As the term "design pattern" had not been coined at that time, it was called the MVC paradigm.

An application implementing the MVC pattern consists of three modules: model, view, and controller. The view takes care of the display of the application. The model encapsulates the application data and business logic. The controller receives user input and commands the model and/or the view to change accordingly.

Note
The paper entitled *Applications Programming in Smalltalk-80(TM): How to use Model-View-Controller (MVC)* by Steve Burbeck, Ph.D. talks about the MVC pattern. You can find it at
http://st-www.cs.illinois.edu/users/smarch/st-docs/mvc.html.

In Model 2, you have a servlet or a filter acting as controller. All modern web frameworks are Model 2 implementations. Frameworks such as Struts 1 and Spring MVC employ a servlet controller in their MVC architectures, whereas Struts 2, another popular framework, uses a filter. Generally JSP pages are employed as the views of the application, even though other view technologies are supported. As the models, you use POJOs (POJO is an acronym for Plain Old Java Object). POJOs are ordinary objects, as opposed to Enterprise JavaBeans (EJB) or other special objects. Many people choose to use a JavaBean (plain JavaBean, not EJB) to store the states of a model object and move business logic to an action class. A JavaBean must have a no-argument constructor and get/set methods for accessing properties. In addition, it should be serializable.

Figure 10.1 shows the diagram of a Model 2 application.

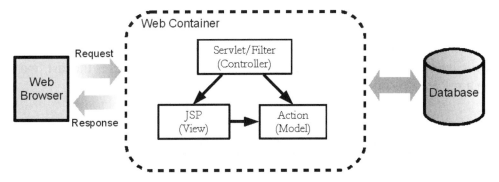

Figure 10.1: Model 2 architecture

In a Model 2 application, every HTTP request must be directed to the controller. The request's Uniform Request Identifier (URI) tells the controller what action to invoke. The term "action" refers to an operation that the application is able to perform. The Java object associated with an action is called an action object. A single action class may be used to serve different actions (as in Struts 2 and Spring MVC) or a single action (as in Struts 1).

A seemingly trivial operation may take more than one action. For instance, adding a product to a database would require two actions:

1. Display an "Add Product" form for the user to enter product information.
2. Save the product information in the database.

As mentioned above, you use the URI to tell the controller which action to invoke. For instance, to get the application to send the "Add Product" form, you would use a URI like this:

http://*domain*/*appName*/product_input

To get the application to save a product, the URI would be:

http://*domain*/*appName*/product_save

The controller examines the URI to decide what action to invoke. It also stores the model object in a place that can be accessed from the view, so that server-side values can be displayed on the browser. Finally, the controller uses a **RequestDispatcher** to forward to a view (JSP page). In the JSP page, you use the Expression Language expressions and custom tags to display values.

Note that calling **RequestDispatcher.forward()** does not prevent the code below it from being executed. Therefore, unless the call is the last line in a method, you need to return explicitly.

Model 2 with A Servlet Controller

This section presents a simple Model 2 application to give you a general idea of what a Model 2 application looks like. In real life, Model 2 applications are far more complex than this.

The application can be used to enter product information and is named **app10a**. The user fills in a form like the one in Figure 10.2 and submits it. The application then sends a confirmation page to the user and display the details of the saved product. (See Figure 10.3)

Figure 10.2: The Product form

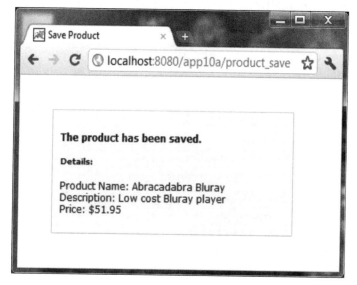

Figure 10.3: The product details page

The application is capable of performing these two actions:

1. Display the "Add Product" form. This action sends the entry form in Figure 10.2 to the browser. The URI to invoke this action must contain the string **product_input**.
2. Save the product and returns the confirmation page in Figure 10.3. The URI to invoke this action must contain the string **product_save**.

The application consists of the following components:

1. A **Product** class that is the template for the model objects. An instance of this class contains product information.
2. A **ProductForm** class, which encapsulates the fields of the HTML form for inputting a product. The properties of a **ProductForm** are used to populate a **Product**.
3. A **ControllerServlet** class, which is the controller of this Model 2 application.
4. An action class named **SaveProductAction**.
5. Two JSP pages (**ProductForm.jsp** and **ProductDetails.jsp**) as the views.

6. A CSS file that defines the styles of the views. This is a static resource.

The directory structure of this application is shown in Figure 10.4.

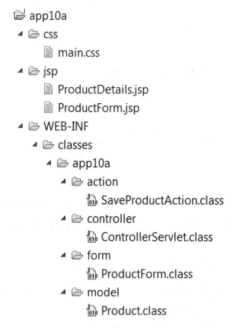

Figure 10.4: app10a directory structure

Let's take a closer look at each component in **app10a**.

The Product Class

A **Product** instance is a JavaBean that encapsulates product information. The **Product** class (shown in Listing 10.1) has three properties: **productName**, **description**, and **price**.

Listing 10.1: The Product class

```
package app10a.model;
import java.io.Serializable;

public class Product implements Serializable {
    private static final long serialVersionUID = 748392348L;
```

```
        private String name;
        private String description;
        private float price;

        public String getName() {
            return name;
        }
        public void setName(String name) {
            this.name = name;
        }
        public String getDescription() {
            return description;
        }
        public void setDescription(String description) {
            this.description = description;
        }
        public float getPrice() {
            return price;
        }
        public void setPrice(float price) {
            this.price = price;
        }
}
```

The **Product** class implements **java.io.Serializable** so that its instances can be stored safely in **HttpSession** objects. As an implementation of **Serializable**, **Product** should have a **serialVersionUID** field.

The ProductForm Class

A form class is mapped to an HTML form. It is the representation of the HTML form on the server. The **ProductForm** class, given in Listing 10.2, contains the **String** values of a product. At a glance the **ProductForm** class is similar to the **Product** class and you might question why **ProductForm** needs to exist at all. A form object, as you can see in the section "Validators" later in this chapter, saves passing the **ServletRequest** to other components, such as validators. **ServletRequest** is a servlet-specific type and should not be exposed to other layers of the applications.

The second purpose of a form object is to preserve and redisplay user input in its original form if input validation fails. You will learn how to do this in the section "Validators" later in this chapter.

Note that most of the time a form class does not have to implement **Serializable** as form objects are rarely stored in an **HttpSession**.

Listing 10.2: The ProductForm class

```
package app10a.form;
public class ProductForm {
    private String name;
    private String description;
    private String price;

    public String getName() {
        return name;
    }
    public void setName(String name) {
        this.name = name;
    }
    public String getDescription() {
        return description;
    }
    public void setDescription(String description) {
        this.description = description;
    }
    public String getPrice() {
        return price;
    }
    public void setPrice(String price) {
        this.price = price;
    }
}
```

The ControllerServlet Class

The **ControllerServlet** class (presented in Listing 10.3) extends the **javax.servlet.http.HttpServlet** class. Both its **doGet** and **doPost** methods call the **process** method, which is the brain of the servlet controller.

I am probably raising a few eyebrows here by naming the servlet controller **ControllerServlet**, but I'm following the convention that says all servlet classes should be suffixed with **Servlet**.

Listing 10.3: The ControllerServlet Class

```java
package app10a.controller;
import java.io.IOException;
import javax.servlet.RequestDispatcher;
import javax.servlet.ServletException;
import javax.servlet.annotation.WebServlet;
import javax.servlet.http.HttpServlet;
import javax.servlet.http.HttpServletRequest;
import javax.servlet.http.HttpServletResponse;
import app10a.action.SaveProductAction;
import app10a.form.ProductForm;
import app10a.model.Product;

@WebServlet(name = "ControllerServlet", urlPatterns = {
        "/product_input", "/product_save" })
public class ControllerServlet extends HttpServlet {
    private static final long serialVersionUID = 1579L;

    @Override
    public void doGet(HttpServletRequest request,
            HttpServletResponse response)
            throws IOException, ServletException {
        process(request, response);
    }

    @Override
    public void doPost(HttpServletRequest request,
            HttpServletResponse response)
            throws IOException, ServletException {
        process(request, response);
    }

    private void process(HttpServletRequest request,
            HttpServletResponse response)
            throws IOException, ServletException {

        String uri = request.getRequestURI();
        /*
         * uri is in this form: /contextName/resourceName,
         * for example: /app10a/product_input.
         * However, in the event of a default context, the
         * context name is empty, and uri has this form
         * /resourceName, e.g.: /product_input
         */
```

```
        int lastIndex = uri.lastIndexOf("/");
        String action = uri.substring(lastIndex + 1);
        // execute an action
        if (action.equals("product_input")) {
            // no action class, there is nothing to be done
        } else if (action.equals("product_save")) {
            // create form
            ProductForm productForm = new ProductForm();
            // populate action properties
            productForm.setName(request.getParameter("name"));
            productForm.setDescription(
                    request.getParameter("description"));
            productForm.setPrice(request.getParameter("price"));

            // create model
            Product product = new Product();
            product.setName(productForm.getName());
            product.setDescription(product.getDescription());
            try {
                product.setPrice(Float.parseFloat(
                        productForm.getPrice()));
            } catch (NumberFormatException e) {
            }
            // execute action method
            SaveProductAction saveProductAction =
                    new SaveProductAction();
            saveProductAction.save(product);

            // store model in a scope variable for the view
            request.setAttribute("product", product);
        }

        // forward to a view
        String dispatchUrl = null;
        if (action.equals("product_input")) {
            dispatchUrl = "/jsp/ProductForm.jsp";
        } else if (action.equals("product_save")) {
            dispatchUrl = "/jsp/ProductDetails.jsp";
        }
        if (dispatchUrl != null) {
            RequestDispatcher rd =
                    request.getRequestDispatcher(dispatchUrl);
            rd.forward(request, response);
        }
    }
}
```

The **process** method in the **ControllerServlet** class processes all incoming requests. It starts by obtaining the request URI and the action name.

```
String uri = request.getRequestURI();
int lastIndex = uri.lastIndexOf("/");
String action = uri.substring(lastIndex + 1);
```

The value of **action** in this application can be either **product_input** or **product_save**.

The **process** method then continues by performing these steps:

1. Instantiate a relevant action class, if any.
2. If an action object exists, create and populate a form object with request parameters. There are three properties in the **product_save** action: **name**, **description**, and **price**. Next, create a model object and populate its properties from the form object.
3. If an action object exists, call the action method.
4. Forward the request to a view (JSP page).

The part of the **process** method that determines what action to perform is in the following **if** block:

```
    // execute an action
    if (action.equals("product_input")) {
        // there is nothing to be done
    } else if (action.equals("product_save")) {
        // instantiate action class
        ...
    }
```

There is no action class to instantiate for action **product_input**. For **product_save**, the **process** method creates a **ProductForm** and a **Product** and copies values from the former to the latter. At this stage, there's no guarantee all non-string properties, such as price, can be copied successfully, but we'll deal with this later in the section "Validators." The **process** method then instantiates the **SaveProductAction** class and calls its **save** method.

```
        // create form
        ProductForm productForm = new ProductForm();
        // populate action properties
        productForm.setName(request.getParameter("name"));
```

```
productForm.setDescription(
        request.getParameter("description"));
productForm.setPrice(request.getParameter("price"));

// create model
Product product = new Product();
product.setName(productForm.getName());
product.setDescription(product.getDescription());
try {
    product.setPrice(Float.parseFloat(
            productForm.getPrice()));
} catch (NumberFormatException e) {

}
// execute action method
SaveProductAction saveProductAction =
        new SaveProductAction();
saveProductAction.save(product);

// store model in a scope variable for the view
request.setAttribute("product", product);
```

The **Product** is then stored in the **HttpServletRequest** so that the view can access it.

```
// store action in a scope variable for the view
request.setAttribute("product", product);
```

The **process** method concludes by forwarding to a view. If **action** equals **product_input**, control is forwarded to the **ProductForm.jsp** page. If **action** is **product_save**, control is forwarded to the **ProductDetails.jsp** page.

```
// forward to a view
String dispatchUrl = null;
if (action.equals("Product_input")) {
    dispatchUrl = "/jsp/ProductForm.jsp";
} else if (action.equals("Product_save")) {
    dispatchUrl = "/jsp/ProductDetails.jsp";
}
if (dispatchUrl != null) {
    RequestDispatcher rd =
            request.getRequestDispatcher(dispatchUrl);
    rd.forward(request, response);
}
```

The Action Class

There is only one action class in the application, which is responsible for saving a product to some storage, such as a database. The action class is named **SaveProductAction** and is given in Listing 10.4.

Listing 10.4: The SaveProductAction class

```
package app10a.action;

public class SaveProductAction {
    public void save(Product product) {
        // insert Product to the database
    }
}
```

In this example, the **SaveProductAction** class does not have implementation for its **save** method. You will provide an implementation in the next examples in this chapter.

The Views

The application utilizes two JSP pages for the views of the application. The first page, **ProductForm.jsp**, is displayed if the action is **product_input**. The second page, **ProductDetails.jsp**, is shown for **product_save**. **ProductForm.jsp** is given in Listing 10.5 and **ProductDetails.jsp** in Listing 10.6.

Listing 10.5: The ProductForm.jsp page

```
<!DOCTYPE HTML>
<html>
<head>
<title>Add Product Form</title>
<style type="text/css">@import url(css/main.css);</style>
</head>
<body>
<div id="global">
    <h3>Add a product</h3>
    <form method="post" action="product_save">
    <table>
    <tr>
```

```
        <td>Product Name:</td>
        <td><input type="text" name="name"/></td>
    </tr>
    <tr>
        <td>Description:</td>
        <td><input type="text" name="description"/></td>
    </tr>
    <tr>
        <td>Price:</td>
        <td><input type="text" name="price"/></td>
    </tr>
    <tr>
        <td><input type="reset"/></td>
        <td><input type="submit" value="Add Product"/></td>
    </tr>
    </table>
    </form>
</div>
</body>
</html>
```

Listing 10.6: The ProductDetails.jsp page

```
<!DOCTYPE HTML>
<html>
<head>
<title>Save Product</title>
<style type="text/css">@import url(css/main.css);</style>
</head>
<body>
<div id="global">
    <h4>The product has been saved.</h4>
    <p>
        <h5>Details:</h5>
        Product Name: ${product.name}<br/>
        Description: ${product.description}<br/>
        Price: $${product.price}
    </p>
</div>
</body>
</html>
```

The **ProductForm.jsp** page contains an HTML form for entering product details. The **ProductDetails.jsp** page uses the Expression Language (EL) to access the **product** scoped-object in the **HttpServletRequest**.

In this application, as is the case for most Model 2 applications, you need to prevent the JSP pages from being accessed directly from the browser. There are a number of ways to achieve this, including:

- Putting the JSP pages under **WEB-INF**. Anything under **WEB-INF** or a subdirectory under **WEB-INF** is protected. If you put your JSP pages under **WEB-INF** you cannot access them directly from the browser, but the controller can still dispatch requests to those pages. However, this is not a recommended approach since not all containers implement this feature.
- Using a servlet filter and filter out requests for JSP pages.
- Using security restriction in the deployment descriptor. This is easier than using a filter since you do not have to write a filter class. This method is chosen for this application.

Testing the Application

Assuming you are running the application on your local machine on port 8080, you can invoke the application using the following URL:

```
http://localhost:8080/app10a/product_input
```

You will see something similar to Figure 10.2 in your browser.

When you submit the form, the following URL will be sent to the server:

```
http://localhost:8080/app10a/product_save
```

Using a servlet controller allows you to use the servlet as a welcome page. This is an important feature since you can then configure your application so that the servlet controller will be invoked simply by typing your domain name (such as http://example.com) in the browser's address box. You can't do this with a filter.

Model 2 with A Filter Dispatcher

While a servlet is the most common controller in a Model 2 application, a filter can act as a controller too. Note, however, that a filter does not have the privilege to act as a welcome page. Simply typing the domain name won't invoke a filter dispatcher. Struts 2 uses a filter as a controller because the filter is used to serve static contents too.

The following example (**app10b**) is a Model 2 application that uses a filter dispatcher. The directory structure of **app10b** is shown in Figure 10.5.

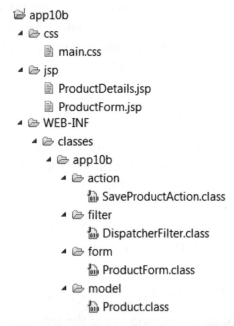

Figure 10.5: app10b directory structure

The JSP pages and the **Product** class are the same as the ones in **app10a**. However, instead of a servlet as controller, you have a filter called **FilterDispatcher** (given in Listing 10.7).

Listing 10.7: The DispatcherFilter class

```
package app10b.filter;
import java.io.IOException;
import javax.servlet.Filter;
```

```java
import javax.servlet.FilterChain;
import javax.servlet.FilterConfig;
import javax.servlet.RequestDispatcher;
import javax.servlet.ServletException;
import javax.servlet.ServletRequest;
import javax.servlet.ServletResponse;
import javax.servlet.annotation.WebFilter;
import javax.servlet.http.HttpServletRequest;

import app10b.action.SaveProductAction;
import app10b.form.ProductForm;
import app10b.model.Product;

@WebFilter(filterName = "DispatcherFilter",
        urlPatterns = { "/*" })
public class DispatcherFilter implements Filter {

    @Override
    public void init(FilterConfig filterConfig)
            throws ServletException {
    }

    @Override
    public void destroy() {
    }

    @Override
    public void doFilter(ServletRequest request,
            ServletResponse response, FilterChain filterChain)
            throws IOException, ServletException {
        HttpServletRequest req = (HttpServletRequest) request;
        String uri = req.getRequestURI();
        /*
         * uri is in this form: /contextName/resourceName, for
         * example /app01b/product_input. However, in the
         * case of a default context, the context name is empty,
         * and uri has this form /resourceName, e.g.:
         * /product_input
         */
        // action processing
        int lastIndex = uri.lastIndexOf("/");
        String action = uri.substring(lastIndex + 1);
        if (action.equals("product_input")) {
            // do nothing
        } else if (action.equals("product_save")) {
```

```
// create form
ProductForm productForm = new ProductForm();
// populate action properties
productForm.setName(request.getParameter("name"));
productForm.setDescription(
        request.getParameter("description"));
productForm.setPrice(request.getParameter("price"));

// create model
Product product = new Product();
product.setName(productForm.getName());
product.setDescription(product.getDescription());
try {
    product.setPrice(Float.parseFloat(
            productForm.getPrice()));
} catch (NumberFormatException e) {
}
// execute action method
SaveProductAction saveProductAction =
        new SaveProductAction();
saveProductAction.save(product);

// store model in a scope variable for the view
request.setAttribute("product", product);
}

// forward to a view
String dispatchUrl = null;
if (action.equals("product_input")) {
    dispatchUrl = "/jsp/ProductForm.jsp";
} else if (action.equals("product_save")) {
    dispatchUrl = "/jsp/ProductDetails.jsp";
}
if (dispatchUrl != null) {
    RequestDispatcher rd = request
            .getRequestDispatcher(dispatchUrl);
    rd.forward(request, response);
} else {
    // let static contents pass
    filterChain.doFilter(request, response);
}
}
}
```

The **doFilter** method performs what the **process** method in **app10a** did.

Since the filter targets all URLs including static contents, you need to call **filterChain.doFilter()** if no action is invoked.

```
    } else {
        // let static contents pass
        filterChain.doFilter(request, response);
    }
```

To test the application, direct your browser to this URL:

```
http://localhost:8080/app10b/product_input
```

Validators

Input validation is an important step in performing an action. Validation ranges from simple tasks like checking if an input field has a value to more complex ones like verifying a credit card number. In fact, validation play such an important role that the Java community has published JSR 303, "Bean Validation" to standardize input validation in Java. Modern MVC frameworks often offer both programmatic and declarative validation methods. In programmatic validation, you write code to validate user input. In declarative validation, you provide validation rules in XML documents or properties files.

The following example features a new application (**app10c**) that extends the servlet controller-based Model 2 application in **app10a**. The new application incorporates a product validator whose class is given in Listing 10.8.

Listing 10.8: The ProductValidator class

```
package app10c.validator;
import java.util.ArrayList;
import java.util.List;
import app10c.form.ProductForm;

public class ProductValidator {

    public List<String> validate(ProductForm productForm) {
        List<String> errors = new ArrayList<String>();
        String name = productForm.getName();
```

```
        if (name == null || name.trim().isEmpty()) {
            errors.add("Product must have a name");
        }
        String price = productForm.getPrice();
        if (price == null || price.trim().isEmpty()) {
            errors.add("Product must have a price");
        } else {
            try {
                Float.parseFloat(price);
            } catch (NumberFormatException e) {
                errors.add("Invalid price value");
            }
        }
        return errors;
    }
}
```

The **ProductValidator** class in Listing 10.8 offers a **validate** method that works on a **ProductForm**. The validator makes sure that a product has a non-empty name and its price is a valid number. The **validate** method returns a **List** of **String**s containing validation error messages. An empty **List** means successful validation.

Now that you have a validator, you need to tell the controller to use it. Listing 10.9 presents the revised version of **ControllerServlet**. Pay special attention to the lines in bold.

Listing 10.9: The ControllerServlet class in app10c

```
package app10c.controller;
import java.io.IOException;
import java.util.List;
import javax.servlet.RequestDispatcher;
import javax.servlet.ServletException;
import javax.servlet.annotation.WebServlet;
import javax.servlet.http.HttpServlet;
import javax.servlet.http.HttpServletRequest;
import javax.servlet.http.HttpServletResponse;
import app10c.action.SaveProductAction;
import app10c.form.ProductForm;
import app10c.model.Product;
import app10c.validator.ProductValidator;

@WebServlet(name = "ControllerServlet", urlPatterns = {
        "/product_input", "/product_save" })
```

```
public class ControllerServlet extends HttpServlet {

    private static final long serialVersionUID = 98279L;

    @Override
    public void doGet(HttpServletRequest request,
            HttpServletResponse response)
            throws IOException, ServletException {
        process(request, response);
    }

    @Override
    public void doPost(HttpServletRequest request,
            HttpServletResponse response)
            throws IOException, ServletException {
        process(request, response);
    }

    private void process(HttpServletRequest request,
            HttpServletResponse response)
            throws IOException, ServletException {

        String uri = request.getRequestURI();
        /*
         * uri is in this form: /contextName/resourceName,
         * for example: /app10a/product_input.
         * However, in the case of a default context, the
         * context name is empty, and uri has this form
         * /resourceName, e.g.: /product_input
         */
        int lastIndex = uri.lastIndexOf("/");
        String action = uri.substring(lastIndex + 1);
        String dispatchUrl = null;

        if (action.equals("product_input")) {
            // no action class, there is nothing to be done
            dispatchUrl = "/jsp/ProductForm.jsp";
        } else if (action.equals("product_save")) {
            // instantiate action class
            ProductForm productForm = new ProductForm();
            // populate action properties
            productForm.setName(
                    request.getParameter("name"));
            productForm.setDescription(
                    request.getParameter("description"));
```

```
        productForm.setPrice(request.getParameter("price"));

        // validate ProductForm
        ProductValidator productValidator = new
                ProductValidator();
        List<String> errors =
                productValidator.validate(productForm);
        if (errors.isEmpty()) {
            // create Product from ProductForm
            Product product = new Product();
            product.setName(productForm.getName());
            product.setDescription(
                    productForm.getDescription());
            product.setPrice(Float.parseFloat(
                    productForm.getPrice()));

            // no validation error, execute action method
            SaveProductAction saveProductAction = new
                    SaveProductAction();
            saveProductAction.save(product);

            // store action in a scope variable for the view
            request.setAttribute("product", product);
            dispatchUrl = "/jsp/ProductDetails.jsp";
        } else {
            request.setAttribute("errors", errors);
            request.setAttribute("form", productForm);
            dispatchUrl = "/jsp/ProductForm.jsp";
        }
    }

    // forward to a view
    if (dispatchUrl != null) {
        RequestDispatcher rd =
                request.getRequestDispatcher(dispatchUrl);
        rd.forward(request, response);
    }
  }
}
```

The new **ControllerServlet** class in Listing 10.9 inserts code that instantiates the **ProductValidator** class and calls its **validate** method on **product_save**.

```
        // validate ProductForm
        ProductValidator productValidator = new
```

```
                ProductValidator();
        List<String> errors =
                productValidator.validate(productForm);
```

The **validate** method takes a **ProductForm**, which encapsulates product information entered to the HTML form. Without a **ProductForm** you would have to pass the **ServletRequest** to the validator.

The **validate** method returns an empty **List** if validation was successful, in which case a **Product** will be created and passed to a **SaveProductAction**. Upon successful validation, the controller stores the **Product** in the **ServletContext** and forwards to the **ProductDetails.jsp** page, which then displays the product's details. If validation failed, the controller stores the **errors List** and the **ProductForm** in the **ServletContext** and forwards back to **ProductForm.jsp**.

```
        if (errors.isEmpty()) {
                // create Product from ProductForm
                Product product = new Product();
                product.setName(productForm.getName());
                product.setDescription(
                        productForm.getDescription());
                product.setPrice(Float.parseFloat(
                        productForm.getPrice()));

                // no validation error, execute action method
                SaveProductAction saveProductAction = new
                        SaveProductAction();
                saveProductAction.save(product);

                // store action in a scope variable for the view
                request.setAttribute("product", product);
                dispatchUrl = "/jsp/ProductDetails.jsp";
        } else {
                request.setAttribute("errors", errors);
                request.setAttribute("form", productForm);
                dispatchUrl = "/jsp/ProductForm.jsp";
        }
```

The **ProductForm.jsp** page in **app10c** has been modified to give it the capability of showing error messages and redisplaying invalid values. Listing 10.10 shows the **ProductForm.jsp** in **app10c**.

Listing 10.10: The ProductForm.jsp page in app10c

```
<%@ taglib uri="http://java.sun.com/jsp/jstl/core" prefix="c" %>
<!DOCTYPE HTML>
<html>
<head>
<title>Add Product Form</title>
<style type="text/css">@import url(css/main.css);</style>
</head>
<body>
<div id="global">
    <h3>Add a product</h3>
    <c:if test="${requestScope.errors != null}">
        <p id="errors">
        Error(s)!
        <ul>
        <c:forEach var="error" items="${requestScope.errors}">
            <li>${error}</li>
        </c:forEach>
        </ul>
        </p>
    </c:if>
    <form method="post" action="product_save">
    <table>
    <tr>
        <td>Product Name:</td>
        <td><input type="text" name="name"
                value="${form.name}"/></td>
    </tr>
    <tr>
        <td>Description:</td>
        <td><input type="text" name="description"
                value="${form.description}"/></td>
    </tr>
    <tr>
        <td>Price:</td>
        <td><input type="text" name="price"
                value="${form.price}"/></td>
    </tr>
    <tr>
        <td><input type="reset"/></td>
        <td><input type="submit" value="Add Product"/></td>
    </tr>
    </table>
    </form>
</div>
```

```
</body>
</html>
```

You can test **app10c** by invoking the **product_input** action:

```
http://localhost:8080/app10c/product_input
```

Unlike the previous examples, if the Product form contains an invalid value when you submit it, an error message will be displayed along with the incorrect value. Figure 10.6 shows two validation error messages.

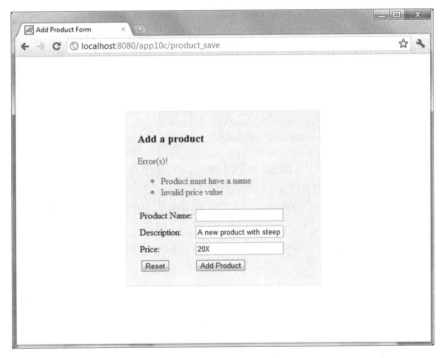

Figure 10.6: The ProductForm with error mesages

Database Access

Most web applications use data from a database. It is therefore important that you know how to access and manipulate data using the Java Database Connectivity (JDBC) API. This section does not cover JDBC and I assume you have some working knowledge of it. Instead, this section explains the two important topics when working with the database: connection pooling and the Data Access Object pattern. An sample application (**app10d**) is given at the end of this section.

Connection Pooling

The most crucial and time consuming operation in accessing data in a database is often trying to establish a connection. As a rule, in well-designed applications database connections are always pooled. While managing connections can be complex and challenging, fortunately there are Java libraries that do that well. The following are examples of Java database connection libraries.

- Apache Commons DBCP (http://commons.apache.org/dbcp)
- C3P0 (http://sourceforge.net/projects/c3p0)
- Tomcat JDBC Connection Pool in Tomcat 7

Apache Commons DBCP, especially the older versions, has in the past been criticized for its complexity and sluggishness. As such, it looks like C3P0 is a more sensible choice. If you're using Tomcat 7, however, connection pool comes built-in with it.

Until a few years ago, the most popular method for managing a connection pool is to not manage it yourself and let the servlet/JSP container manage it for you. Here is code for obtaining a JDBC connection from a container-managed pool, using Java Naming and Directory Interface (JNDI) lookup.

```
import javax.naming.Context;
import javax.naming.InitialContext;
import javax.naming.NamingException;
import javax.sql.DataSource;
import java.sql.Connection;
import java.sql.SQLException;

    ...

    Connection connection = null;
    try {
        Context context = new InitialContext();
```

```
        DataSource dataSource = (DataSource)
                context.lookup(jndiName);
        connection = dataSource.getConnection();
    } catch (NamingException e) {
        ...
    } catch (SQLException e) {
        ...
    } catch (Exception e) {
        ...
    }
```

Calling the **getConnection** method on a **DataSource** is fast because connections are never closed; closing a connection simply returns the connection to the pool. However, JNDI lookups are slow and, as such, the returned **DataSource** is often cached.

To tell the servlet container to manage a connection pool, you need to configure the container. In Tomcat, this is done by declaring a **Resource** element under the **Context** element of the application. For example, the following Tomcat context contains a **DataSource** resource with an internal connection pool.

```
<Context path="/appName" docBase="...">
    <Resource name="jdbc/dataSourceName"
        auth="Container"
        type="javax.sql.DataSource"
        username="..."
        password="..."
        driverClassName="..."
        url="..."
    />
</Context>
```

You need to enter the correct database user name and password in the **username** and **password** attributes, respectively. You also need to supply the JDBC driver class name and the database URL in the **driverClassName** and **url** attributes, respectively. In addition, you need to include the JDBC driver library in the **WEB-INF/lib** directory of your application directory. More information on configuring a resource can be found in Appendix A, "Tomcat."

For example, the following Tomcat **Context** declaration defines an application (**app10d**) with a **DataSource** resource that maintains a connection pool to a MySQL database named **test**. The JNDI name for the **DataSource** is **jdbc/myDataSource** and the MySQL database is assumed to be in the same computer as the one running Tomcat. The user name and password for accessing the database is **testuser** and **secret**, respectively.

```
<Context path="/app10d" docBase="/path/to/app" reloadable="true">
    <Resource name="jdbc/myDataSource"
        auth="Container"
        type="javax.sql.DataSource"
        username="testuser"
        password="secret"
        driverClassName="com.mysql.jdbc.Driver"
        url="jdbc:mysql://localhost:3306/test"/>
</Context>
```

Even though more recent applications tend to use a dependency injection framework to manage database connections, many applications running today still depend on the older method of JNDI lookup, which is why we give it a try in the **app10d** application.

The Data Access Object (DAO) Pattern

A good approach to accessing data in a database is by using a separate module for managing the complexity of obtaining a connection and building SQL statements. The DAO design pattern is a simple pattern that does this job very well. There are a few variants of this pattern, but one of the simplest is depicted in Figure 10.7.

With this pattern, you write a class for each type of object you need to persist. For example, if your application needs to persist three types of objects—**Product**, **Customer**, and **Order**—you need three DAO classes, each of which takes care of an object type. Therefore, you would have the following classes: **ProductDAO**, **CustomerDAO**, and **OrderDAO**. The DAO suffix at the end of the class name indicates that the class is a DAO class. It is a convention that you should follow unless you have compelling reasons not to do so.

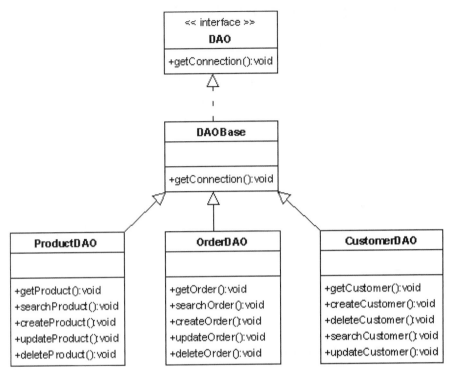

Figure 10.7: The DAO pattern

A typical DAO class takes care of the addition, deletion, modification, and retrieval of an object, and the searching for those objects. For example, a **ProductDAO** class may support the following methods:

```
void addProduct(Product product)

void updateProduct(Product product)

void deleteProduct(int productId)

Product getProduct(int productId)

List<Product> findProducts(SearchCriteria searchCriteria)
```

In your DAO implementation classes, you can either write SQL statements manually or use a Java Persistence API (JPA) implementation such as Hibernate to take care of database data. JPA is unfortunately outside the scope of this book, but you should know that it is a popular technology and many people would choose JPA for their data access needs.

A Model 2 Application with Database Access

The **app10d** application is an example of Model 2 with database access, It was built on top of the previous example (**app10c**) to access a MySQL database called **test** containing a **products** table. The revised application also has an additional action, **product_list**, that displays all products in the database. In addition, it comes with a **web.xml** file that declares a welcome page.

The SQL statement for creating the database and the table is given in Listing 10.11.

Listing 10.11: The SQL statement for creating the database and table

```
CREATE DATABASE /*!32312 IF NOT EXISTS*/`test` /*!40100 DEFAULT
      CHARACTER SET latin1 */;
USE `test`;
DROP TABLE IF EXISTS `products`;

CREATE TABLE `products` (
    `id` int(11) NOT NULL auto_increment,
    `name` varchar(255) NOT NULL,
    `description` varchar(1000) default NULL,
    `price` decimal(10,0) NOT NULL,
    PRIMARY KEY (`id`)
) ENGINE=MyISAM AUTO_INCREMENT=6 DEFAULT CHARSET=utf8;
```

A DAO module has been added to **app10d** and this module consists of the following interfaces and classes.

- The **DAO** interface in Listing 10.12, which all DAO interfaces are derived from.
- The **BaseDAO** class in Listing 10.13, which provides basic implementation for all DAO classes.
- The **DataSourceCache** class in Listing 10.14, a utility class that looks up the container-managed **DataSource** and caches it.
- The **DAOFactory** class in Listing 10.15, a factory class that creates various DAO implementations.
- The **DAOException** class in Listing 10.16 that a DAO method throws in the event of a runtime exception.

- **ProductDAO** interface in Listing 10.17 and **ProductDAOImpl** class in Listing 10.18. Both provide methods for persisting **Product** instances and retrieving them from the database.

Listing 10.12: The DAO interface

```
package app10d.dao;
import java.sql.Connection;

public interface DAO {
    Connection getConnection() throws DAOException;
}
```

Listing 10.13: The BaseDAO class

```
package app10d.dao;
import java.sql.Connection;
import java.sql.ResultSet;
import java.sql.Statement;
import javax.sql.DataSource;

public class BaseDAO implements DAO {

    public Connection getConnection() throws DAOException {
        DataSource dataSource =
                DataSourceCache.getInstance().getDataSource();
        try {
            return dataSource.getConnection();
        } catch (Exception e) {
            e.printStackTrace();
            throw new DAOException();
        }
    }

    protected void closeDBObjects(ResultSet resultSet, Statement
        statement,
            Connection connection) {
        if (resultSet != null) {
            try {
                resultSet.close();
            } catch (Exception e) {
            }
        }
        if (statement != null) {
            try {
```

```
                    statement.close();
            } catch (Exception e) {
            }
        }
        if (connection != null) {
            try {
                connection.close();
            } catch (Exception e) {
            }
        }
    }
}
```

Listing 10.14: The DataSourceCache class

```
package app10d.dao;
import javax.naming.Context;
import javax.naming.InitialContext;
import javax.naming.NamingException;
import javax.sql.DataSource;

public class DataSourceCache {
    private static DataSourceCache instance;
    private DataSource dataSource;
    static {
        instance = new DataSourceCache();
    }

    private DataSourceCache() {
        Context context = null;
        try {
            context = new InitialContext();
            dataSource = (DataSource) context.lookup(
                    "java:comp/env/jdbc/myDataSource");
        } catch (NamingException e) {
        }
    }

    public static DataSourceCache getInstance() {
        return instance;
    }

    public DataSource getDataSource() {
        return dataSource;
    }
}
```

Listing 10.15: The DAOFactory class

```
package app10d.dao;
public class DAOFactory {
    public static ProductDAO getProductDAO() {
        return new ProductDAOImpl();
    }
}
```

Listing 10.16: The DAOException class

```
package app10d.dao;

public class DAOException extends Exception {
    private static final long serialVersionUID = 19192L;

    public DAOException() {
    }
    public DAOException(String message) {
        this.message = message;
    }
    public String getMessage() {
        return message;
    }
    public void setMessage(String message) {
        this.message = message;
    }
    private String message;

    public String toString() {
        return message;
    }
}
```

Listing 10.17: The ProductDAO interface

```
package app10d.dao;
import java.util.List;
import app10d.model.Product;

public interface ProductDAO extends DAO {
    List<Product> getProducts() throws DAOException;
    void insert(Product product) throws DAOException;
}
```

Listing 10.18: The ProductDAOImpl class

```
package app10d.dao;
import java.sql.Connection;
import java.sql.PreparedStatement;
import java.sql.ResultSet;
import java.sql.SQLException;
import java.util.ArrayList;
import java.util.List;
import app10d.model.Product;

public class ProductDAOImpl extends BaseDAO implements ProductDAO {

    private static final String GET_PRODUCTS_SQL =
            "SELECT name, description, price FROM products";
    public List<Product> getProducts() throws DAOException {
        List<Product> products = new ArrayList<Product>();
        Connection connection = null;
        PreparedStatement pStatement = null;
        ResultSet resultSet = null;
        try {
            connection = getConnection();
            pStatement = connection.prepareStatement(
                    GET_PRODUCTS_SQL);
            resultSet = pStatement.executeQuery();
            while (resultSet.next()) {
                Product product = new Product();
                product.setName(resultSet.getString("name"));
                product.setDescription(
                        resultSet.getString("description"));
                product.setPrice(resultSet.getFloat("price"));
                products.add(product);
            }
        } catch (SQLException e) {
            throw new DAOException("Error getting products. "
                    + e.getMessage());
        } finally {
            closeDBObjects(resultSet, pStatement, connection);
        }
        return products;
    }

    private static final String INSERT_PRODUCT_SQL =
            "INSERT INTO products " +
            "(name, description, price) " +
            "VALUES (?, ?, ?)";
```

```
    public void insert(Product product)
            throws DAOException {
        Connection connection = null;
        PreparedStatement pStatement = null;
        try {
            connection = getConnection();
            pStatement = connection.prepareStatement(
                    INSERT_PRODUCT_SQL);
            pStatement.setString(1, product.getName());
            pStatement.setString(2,
                    product.getDescription());
            pStatement.setFloat(3, product.getPrice());
            pStatement.execute();
        } catch (SQLException e) {
            throw new DAOException("Error adding product. "
                    + e.getMessage());
        } finally {
            closeDBObjects(null, pStatement, connection);
        }
    }
}
```

All of these DAO interfaces and classes are self-explanatory. Now that you
have a DAO module for database access, the **SaveProductAction** class can
finally do what it's supposed to do: saving a product. The
SaveProductAction class in **app10d** is presented in Listing 10.19.

Listing 10.19: The SaveProductAction class in app10d

```
package app10d.action;
import app10d.dao.DAOException;
import app10d.dao.DAOFactory;
import app10d.dao.ProductDAO;
import app10d.model.Product;

public class SaveProductAction {
    public void save(Product product) {
        ProductDAO productDAO = DAOFactory.getProductDAO();
        try {
            productDAO.insert(product);
        } catch (DAOException e) {
            e.printStackTrace();
        }
    }
```

```
}
```

Thanks to the DAO pattern, the **save** method in **SaveProductAction** can be kept very clean. It simply obtains a **ProductDAO** from **DAOFactory** and calls the **insert** method on the **ProductDAO**.

A new action in **app10d**, **product_list**, is based on the **GetProductsAction** class in Listing 10.20. It has a **getProducts** method that returns a **List** of **Product**s.

Listing 10.20: The GetProductsAction class

```
package app10d.action;
import java.util.List;
import app10d.dao.DAOException;
import app10d.dao.DAOFactory;
import app10d.dao.ProductDAO;
import app10d.model.Product;

public class GetProductsAction {
    public List<Product> getProducts() {
        ProductDAO productDAO = DAOFactory.getProductDAO();
        List<Product> products = null;
        try {
            products = productDAO.getProducts();
        } catch (DAOException e) {

        }
        return products;
    }
}
```

The **getProducts** method obtains a **ProductDAO** and calls its **getProducts** method.

The last piece of **app10d** worth mentioning is the deployment descriptor in Listing 10.21.

Listing 10.21: The deployment descriptor for app10d

```
<?xml version="1.0" encoding="ISO-8859-1"?>
<web-app xmlns="http://java.sun.com/xml/ns/javaee"
    xmlns:xsi="http://www.w3.org/2001/XMLSchema-instance"
    xsi:schemaLocation="http://java.sun.com/xml/ns/javaee
➥http://java.sun.com/xml/ns/javaee/web-app_3_0.xsd"
    version="3.0"
```

```
>
    <welcome-file-list>
        <welcome-file>product_list</welcome-file>
    </welcome-file-list>
</web-app>
```

Also, note that the controller servlet has a new URL pattern (**/product_list**) added to it, which means the welcome file actually references the controller servlet.

```
@WebServlet(name = "ControllerServlet", urlPatterns = {
        "/product_input", "/product_save", "/product_list" })
public class ControllerServlet extends HttpServlet {
```

To test **app10d**, use this URL. Since a welcome file is defined in the deployment descriptor, there's no need to specify a resource.

```
http://localhost:8080/app10d
```

Figure 10.8 shows all products in the database. Initially, you should see an empty list because you still have to insert products. So, do it now and revisit this page afterwards.

Dependency Injection

Dependency injection has been widely used in the past few years as a solution to, among others, code testability. In fact, dependency injection is behind great frameworks such as Spring and Struts 2. So, what is dependency injection?

Martin Fowler wrote an excellent article on this subject:

```
http://martinfowler.com/articles/injection.html
```

Before Fowler coined the term "dependency injection," the phrase "inversion of control" was often used to mean the same thing. As Fowler notes in his article, the two are not exactly the same.

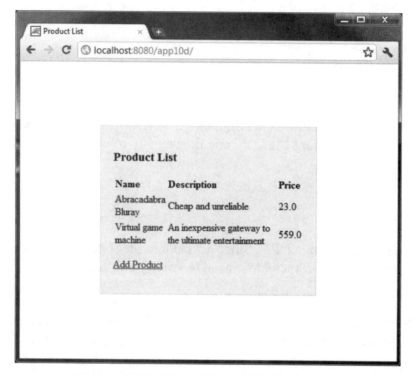

Figure 10.8: The welcome file in app10d

If you have two components, **A** and **B**, and **A** depends on **B**, you can say **A** is dependent on **B** or **B** is a dependency of **A**. Suppose **A** has a method, **importantMethod**, that uses **B** as defined in the following code fragment:

```
public class A {
    public void importantMethod() {
        B b = ... // get an instance of B
        b.usefulMethod();
        ...
    }
    ...
}
```

A must obtain an instance of **B** before it can use **B**. While it is as straightforward as using the **new** keyword if **B** is a Java concrete class, it can be problematic if **B** is not and there are various implementations of **B**. You will have to choose an implementation of **B** and by doing so you reduce the reusability of A because you cannot use **A** with implementations of **B** that you did not choose.

Take the **ProductDAO** interface in **app10d** (shown in Listing 10.17) as a more concrete example. Its implementation, **ProductDAOImpl** in Listing 10.18, depends on the **getConnection** method of its parent, **BaseDAO**, to obtain a connection. The problem is the connection comes from a JNDI object maintained by the container. How do you test **ProductDAO** outside the container? You can't without changing the **BaseDAO** class. The testability of **ProductDAO** (and all DAO implementations that may be added) has been reduced because of its dependency on another object. To test a DAO object in **app10d** you have to first deploy the whole application in a container and use a browser to enter values for the DAO object. How much productivity is lost?

With dependency injection every component has its dependencies injected to it and this makes testing each component easier. Far easier. For a class to be used in a dependency injection environment, you have to make it inject-ready. One way to do it is to create a set method for each dependency. For example, the **SaveProductAction** class in Listing 10.22 and **GetProductsAction** class in 10.23 are part of the **app10e** application. What differentiates this class from its predecessors in the previous example is that they have a **setProductDAO** method that a dependency injection framework can call to inject a **ProductDAO**. Injection can also occur through a constructor or a class field, but I will stick with set methods in this book.

Listing 10.22: The modified SaveProductAction that is inject-ready

```
package app10e.action;
import app10e.dao.DAOException;
import app10e.dao.ProductDAO;
import app10e.model.Product;

public class SaveProductAction {

    private ProductDAO productDAO;
    public void setProductDAO(ProductDAO productDAO) {
        this.productDAO = productDAO;
    }
```

```
public void save(Product product) {
    try {
        productDAO.insert(product);
    } catch (DAOException e) {
        e.printStackTrace();
    }
}
}
```

Listing 10.23: The GetProductsAction class

```
package app10e.action;
import java.util.List;
import app10e.dao.DAOException;
import app10e.dao.ProductDAO;
import app10e.model.Product;

public class GetProductsAction {
    private ProductDAO productDAO;
    public void setProductDAO(ProductDAO productDAO) {
        this.productDAO = productDAO;
    }

    public List<Product> getProducts() {
        List<Product> products = null;
        try {
            products = productDAO.getProducts();
        } catch (DAOException e) {

        }
        return products;
    }
}
```

Once all your classes are inject-ready, you can choose a dependency injection framework and import it to your project. Spring Framework, Google Guice, Weld, and PicoContainer are some good ones.

Note

Dependency injection in Java is specified in JSR 330 and JSR 299, both outside the scope of this book.

Enough theory, now let's see dependency injection in action in **app10e**.

To make it easy to understand, the **app10e** application uses the **DependencyInjector** class in 10.24 in lieu of a dependency injection framework. (In a real-world application, of course you would use a proper framework.) This class has been designed to work with **app10e** alone and can be instantiated easily, with or without a container. Once instantiated, its **start** method must be called that will prepare a C3P0 connection pool to be used by other components. After use, its **shutdown** method should be called to release resources.

Listing 10.24: The DependencyInjector class

```
package app10e.util;
import javax.sql.DataSource;
import app10e.action.GetProductsAction;
import app10e.action.SaveProductAction;
import app10e.dao.ProductDAO;
import app10e.dao.ProductDAOImpl;
import app10e.validator.ProductValidator;
import com.mchange.v2.c3p0.ComboPooledDataSource;
import com.mchange.v2.c3p0.DataSources;

public class DependencyInjector {
    private DataSource dataSource;

    public void start() {
        // create dataSource
        ComboPooledDataSource cpds = new ComboPooledDataSource();
        try {
            cpds.setDriverClass("com.mysql.jdbc.Driver");
        } catch (Exception e) {
            e.printStackTrace();
        }
        cpds.setJdbcUrl("jdbc:mysql://localhost:3306/test");
        cpds.setUser("testuser");
        cpds.setPassword("secret");

        // to override default settings:
        cpds.setMinPoolSize(5);
        cpds.setAcquireIncrement(5);
        cpds.setMaxPoolSize(20);
        dataSource = cpds;
    }

    public void shutDown() {
        // destroy dataSource
        try {
```

```
                DataSources.destroy(dataSource);
            } catch (Exception e) {
                e.printStackTrace();
            }
        }

        /*
         * Returns an instance of type. type is of type Class
         * and not String because it's easy to misspell a class name
         */
        public Object getObject(Class type) {
            if (type == ProductValidator.class) {
                return new ProductValidator();
            } else if (type == ProductDAO.class) {
                return createProductDAO();
            } else if (type == GetProductsAction.class) {
                return createGetProductsAction();
            } else if (type == SaveProductAction.class) {
                return createSaveProductAction();
            }
            return null;
        }

        private GetProductsAction createGetProductsAction() {
            GetProductsAction getProductsAction = new
          GetProductsAction();
            // inject a ProductDAO to getProductsAction
            getProductsAction.setProductDAO(createProductDAO());
            return getProductsAction;
        }

        private SaveProductAction createSaveProductAction() {
            SaveProductAction saveProductAction = new
                    SaveProductAction();
            // inject a ProductDAO to saveProductAction
            saveProductAction.setProductDAO(createProductDAO());
            return saveProductAction;
        }

        private ProductDAO createProductDAO() {
            ProductDAO productDAO = new ProductDAOImpl();
            // inject a DataSource to productDAO
            productDAO.setDataSource(dataSource);
            return productDAO;
        }
    }
}
```

The **DependencyInjector** class hard-codes many of its values, including the JDBC URL and the database user name and password. In a framework, property values normally come from an editable configuration file, which most of the time takes the form of an XML document. Let's keep it simple this time.

To obtain an object from the **DependencyInjector**, call its **getObject** method, passing the **Class** of the expected object. **DependencyInjector** supports the following types in **app10e**: **ProductValidator**, **ProductDAO**, **GetProductsAction**, and **SaveProductAction**. For example, to get an instance of **ProductDAO**, you would call **getObject** by passing **ProductDAO.class**:

```
ProductDAO productDAO = (ProductDAO)
        dependencyInjector.getObject(ProductDAO.class);
```

The beauty of **DependencyInjector** (and all dependency injection frameworks) is that the object it returns comes injected with dependencies. If a dependency has dependencies, the dependency is also injected with its own dependencies.

The servlet controller in **app10e** is given in Listing 10.25. Note that it instantiates the **DependencyInjector** in its **init** method and calls the **DependencyInjector**'s **shutdown** method in its **destroy** method. The servlet no longer creates a dependency on its own. Instead, it obtains it from the **DependencyInjector**.

Listing 10.25: The ControllerServlet class in app10e

```
package app10e.servlet;
import java.io.IOException;
import java.util.List;
import javax.servlet.RequestDispatcher;
import javax.servlet.ServletException;
import javax.servlet.annotation.WebServlet;
import javax.servlet.http.HttpServlet;
import javax.servlet.http.HttpServletRequest;
import javax.servlet.http.HttpServletResponse;
import app10e.util.DependencyInjector;
import app10e.action.GetProductsAction;
import app10e.action.SaveProductAction;
import app10e.form.ProductForm;
import app10e.model.Product;
```

```java
import app10e.validator.ProductValidator;

@WebServlet(name = "ControllerServlet", urlPatterns = {
        "/product_input", "/product_save", "/product_list" })
public class ControllerServlet extends HttpServlet {

    private static final long serialVersionUID = 6679L;
    private DependencyInjector dependencyInjector;

    @Override
    public void init() {
        dependencyInjector = new DependencyInjector();
        dependencyInjector.start();
    }

    @Override
    public void destroy() {
        dependencyInjector.shutDown();
    }

    @Override
    public void doGet(HttpServletRequest request,
            HttpServletResponse response)
            throws IOException, ServletException {
        process(request, response);
    }

    @Override
    public void doPost(HttpServletRequest request,
            HttpServletResponse response)
            throws IOException, ServletException {
        process(request, response);
    }

    private void process(HttpServletRequest request,
            HttpServletResponse response)
            throws IOException, ServletException {

        String uri = request.getRequestURI();
        /*
         * uri is in this form: /contextName/resourceName,
         * for example: /app10a/product_input.
         * However, in the case of a default context, the
         * context name is empty, and uri has this form
         * /resourceName, e.g.: /product_input
         */
```

```
int lastIndex = uri.lastIndexOf("/");
String action = uri.substring(lastIndex + 1);
String dispatchUrl = null;

if (action.equals("product_input")) {
    // no action class, there is nothing to be done
    dispatchUrl = "/jsp/ProductForm.jsp";
} else if (action.equals("product_save")) {
    // instantiate action class
    ProductForm productForm = new ProductForm();
    // populate action properties
    productForm.setProductName(
            request.getParameter("productName"));
    productForm.setDescription(
            request.getParameter("description"));
    productForm.setPrice(request.getParameter("price"));

    // validate ProductForm
    ProductValidator productValidator = (ProductValidator)
            dependencyInjector.getObject(
                    ProductValidator.class);
    List<String> errors =
            productValidator.validate(productForm);
    if (errors.isEmpty()) {
        // create Product from ProductForm
        Product product = new Product();
        product.setProductName(
                productForm.getProductName());
        product.setDescription(
                productForm.getDescription());
        product.setPrice(Float.parseFloat(
                productForm.getPrice()));

        // no validation error, execute action method
        SaveProductAction saveProductAction =
                (SaveProductAction)
                dependencyInjector.getObject(
                SaveProductAction.class);
        saveProductAction.save(product);

        // store action in a scope variable for the view
        request.setAttribute("product", product);
        dispatchUrl = "/jsp/ProductDetails.jsp";
    } else {
        request.setAttribute("errors", errors);
```

```
                dispatchUrl = "/jsp/ProductForm.jsp";
        }
    } else if (action.equals("product_list") ||
                action.isEmpty()) {
        GetProductsAction getProductsAction =
                (GetProductsAction)
                dependencyInjector.getObject(
                GetProductsAction.class);
        List<Product> products =
                getProductsAction.getProducts();
        request.setAttribute("products", products);
        dispatchUrl = "/jsp/ProductList.jsp";
    }

    // forward to a view
    if (dispatchUrl != null) {
        RequestDispatcher rd =
                request.getRequestDispatcher(dispatchUrl);
        rd.forward(request, response);
    }
    }
}
```

Note that in **app10e** you write your own dependency injector and instantiate it when the servlet initializes. If you are using a Java 6 EE container, such as Glassfish, it is possible to have the container inject dependencies to a servlet. Your servlet would look like this:

```
public class ControllerServlet extends HttpServlet {
    @Inject ProductValidator productValidator;
    @Inject GetProductsAction getProductsAction;
    @Inject SaveProductAction saveProductAction;
    ...

    @Override
    public void doGet(HttpServletRequest request,
            HttpServletResponse response) throws IOException,
            ServletException {
        ...
    }

    @Override
    public void doPost(HttpServletRequest request,
            HttpServletResponse response) throws IOException,
            ServletException {
```

```
        ...
    }
}
```

To run **app10e**, your Tomcat **Context** does not need a **Resource** declaration. It should look simply like this.

```
<Context path="/app10e" docBase="/path/to/app">
</Context>
```

You can test **app10e** by invoking this URL:

```
http://localhost:8080/app10e
```

Thanks to the dependency injector, each component in **app10e** can be tested independently. For example, the **ProductDAOTest** class in Listing 10.26 can be run to test the **ProductDAO**'s **insert** method.

Listing 10.26: The ProductDAOTest class

```
package test.app10e.dao;
import util.DependencyInjector;
import app10e.dao.DAOException;
import app10e.dao.ProductDAO;
import app10e.model.Product;

public class ProductDAOTest {

    public static void main(String[] args) {
        DependencyInjector injector = new DependencyInjector();
        try {
            injector.start();
            ProductDAO productDAO = (ProductDAO)
                    injector.getObject(ProductDAO.class);
            Product product = new Product();
            product.setName("New Product");
            product.setDescription("Testing");
            product.setPrice(20.20f);
            try {
                productDAO.insert(product);
            } catch (DAOException e) {
                e.printStackTrace();
            }
        } finally {
            injector.shutDown();
```

```
            }
        }
    }
```

To run the **ProductDAOTest** class successfully, you have to include the C3P0 library and the MySQL JDBC driver in your classpath. And yes, you should use a test framework (such as JUnit) for unit testing.

Summary

In this chapter you have learned about the Model 2 architecture, which is based on the MVC pattern, and how to write Model 2 applications using either a servlet controller or a filter dispatcher. These two types of Model 2 applications were demonstrated in **app10a** and **app10b**, respectively. One clear advantage of using a servlet as the controller over a filter is that you can configure the servlet as a welcome page. In a Model 2 application, JSP pages are often used as the view, even though other technologies such as Apache Velocity and FreeMarker can also be used. If JSP pages are used as the view in a Model 2 architecture, those pages are used to display values only and no scripting elements should be present in them.

In this chapter you have also built a simple MVC framework incorporating such components as a validator and a dependency injection framework. While the homemade framework serves as a good educational tool, going forward you should base your MVC projects on a mature MVC framework like Struts 2 or Spring MVC and not try to reinvent the wheel.

Chapter 11
File Upload

Once upon a time not long after Servlet technology had emerged, file upload programming was still a challenging task that involved parsing raw HTTP responses on the server side. To alleviate the pain, developers would resort to commercial file upload components, some of which cost an arm and a leg. Fortunately, in 2003 the Apache Software Foundation released its open source Commons FileUpload component, which soon became a hit with servlet/JSP programmers worldwide.

It took years before the designers of Servlet realized that file upload was essential, but file upload was finally a built-in feature in Servlet 3. Servlet 3 developers do not have to import the Commons FileUpload component into their projects anymore.

This chapter shows how to make use of the Servlet 3 file upload feature and what you need to do on the client side. It also demonstrates how you can enhance user experience with HTML 5.

Client Side Programming

To upload a file, you must set the value of the **enctype** attribute of your HTML form with **multipart/form-data**, like this:

```
<form action="action" enctype="multipart/form-data" method="post">
    Select a file <input type="file" name="fieldName"/>
    <input type="submit" value="Upload"/>
</form>
```

The form must contain an input element of type **file**, which will be rendered as a button that, when clicked, opens a dialog to select a file. The form may also contain other field types such as a text area or a hidden field.

Prior to HTML 5, if you wanted to upload multiple files, you had to use multiple file **input** elements. HTML 5, however, makes multiple file uploads simpler by introducing the **multiple** attribute in the **input** element. You can write one of the following in HTML 5 to generate a button for selecting multiple files:

```
<input type="file" name="fieldName" multiple/>

<input type="file" name="fieldName" multiple="multiple"/>

<input type="file" name="fieldName" multiple=""/>
```

Server Side Programming

Server side file upload programming in Servlet centers around the **MultipartConfig** annotation type and the **javax.servlet.http.Part** interface. Servlets that handle uploaded files must be annotated **@MultipartConfig**. **MultipartConfig** may have the following attributes, all of which optional.

- **maxFileSize**. The maximum size for uploaded files. Files larger than the specified value will be rejected. By default, the value of **maxFileSize** is -1, which means unlimited.
- **maxRequestSize**. The maximum size allowed for multipart HTTP requests. By default, the value is -1, which translates into unlimited.
- **location**. The save location when the uploaded file is saved to disk by calling the **write** method on the **Part**.
- **fileSizeThreshold**. The size threshold after which the uploaded file will be written to disk.

In a multipart request, every form field, including non-file fields, is converted into a **Part**. The **HttpServletRequest** interface defines the following methods for working with multipart requests:

```
Part getPart(java.lang.String name)
```
Returns the **Part** associated with the specified name.

```
java.util.Collection<Part> getParts()
```

Returns all **Part**s in this request.

And, these are the methods in the **Part** interface.

```
java.lang.String getName()
```
Retrieves the name of this part, i.e. the name of the associated form field.

```
java.lang.String getContentType()
```
If the **Part** if a file, returns the content type of the **Part**. Otherwise, returns null.

```
java.util.Collection<java.lang.String> getHeaderNames()
```
Returns all header names in this **Part**.

```
java.lang.String getHeader(java.lsng.String headerName)
```
Returns the value of the specified header name.

```
java.util.Collection<java.lang.String> getHeaders(java.lang.String
      headerName)
```
Returns the values of the **Part** header.

```
void write(java.lang.String path)
```
Writes the uploaded file to the disk. If path is an absolute path, writes to the specified path. If path is a relative path, write to the path specified path relative to the value of the location attribute of the **MultiConfig** annotation.

```
void delete()
```
Deletes the underlying storage for this file including the associated temporary file.

```
java.io.InputStream getInputStream()
```
Returns the content of the uploaded file as an **InputStream**.

A **Part** returns these headers if the corresponding HTML input is a file **input** element:

```
content-type:contentType
content-disposition:form-data; name="fieldName"; filename="fileName"
```

For example, uploading a **note.txt** file in an input field called **document** will cause the associated part to have these headers:

```
content-type:text/plain
```

```
content-disposition:form-data; name="document"; filename="note.txt"
```

If no file is selected, a **Part** will still be created for the file field, but the associated headers will be as follows.

```
content-type:application/octet-stream
content-disposition:form-data; name="document"; filename=""
```

The **getName** of the **Part** interface returns the field name associated with this part, not the name of the uploaded file. To get the latter, you need to parse the **content-disposition** header.

For a non-file field, a **Part** will only have a **content-disposition** header, which is of the following format:

```
content-disposition:form-data; name="fieldName"
```

When processing uploaded files in a servlet, you need to

- check if a **Part** is an ordinary form field or a file field by checking whether the **content-type** header exists. You can do this by calling the **getContentType** method or **getHeader("content-type")** on the **Part**.
- If the **content-type** header exists, check if the uploaded file name is empty. An empty file name indicates the presence of a field of file type but no file was selected for upload.
- If a file exists, you can write to the disk by calling the **write** method on the **Part**, passing an absolute path or a path relative to the location attribute of the **MultipartConfig** annotation.

Upload Servlet Example

The following is an example of how to write a multipart servlet. The servlet class, called **SingleUploadServlet** and printed in Listing 11.1, can handle a single file upload and is annotated with **@MultipartConfig**.

Listing 11.1: The SingleUploadServlet class

```
package app11a.servlet;
import java.io.IOException;
import java.io.PrintWriter;
```

```java
import javax.servlet.ServletException;
import javax.servlet.annotation.MultipartConfig;
import javax.servlet.annotation.WebServlet;
import javax.servlet.http.HttpServlet;
import javax.servlet.http.HttpServletRequest;
import javax.servlet.http.HttpServletResponse;
import javax.servlet.http.Part;

@WebServlet(urlPatterns = { "/singleUpload" })
@MultipartConfig
public class SingleUploadServlet extends HttpServlet {

    private static final long serialVersionUID = 8593038L;

    private String getFilename(Part part) {
        String contentDispositionHeader =
                part.getHeader("content-disposition");
        String[] elements = contentDispositionHeader.split(";");
        for (String element : elements) {
            if (element.trim().startsWith("filename")) {
                return element.substring(element.indexOf('=') + 1)
                        .trim().replace("\"", "");
            }
        }
        return null;
    }

    public void doPost(HttpServletRequest request,
            HttpServletResponse response) throws ServletException,
            IOException {

        // save uploaded file to WEB-INF
        Part part = request.getPart("filename");
        String fileName = getFilename(part);
        if (fileName != null && !fileName.isEmpty()) {
            part.write(getServletContext().getRealPath(
                    "/WEB-INF") + "/" + fileName);
        }

        // write to browser
        response.setContentType("text/html");
        PrintWriter writer = response.getWriter();
        writer.print("<br/>Uploaded file name: " + fileName);
        writer.print("<br/>Size: " + part.getSize());
```

```
            String author = request.getParameter("author");
            writer.print("<br/>Author: " + author);
        }
    }
```

One crucial method in the multipart servlet is the **getFilename** method that returns the name of the uploaded file. Note that the **getName** method of the **Part** interface returns the field name, not the uploaded file name.

The **getFilename** method retrieves the **content-disposition** header and splits it and then loops through the elements until it find one named **filename**.

```
    private String getFilename(Part part) {
        String contentDispositionHeader =
                part.getHeader("content-disposition");
        String[] elements = contentDispositionHeader.split(";");
        for (String element : elements) {
            if (element.trim().startsWith("filename")) {
                return element.substring(element.indexOf('=') + 1)
                        .trim().replace("\"", "");
            }
        }
        return null;
    }
```

To test the multipart servlet, invoke the **singleUpload.jsp** page in Listing 11.2 with this URL:

```
http://localhost:8080/app11a/singleUpload.jsp
```

Listing 11.2: The singleUpload.jsp page

```
<!DOCTYPE HTML>
<html>
<body>
<h1>Select a file to upload</h1>
<form action="singleUpload" enctype="multipart/form-data"
        method="post">
    Author: <input type="text" name="author"/><br/>
    Select file to upload <input type="file" name="filename"/><br/>
    <input type="submit" value="Upload"/>
</form>
</body>
</html>
```

Figure 11.1 shows the rendered page. Note that the file **input** element is rendered as a clickable button that opens an Open File dialog. The button label is different from one browser to another. In Chrome, it is Choose File. In Internet Explorer and Firefox, it's Browse. Also, Chrome prints the selected file to the right of the button, but Firefox and IE do not.

Figure 11.1: File upload form

Now select a file, enter a value in the Author field and clicks Upload. You will see the uploaded file name and size printed in your browser, as shown in Figure 11.2.

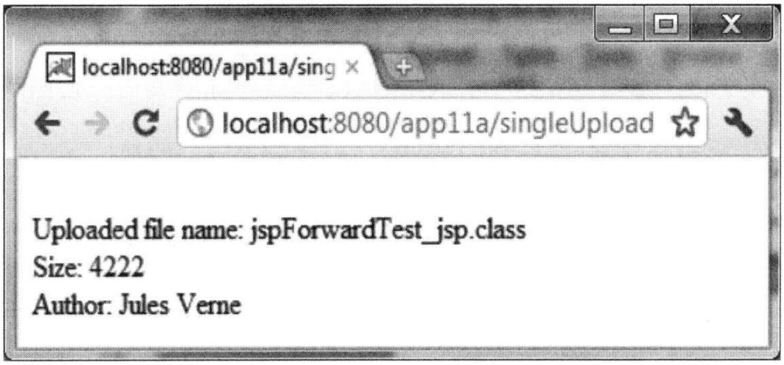

Figure 11.2: The output of SingleUploadServlet

Multiple Uploads

As another example, the **MultipleUploadsServlet** in Listing 11.3 shows off
how you can upload more than one file at a time. The servlet is similar to
the previous example except that it loops through the **Part** collection and
tries to figure out if a **Part** contains a file or a field value.

Listing 11.3: The MultipleUploadsServlet class

```
package app11a.servlet;
import java.io.IOException;
import java.io.PrintWriter;
import java.util.Collection;
import javax.servlet.ServletException;
import javax.servlet.annotation.MultipartConfig;
import javax.servlet.annotation.WebServlet;
import javax.servlet.http.HttpServlet;
import javax.servlet.http.HttpServletRequest;
import javax.servlet.http.HttpServletResponse;
import javax.servlet.http.Part;

@WebServlet(urlPatterns = { "/multipleUploads" })
@MultipartConfig
public class MultipleUploadsServlet extends HttpServlet {

    private static final long serialVersionUID = 9991L;

    private String getFilename(Part part) {
        String contentDispositionHeader =
                part.getHeader("content-disposition");
        String[] elements = contentDispositionHeader.split(";");
        for (String element : elements) {
            if (element.trim().startsWith("filename")) {
                return element.substring(element.indexOf('=') + 1)
                        .trim().replace("\"", "");
            }
        }
        return null;
    }

    public void doPost(HttpServletRequest request,
            HttpServletResponse response) throws ServletException,
            IOException {
```

```
        response.setContentType("text/html");
        PrintWriter writer = response.getWriter();

        Collection<Part> parts = request.getParts();
        for (Part part : parts) {
            if (part.getContentType() != null) {
                // save file Part to disk
                String fileName = getFilename(part);
                if (fileName != null && !fileName.isEmpty()) {
                    part.write(getServletContext().getRealPath(
                            "/WEB-INF") + "/" + fileName);
                    writer.print("<br/>Uploaded file name: " +
                            fileName);
                    writer.print("<br/>Size: " + part.getSize());
                }
            } else {
                // print field name/value
                String partName = part.getName();
                String fieldValue = request.getParameter(partName);
                writer.print("<br/>" + partName + ": " +
                        fieldValue);
            }
        }
    }
}
```

The **doPost** method of the **MultipleUploadsServlet** class starts by getting all **Part**s in the **HttpServletRequest**.

```
        Collection<Part> parts = request.getParts();
```

It then iterates over the collection and for each **Part** checks if there exists a **content-type** header by calling the **getContentType** method.

```
        for (Part part : parts) {
            if (part.getContentType() != null) {
                ...
            }
        }
```

A content type denotes the presence of a file **input** element at the client side, and you can try to find out if a file was uploaded. If a file is found, the **doPost** method writes the content of the file to the disk and sends some information to the browser.

```
// save file Part to disk
String fileName = getFilename(part);
if (fileName != null && !fileName.isEmpty()) {
    part.write(getServletContext().getRealPath(
            "/WEB-INF") + "/" + fileName);
    writer.print("<br/>Uploaded file name: " +
            fileName);
    writer.print("<br/>Size: " + part.getSize());
}
```

The absence of content type indicates that the **Part** represents a non-file field and you can retrieve the field value by calling the **getParameter** method on the **HttpServletRequest**:

```
// print field name/value
String partName = part.getName();
String fieldValue = request.getParameter(partName);
writer.print("<br/>" + partName + ": " +
        fieldValue);
```

To test the multiple upload servlet, invoke the **multipleUploads.jsp** page in Listing 11.4 using this URL:

```
http://localhost:8080/app11a/multipleUploads.jsp
```

Listing 11.4: The multipleUploads.jsp page

```
<!DOCTYPE HTML>
<html>
<body>
<h1>Select a file to upload</h1>
<form action="multipleUploads" enctype="multipart/form-data"
        method="post">
    Author : <input name="author"/><br/>
    First file to upload <input type="file" name="filename"/>
    <br/>
    Second file to upload <input type="file" name="filename"/>
    <br/>
    <input type="submit" value="Upload"/>
</form>
</body>
</html>
```

Upload Clients

While the file upload feature in Servlet 3 makes file upload a breeze to program on the server side, it does nothing to enhance user experience. An HTML form alone will not let you display a progress bar or show the number of files successfully uploaded. Developers have used different techniques to improve the user interface, such as by inquiring the server using a separate browser thread so that upload progress can be reported, or by using third-party technologies such as Java applets, Adobe Flash, or Microsoft Silverlight.

The third-party technologies work. To some extent and with limitation. The first disadvantage of using one of these technologies is that there is no built-in support for them in all major browsers. For example, Java applets can only run if the user has installed Java on his/her computer. While some computer makers, such as Dell and HP, ship their products with Java installed, some others, such as Lenovo, do not. While there are ways to detect if Java is installed on the user's machine and direct the user to install one if none exists, this is a disruption that not all users are willing to tolerate. On top of that, Java applets by default have very restricted access to the local file system unless they are signed. These obviously add costs and complexity to the program.

Flash has the same issues as applets. Flash programs need a player to run and not all platforms support Flash. The user will have to install a Flash player to run Flash programs inside a browser. Besides, Apple won't allow Flash to run on iPad and iPhone and Adobe has finally discontinued Flash on mobile platforms.

Microsoft Silverlight also needs a player to run and non-IE browsers do not ship with one. So, basically Silverlight programmers have more or less the same problems as those encountered by applet and Flash developers.

Luckily for us, HTML 5 comes to the rescue.

HTML 5 adds a File API to its DOM to allow local file access. Compared to applets, Flash, and Silverlight, HTML 5 seems ideal as the perfect solution to client side file upload limitations. At time of writing, unfortunately, Internet Explorer 9 does not yet fully support this API. You can test the following example with the latest version of Firefox, Chrome and Opera, however.

To demonstrate the power of HTML 5, the **html5.jsp** page in **app11b** (given in Listing 11.5) uses JavaScript and the HTML 5 File API to provide a progress bar that reports the upload progress. The **app11b** application also contains a copy of the **MultipleUploadsServlet** class to save uploaded files on the server. However, as Javascript is beyond the scope of this book, explanation will only be given cursorily.

In short, we're interested in the **change** event of the HTML 5 **input** element, which is triggered when the value of an **input** element changes. We're also interested in the **progress** event added to the **XMLHttpRequest** object in HTML 5. **XMLHttpRequest** is of course the backbone of AJAX. When the **XMLHttpRequest** object is used asynchronously to upload a file, it triggers the **progress** event continuously until the upload process is complete or canceled or until the process is halted by an error. By listening to the **progress** event, you can easily monitor the progress of a file upload operation.

Listing: 11.5: The html5.jsp page

```
<!DOCTYPE HTML>
<html>
<head>
<script>
    var totalFileLength, totalUploaded, fileCount, filesUploaded;

    function debug(s) {
        var debug = document.getElementById('debug');
        if (debug) {
            debug.innerHTML = debug.innerHTML + '<br/>' + s;
        }
    }

    function onUploadComplete(e) {
        totalUploaded += document.getElementById('files').
                files[filesUploaded].size;
        filesUploaded++;
        debug('complete ' + filesUploaded + " of " + fileCount);
        debug('totalUploaded: ' + totalUploaded);
        if (filesUploaded < fileCount) {
            uploadNext();
        } else {
```

```
            alert('Finished uploading file(s)');
        }
}

function onFileSelect(e) {
    var files = e.target.files; // FileList object
    var output = [];
    fileCount = files.length;
    totalFileLength = 0;
    for (var i=0; i<fileCount; i++) {
        var file = files[i];
        output.push(file.name, ' (',
                file.size, ' bytes, ',
                file.lastModifiedDate.toLocaleDateString(), ')'
        );
        output.push('<br/>');
        debug('add ' + file.size);
        totalFileLength += file.size;
    }
    document.getElementById('selectedFiles').innerHTML =
        output.join('');
    debug('totalFileLength:' + totalFileLength);
}

function onUploadProgress(e) {
    if (e.lengthComputable) {
        var percentComplete = parseInt(
                (e.loaded + totalUploaded) * 100
                / totalFileLength);
        var bar = document.getElementById('bar');
        bar.style.width = percentComplete + '%';
        bar.innerHTML = percentComplete + ' % complete';
    } else {
        debug('unable to compute');
    }
}

function onUploadFailed(e) {
    alert("Error uploading file");
}

function uploadNext() {
    var xhr = new XMLHttpRequest();
    var fd = new FormData();
    var file = document.getElementById('files').
```

```
                    files[filesUploaded];
        fd.append("fileToUpload", file);
        xhr.upload.addEventListener(
                "progress", onUploadProgress, false);
        xhr.addEventListener("load", onUploadComplete, false);
        xhr.addEventListener("error", onUploadFailed, false);
        xhr.open("POST", "multipleUploads");
        debug('uploading ' + file.name);
        xhr.send(fd);
    }

    function startUpload() {
        totalUploaded = filesUploaded = 0;
        uploadNext();
    }
    window.onload = function() {
        document.getElementById('files').addEventListener(
                'change', onFileSelect, false);
        document.getElementById('uploadButton').
                addEventListener('click', startUpload, false);
    }
</script>
</head>
<body>
<h1>Multiple file uploads with progress bar</h1>
<div id='progressBar' style='height:20px;border:2px solid green'>
    <div id='bar'
            style='height:100%;background:#33dd33;width:0%'>
    </div>
</div>
<form id='form1' action="multipleUploads"
        enctype="multipart/form-data" method="post">
    <input type="file" id="files" multiple/>
    <br/>
    <output id="selectedFiles"></output>
    <input id="uploadButton" type="button" value="Upload"/>
</form>
<div id='debug'
    style='height:100px;border:2px solid green;overflow:auto'>
</div>
</body>
</html>
```

The user interface in the **html5.jsp** page consists mainly of a **div** element called **progressBar**, a form, and another **div** element called **debug**. You guessed it right that the **progressBar div** is for showing the upload progress and **debug** is for debugging info. The form has an **input** element of type file and a button.

There are two things to note from the form. First, the **input** element identified as **files** has a **multiple** attribute to support multiple file selection. Second, the button is not a submit button. So, clicking it will not submit the containing form. In fact, the script uses the **XMLHttpRequest** object to do the upload.

Now, let's look at the Javascript code. This assumes some knowledge of the scripting language.

When the script is executed, the first thing it does is allocate space for four variables.

```
var totalFileLength, totalUploaded, fileCount, filesUploaded;
```

The **totalFileLength** variable holds the total length of the files to be uploaded. **totalUploaded** is the number of bytes uploaded so far. **fileCount** contains the number of files to be uploaded, and **filesUploaded** indicates the number of files that have been uploaded.

Then the function assigned to **window.onload** is called after the window completely loads.

```
window.onload = function() {
    document.getElementById('files').addEventListener(
            'change', onFileSelect, false);
    document.getElementById('uploadButton').
            addEventListener('click', startUpload, false);
}
```

This maps the **files input** element's **change** event with the **onFileSelect** function and the button's **click** event with **startUpload**.

The **change** event occurs every time the user changes a different set of files from a local directory. The event handler attached to this event simply prints the names and sizes of the selected files to an output element. Here is the event handler again:

```
function onFileSelect(e) {
    var files = e.target.files; // FileList object
```

```
var output = [];
fileCount = files.length;
totalFileLength = 0;
for (var i=0; i<fileCount; i++) {
    var file = files[i];
    output.push(file.name, ' (',
            file.size, ' bytes, ',
            file.lastModifiedDate.toLocaleDateString(), ')'
    );
    output.push('<br/>');
    debug('add ' + file.size);
    totalFileLength += file.size;
}
document.getElementById('selectedFiles').innerHTML =
    output.join('');
debug('totalFileLength:' + totalFileLength);
}
```

When the user clicks the Upload button, the **startUpload** function is called
and it in turns calls the **uploadNext** function. **uploadNext** uploads the next
file in the selected file collection. It starts by creating an **XMLHttpRequest**
object and a **FormData** object to which the file to be uploaded next is
appended to.

```
var xhr = new XMLHttpRequest();
var fd = new FormData();
var file = document.getElementById('files').
        files[filesUploaded];
fd.append("fileToUpload", file);
```

The **uploadNext** function then attaches the **progress** event of the
XMLHttpRequest object to the **onUploadProgress** and the **load** event and
the **error** event to **onUploadComplete** and **onUploadFailed**, respectively.

```
xhr.upload.addEventListener(
        "progress", onUploadProgress, false);
xhr.addEventListener("load", onUploadComplete, false);
xhr.addEventListener("error", onUploadFailed, false);
```

Next, it opens a connection to the server and sends the **FormData**.

```
xhr.open("POST", "multipleUploads");
debug('uploading ' + file.name);
xhr.send(fd);
```

During the upload progress, the **onUploadProgress** function is called repeatedly, giving it the opportunity to update the progress bar. An update involves calculating the ratio of the total bytes already uploaded and the number of bytes of the selected files as well as widening the **div** element within the **progressBar div** element.

```
function onUploadProgress(e) {
    if (e.lengthComputable) {
        var percentComplete = parseInt(
                (e.loaded + totalUploaded) * 100
                / totalFileLength);
        var bar = document.getElementById('bar');
        bar.style.width = percentComplete + '%';
        bar.innerHTML = percentComplete + ' % complete';
    } else {
        debug('unable to compute');
    }
}
```

At the completion of an upload, the **onUploadComplete** function is invoked. This event handler adds to **totalUploaded** the size of the file that has just finished uploading and increments **filesUploaded**. It then checks if all selected files have been uploaded. If yes, a message is displayed telling the user that uploading has completed successfully. If not, it calls **uploadNext** again. The **onUploadComplete** function is reprinted here for reading convenience.

```
function onUploadComplete(e) {
    totalUploaded += document.getElementById('files').
            files[filesUploaded].size;
    filesUploaded++;
    debug('complete ' + filesUploaded + " of " + fileCount);
    debug('totalUploaded: ' + totalUploaded);
    if (filesUploaded < fileCount) {
        uploadNext();
    } else {
        alert('Finished uploading file(s)');
    }
}
```

You can test the application using this URL:

```
http://localhost:8080/app11b/html5.jsp
```

Select a couple of files and click the Upload button. You'll see a progress bar and the information on the uploaded files like the screen shot in Figure 11.3.

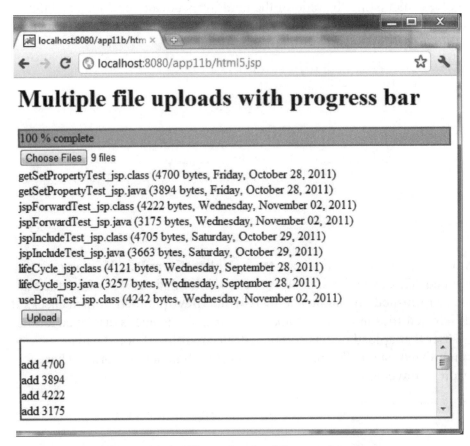

Figure 11.3: File upload with progress bar

Summary

In this chapter you have learned how file upload support in Servlet 3 works. Of particular importance is the **MultipartConfig** annotation type that all multipart servlets must be annotated with and the **Part** interface. A **Part** represents an HTML input field and in the case of a **Part** that corresponds to a file **input** element, **Part** exposes various properties of the uploaded file, such as the file name and size. **Part** also allows you to easily write the file to the disk.

While the new feature is an excellent addition to Servlet 3.0, it does not address the lack of useful user interface in the browser. For this you can use HTML 5. This chapter showed how you can utilize the File API in HTML 5 to render and update a progress bar.

Chapter 12
File Download

A static resource, such as an image or an HTML file, can be downloaded by simply pointing the browser at the right URL. As long as the resource is located in the application directory or a subdirectory under it and not under **WEB-INF**, the servlet/JSP container will send the resource to the browser. However, sometimes a static resource is stored outside the application directory or in a database, or sometimes you want to control over who can see it and prevent other websites from cross-referencing it. In any of these scenarios applies to you, then you have to send the resource programmatically.

In short, programmatic file download lets you selectively send a file to the browser. This chapter explains what it takes to programmatically send a resource to the browser and presents two examples.

File Download Overview

To send a resource such as a file to the browser, you need to do the following in your servlet. It is uncommon to use JSP pages as you're sending a binary and there's nothing to display in the browser.

1. Set the response's content type to the file's content type. The **Content-Type** header specifies the type of the data in the body of an entity and consists of the media type and subtype identifiers. Visit http://www.iana.org/assignments/media-types for standard content types. If you do not know what the content type is or want the browser to always display the Save As dialog, set it to **APPLICATION/OCTET-STREAM**. This value is not case sensitive.

2. Add an HTTP response header named **Content-Disposition** and give it the value **attachment; filename=***fileName*, where *fileName* is the default file name that appears in the File Download dialog box. This is normally the same name as the file, but does not have to be so.

For instance, this code sends a file to the browser.

```
FileInputStream fis = new FileInputStream(file);
BufferedInputStream bis = new BufferedInputStream(fis);
byte[] bytes = new byte[bis.available()];
response.setContentType(contentType);
OutputStream os = response.getOutputStream();
bis.read(bytes);
os.write(bytes);
```

To send a file programmatically tot he browser, first you read the file as a **FileInputStream** and load the content to a byte array. Then, you obtain the **HttpServletResponse**'s **OutputStream** and call its **write** method, passing the byte array.

Warning

Make sure you do not inadvertently send any characters other than the actual file content. This could happen without your realizing it. For example, if you need to write use the **page** directive in a JSP page, you might write the directive like this:

```
<%@ page import="java.io.FileInputStream"%>
<jsp:useBean id="DBBeanId" scope="page" class="MyBean" />
```

Without you realizing it, the carriage return at the end of the **page** directive will be sent to the browser. To prevent extra characters from being sent, write the directive as follows:

```
<%@ page import="java.io.FileInputStream"
%><jsp:useBean id="DBBeanId" scope="page" class="MyBean" />
```

It looks unusual, but it helps.

Example 1: Hiding A Resource

The **app12a** application demonstrates how to send a file to the browser. In this application we employ a **FileDownloadServlet** servlet to send a

secret.pdf file to the browser. However, only authorized users can view it. If a user has not logged in, the application will forward to the Login page. Here the user can enter a user name and password in a form that will be submitted to another servlet, **LoginServlet**.

The **app12a** application directory structure is shown in Figure 12.1. Note that the

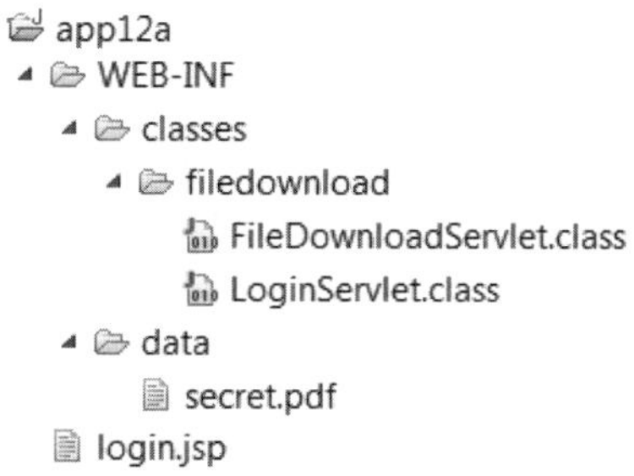

Figure 12.1: The application directory

The **secret.pdf** file is placed under **WEB-INF/data** so that direct access is not possible.

The **FileDownloadServlet** class in Listing 12.1 presents the servlet responsible for sending the **secret.pdf** file. Access is only granted if the user's **HttpSession** contains a **loggedIn** attribute, which indicates the user has successfully logged in.

Listing 12.1: The FileDownloadServlet class

```
package filedownload;
import java.io.BufferedInputStream;
import java.io.File;
import java.io.FileInputStream;
import java.io.IOException;
import java.io.OutputStream;
import javax.servlet.RequestDispatcher;
import javax.servlet.ServletException;
import javax.servlet.annotation.WebServlet;
import javax.servlet.http.HttpServlet;
import javax.servlet.http.HttpServletRequest;
import javax.servlet.http.HttpServletResponse;
import javax.servlet.http.HttpSession;
```

```
@WebServlet(urlPatterns = { "/download" })
public class FileDownloadServlet extends HttpServlet {

    private static final long serialVersionUID = 7583L;

    public void doGet(HttpServletRequest request,
            HttpServletResponse response) throws ServletException,
            IOException {
        HttpSession session = request.getSession();
        if (session == null ||
                session.getAttribute("loggedIn") == null) {
            RequestDispatcher dispatcher =
                    request.getRequestDispatcher("/login.jsp");
            dispatcher.forward(request, response);
            // must return after dispatcher.forward(). Otherwise,
            // the code below will be executed
            return;
        }
        String dataDirectory = request.
                getServletContext().getRealPath("/WEB-INF/data");
        File file = new File(dataDirectory, "secret.pdf");
        if (file.exists()) {
            response.setContentType("application/pdf");
            response.addHeader("Content-Disposition",
                    "attachment; filename=secret.pdf");
            byte[] buffer = new byte[1024];
            FileInputStream fis = null;
            BufferedInputStream bis = null;
            // if you're using Java 7, use try-with-resources
            try {
                fis = new FileInputStream(file);
                bis = new BufferedInputStream(fis);
                OutputStream os = response.getOutputStream();
                int i = bis.read(buffer);
                while (i != -1) {
                    os.write(buffer, 0, i);
                    i = bis.read(buffer);
                }
            } catch (IOException ex) {
                System.out.println (ex.toString());
            } finally {
                if (bis != null) {
                    bis.close();
                }
                if (fis != null) {
                    fis.close();
```

```
                }
            }
        }
    }
}
```

Only the **doGet** method is implemented as the HTTP post method is not permitted. The **doGet** method examines if there is a **loggedIn** attribute in the user session. The absence of one sends the user to the Login page.

```
HttpSession session = request.getSession();
if (session == null ||
        session.getAttribute("loggedIn") == null) {
    RequestDispatcher dispatcher =
            request.getRequestDispatcher("/login.jsp");
    dispatcher.forward(request, response);
    // must return after dispatcher.forward(). Otherwise,
    // the code below will be executed
    return;
}
```

Note that calling **forward** on a **RequestDispatcher** will forward control to a different resource. However, it does not stop the code execution of the calling object. As such, you have to return after forwarding.

If the user has successfully logged in, the **doGet** method opens the intended resource and streams it to the **ServletResponse**'s **OutputStream**.

```
response.setContentType("application/pdf");
response.addHeader("Content-Disposition",
        "attachment; filename=secret.pdf");
byte[] buffer = new byte[1024];
FileInputStream fis = null;
BufferedInputStream bis = null;
// if you're using Java 7, use try-with-resources
try {
    fis = new FileInputStream(file);
    bis = new BufferedInputStream(fis);
    OutputStream os = response.getOutputStream();
    int i = bis.read(buffer);
    while (i != -1) {
        os.write(buffer, 0, i);
        i = bis.read(buffer);
    }
} catch (IOException ex) {
```

```
            System.out.println (ex.toString());
        } finally {
            if (bis != null) {
                bis.close();
            }
            if (fis != null) {
                fis.close();
            }
        }
    }
```

If you're using Java 7, the new try-with-resources feature is a safer way for handling resources.

An unauthorized user will be forwarded to the **login.jsp** page in Listing 12.2. This page contains an HTML form with two input fields, **userName** and **password**.

Listing 12.2: The login.jsp page

```
<html>
<head>
<title>Login</title>
</head>
<body>
<form action="login" method="post">
    <table>
    <tr>
        <td>User Name:</td>
        <td><input name="userName"/></td>
    </tr>
    <tr>
        <td>Password:</td>
        <td><input type="password" name="password"/></td>
    </tr>
    <tr>
        <td colspan="2">
            <input type="submit" value="Login"/>
        </td>
    </tr>
    </table>
</form>
</body>
</html>
```

Submitting the form will invoke the **LoginServlet** whose class is printed in Listing 12.3. Note that for this application the username/password must be ken/secret.

Listing 12.3: The LoginServlet class

```java
package filedownload;
import java.io.IOException;
import javax.servlet.RequestDispatcher;
import javax.servlet.ServletException;
import javax.servlet.annotation.WebServlet;
import javax.servlet.http.HttpServlet;
import javax.servlet.http.HttpServletRequest;
import javax.servlet.http.HttpServletResponse;
import javax.servlet.http.HttpSession;

@WebServlet(urlPatterns = { "/login" })
public class LoginServlet extends HttpServlet {

    private static final long serialVersionUID = -920L;

    public void doPost(HttpServletRequest request,
            HttpServletResponse response) throws ServletException,
            IOException {
        String userName = request.getParameter("userName");
        String password = request.getParameter("password");
        if (userName != null && userName.equals("ken")
                && password != null && password.equals("secret")) {
            HttpSession session = request.getSession(true);
            session.setAttribute("loggedIn", Boolean.TRUE);
            response.sendRedirect("download");
            // must call return or else the code after this if
            // block, if any, will be executed
            return;
        } else {
            RequestDispatcher dispatcher =
                    request.getRequestDispatcher("/login.jsp");
            dispatcher.forward(request, response);
        }
    }
}
```

A successful login will set a **loggedIn** session attribute and forward the user to the **FileDownload** servlet:

```
String userName = request.getParameter("userName");
String password = request.getParameter("password");
if (userName != null && userName.equals("ken")
        && password != null && password.equals("secret")) {
    HttpSession session = request.getSession(true);
    session.setAttribute("loggedIn", Boolean.TRUE);
    response.sendRedirect("download");
    // must call return or else the code after this if
    // block, if any, will be executed
    return;
```

Again, you must return after **HttpServletResponse.sendRedirect** to prevent the next lines of code from getting executed.

A failed login forwards the user to the **login.jsp** page:

```
} else {
    RequestDispatcher dispatcher =
            request.getRequestDispatcher("/login.jsp");
    dispatcher.forward(request, response);
}
```

You can test the **app12a** application by invoking the **FileDownloadServlet** using this URL:

```
http://localhost:8080/app12a/download
```

Example 2: Preventing Cross-Referencing

Competitors might try to "steal" your web assets by cross-referencing them, i.e. displaying your valuables in their websites as if they were theirs. You can prevent this from happening by programmatically sending the resources only if the **referer** header contains your domain name. Of course the most determined thieves will still be able to download your properties. However, they can't do that without sweat.

The **app12b** application uses a servlet to send images to the browser, only if the **referer** header is not null. This will prevent the images from being downloaded directly by typing their URLs in the browser. The servlet, **ImageServlet**, is given in Listing 12.4.

Listing 12.4: The ImageServlet class

```
package filedownload;
import java.io.BufferedInputStream;
import java.io.File;
import java.io.FileInputStream;
import java.io.IOException;
import java.io.OutputStream;
import javax.servlet.ServletException;
import javax.servlet.annotation.WebServlet;
import javax.servlet.http.HttpServlet;
import javax.servlet.http.HttpServletRequest;
import javax.servlet.http.HttpServletResponse;

@WebServlet(urlPatterns = { "/getImage" })
public class ImageServlet extends HttpServlet {

    private static final long serialVersionUID = -99L;

    public void doGet(HttpServletRequest request,
            HttpServletResponse response) throws ServletException,
            IOException {
        String referrer = request.getHeader("referer");
        if (referrer != null) {
            String imageId = request.getParameter("id");
            String imageDirectory = request.getServletContext().
                    getRealPath("/WEB-INF/image");
            File file = new File(imageDirectory,
                    imageId + ".jpg");
            if (file.exists()) {
                response.setContentType("image/jpg");
                byte[] buffer = new byte[1024];
                FileInputStream fis = null;
                BufferedInputStream bis = null;
                // if you're using Java 7, use try-with-resources
                try {
                    fis = new FileInputStream(file);
                    bis = new BufferedInputStream(fis);
                    OutputStream os = response.getOutputStream();
                    int i = bis.read(buffer);
                    while (i != -1) {
                        os.write(buffer, 0, i);
                        i = bis.read(buffer);
                    }
                } catch (IOException ex) {
                    System.out.println (ex.toString());
                } finally {
```

```
                        if (bis != null) {
                            bis.close();
                        }
                        if (fis != null) {
                            fis.close();
                        }
                    }
                }
            }
        }
    }
}
```

In principle the **ImageServlet** class works like **FileDownloadServlet**. However, the **if** statement at the beginning of the **doGet** method makes sure an image will be sent only if the **referer** header is not null.

You can use the **images.html** file in Listing 12.5 to test the application.

Listing 12.5: The images.html file

```
<html>
<head>
    <title>Photo Gallery</title>
</head>
<body>
<img src="getImage?id=1"/>
<img src="getImage?id=2"/>
<img src="getImage?id=3"/>
<img src="getImage?id=4"/>
<img src="getImage?id=5"/>
<img src="getImage?id=6"/>
<img src="getImage?id=7"/>
<img src="getImage?id=8"/>
<img src="getImage?id=9"/>
<img src="getImage?id=10"/>
</body>
</html>
```

To see **ImageServlet** in action, point your browser to this URL:

```
http://localhost:8080/app12b/images.html
```

Figure 12.2 shows the images sent by **ImageServlet**.

Figure 12.2: ImageServlet in action

Summary

In this chapter you have learned how programmatic file download works in servlet/applications. You have also learned how to select a file and sent it to the browser.

Chapter 13
Decorating Requests and
Responses

The Servlet API comes with four wrapper classes that you can use to change the behavior of servlet requests and servlet responses. The wrappers allow you to "wrap" any method in the **ServletRequest** and **ServletResponse** or their HTTP equivalents (**HttpServletRequest** and **HttpServletReponse**, respectively). These wrappers follow the Decorator or Wrapper pattern, and to utilize these wrappers you need to understand what the pattern is.

This chapter starts with an explanation of the Decorator pattern and provides an example of how to change the behavior of **HttpServletRequest** objects by wrapping them. The same technique can be used to wrap **HttpServletResponse** objects.

The Decorator Pattern

The Decorator or Wrapper pattern allows you to decorate or wrap (in plain language, modify the behavior of) an object even if you don't have the source code for the object's class or even if the class is declared final.

The Decorator pattern is suitable for situations where inheritance will not work (for example, if the class of the object in question is final) or you do not create the object yourself but rather get it from another subsystem. For example, the servlet container creates a **ServletRequest** and a **ServletResponse** and pass them to the servlet's **service** method. The only way to change the behavior of the **ServletRequest** and **ServletResponse** is by wrapping them in other objects. The only condition that must be met is that the class of a decorated object implements an interface and the methods that will be wrapped are inherited from that interface.

Consider the UML class diagram in Figure 13.1.

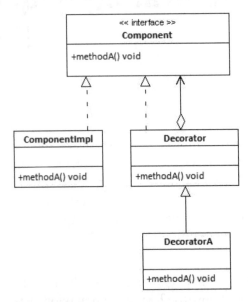

Figure 13.1: The Decorator pattern

The class diagram in Figure 13.1 shows a **Component** interface with an implementation class named **ComponentImpl**. The **Component** interface defines a **methodA** method. To decorate instances of **ComponentImpl**, create a **Decorator** class that implements **Component** and extend **Decorator** to program new behavior in a subclass. In the diagram **DecoratorA** is a subclass of **Decorator**.

Every **Decorator** instance needs to contain an instance of **Component**. The **Decorator** class would look like the code below. (Note that the constructor takes an instance of **Component**, which means you can only create a **Decorator** by passing an instance of **Component**.)

```
public class Decorator implements Component {
    private Component decorated;

    // constructor takes a Component implementation
    public Decorator(Component component) {
        this.decorated = component;
```

```
    }

    // undecorated method
    @Override
    public void methodA(args) {
        decorated.methodA(args);
    }

    // decorated method
    @Override
    public void methodB(args) {
        decorated.methodB(args)
    }
}
```

In the **Decorator** class a decorated method is a method whose behavior will be changed in a subclass. An undecorated method is one that will not be overridden in a subclass. All methods, decorated or otherwise, calls their counterpart methods in **Component**. The **Decorator** class is more of a convenience class that provides default implementation for every method in it. Behavior change is provided by a subclass.

One thing to bear in mind is that the **Decorator** class and the class of the decorated object must implement the same interface. By doing so, you can wrap the decorated object inside the decorator and pass the decorator as an implementation of **Component**. You can pass any implementation of **Component** to a decorator. In fact, you can pass your decorator to another decorator to double decorate an object.

Servlet Wrapper Classes

The Servlet API comes with four classes that are rarely used but could be very powerful, **ServletRequestWrapper** and **ServletResponseWrapper** as well as **HttpServletRequestWrapper** and **HttpServletResponseWrapper**.

The **ServletRequestWrapper** (and the three other wrapper classes) is convenient to use because it provides the default implementation for each method that calls the counterpart method in the wrapped **ServletRequest**. By extending **ServletRequestWrapper**, you just need to override methods

that you want to change. Without **ServletRequestWrapper**, you would
have to implement **ServletRequest** directly and provide the implementation
of every method in the interface.

Figure 13.2 shows the **ServletRequestWrapper** class in the Decorator
pattern. The servlet container creates an instance of **ServletRequest,
ContainerImpl**, every time a servlet's **service** method is invoked. You can
extend **ServletRequestWrapper** to decorate the **ServletRequest**.

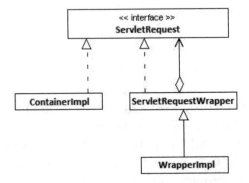

Figure 13.2: Decorating ServletRequest

Example: AutoCorrect Filter

Within a web application the user often enters values with leading or
trailing white spaces and even extra spaces between words. You don't want
to check and remove extra spaces in every servlet in your application. The
AutoCorrect filter featured in this section can help. The filter contains a
subclass of **HttpServletRequestWrapper** named
AutoCorrectHttpServletRequestWrapper and override the following
methods that return parameter value or values: **getParameter,
getParameterValues**, and **getParameterMap**. The filter class is presented
in Listing 13.1.

Listing 13.1: AutoCorrectFilter

```
package filter;
import java.io.IOException;
import java.util.ArrayList;
import java.util.Collection;
```

```java
import java.util.HashSet;
import java.util.Map;
import java.util.Set;

import javax.servlet.Filter;
import javax.servlet.FilterChain;
import javax.servlet.FilterConfig;
import javax.servlet.ServletException;
import javax.servlet.ServletRequest;
import javax.servlet.ServletResponse;
import javax.servlet.annotation.WebFilter;
import javax.servlet.http.HttpServletRequest;
import javax.servlet.http.HttpServletRequestWrapper;

@WebFilter(filterName = "AutoCorrectFilter",
        urlPatterns = { "/*" })
public class AutoCorrectFilter implements Filter {

    @Override
    public void init(FilterConfig filterConfig)
            throws ServletException {
    }

    @Override
    public void destroy() {
    }

    @Override
    public void doFilter(ServletRequest request,
            ServletResponse response, FilterChain filterChain)
            throws IOException, ServletException {
        HttpServletRequest httpServletRequest =
                (HttpServletRequest) request;
        AutoCorrectHttpServletRequestWrapper wrapper = new
                AutoCorrectHttpServletRequestWrapper(
                        httpServletRequest);
        filterChain.doFilter(wrapper, response);
    }

    class AutoCorrectHttpServletRequestWrapper extends
            HttpServletRequestWrapper {
        private HttpServletRequest httpServletRequest;

        public AutoCorrectHttpServletRequestWrapper(
                HttpServletRequest httpServletRequest) {
```

```java
            super(httpServletRequest);
            this.httpServletRequest = httpServletRequest;
        }

        @Override
        public String getParameter(String name) {
            return autoCorrect(
                    httpServletRequest.getParameter(name));
        }

        @Override
        public String[] getParameterValues(String name) {
            return autoCorrect(httpServletRequest
                    .getParameterValues(name));
        }

        @Override
        public Map<String, String[]> getParameterMap() {
            final Map<String, String[]> parameterMap =
                    httpServletRequest.getParameterMap();

            Map<String, String[]> newMap = new Map<String,
                    String[]>() {

                @Override
                public int size() {
                    return parameterMap.size();
                }

                @Override
                public boolean isEmpty() {
                    return parameterMap.isEmpty();
                }

                @Override
                public boolean containsKey(Object key) {
                    return parameterMap.containsKey(key);
                }

                @Override
                public boolean containsValue(Object value) {
                    return parameterMap.containsValue(value);
                }

                @Override
                public String[] get(Object key) {
```

```
        return autoCorrect(parameterMap.get(key));
}

@Override
public void clear() {
    // this will throw an IllegalStateException,
    // but let the user get the original
    // exception
    parameterMap.clear();
}

@Override
public Set<String> keySet() {
    return parameterMap.keySet();
}

@Override
public Collection<String[]> values() {
    return autoCorrect(parameterMap.values());
}

@Override
public Set<Map.Entry<String,
        String[]>> entrySet() {
    return autoCorrect(parameterMap.entrySet());
}

@Override
public String[] put(String key, String[] value) {
    // this will throw an IllegalStateException,
    // but let the user get the original
    // exception
    return parameterMap.put(key, value);
}

@Override
public void putAll(
        Map<? extends String, ? extends
                String[]> map) {
    // this will throw an IllegalStateException,
    // but let
    // the user get the original exception
    parameterMap.putAll(map);
}
```

```
            @Override
            public String[] remove(Object key) {
                // this will throw an IllegalStateException,
                // but let
                // the user get the original exception
                return parameterMap.remove(key);
            }
        };
        return newMap;
    }
}

private String autoCorrect(String value) {
    if (value == null) {
        return null;
    }
    value = value.trim();
    int length = value.length();
    StringBuilder temp = new StringBuilder();
    boolean lastCharWasSpace = false;
    for (int i = 0; i < length; i++) {
        char c = value.charAt(i);
        if (c == ' ') {
            if (!lastCharWasSpace) {
                temp.append(c);
            }
            lastCharWasSpace = true;
        } else {
            temp.append(c);
            lastCharWasSpace = false;
        }
    }
    return temp.toString();
}

private String[] autoCorrect(String[] values) {
    if (values != null) {
        int length = values.length;
        for (int i = 0; i < length; i++) {
            values[i] = autoCorrect(values[i]);
        }
        return values;
    }
    return null;
}
```

```
    private Collection<String[]> autoCorrect(
            Collection<String[]> valueCollection) {
        Collection<String[]> newCollection =
                new ArrayList<String[]>();
        for (String[] values : valueCollection) {
            newCollection.add(autoCorrect(values));
        }
        return newCollection;
    }

    private Set<Map.Entry<String, String[]>> autoCorrect(
            Set<Map.Entry<String, String[]>> entrySet) {
        Set<Map.Entry<String, String[]>> newSet = new
                HashSet<Map.Entry<String, String[]>>();
        for (final Map.Entry<String, String[]> entry
                : entrySet) {
            Map.Entry<String, String[]> newEntry = new
                    Map.Entry<String, String[]>() {
                @Override
                public String getKey() {
                    return entry.getKey();
                }

                @Override
                public String[] getValue() {
                    return autoCorrect(entry.getValue());
                }

                @Override
                public String[] setValue(String[] value) {
                    return entry.setValue(value);
                }
            };
            newSet.add(newEntry);
        }
        return newSet;
    }
}
```

The filter's **doFilter** method is very simple. It creates a decorator for the **ServletRequest** and pass the decorator to the **doFilter** method:

```
        HttpServletRequest httpServletRequest =
                (HttpServletRequest) request;
        AutoCorrectHttpServletRequestWrapper wrapper = new
```

```
        AutoCorrectHttpServletRequestWrapper(
                httpServletRequest);
    filterChain.doFilter(wrapper, response);
```

Any servlet invoked after the filter will get an **HttpServletRequest**
wrapped in an **AutoCorrectHttpServletRequestWrapper**. The wrapper
class is long but easy to understand. Basically, it passes all calls to obtain a
parameter value to this **autoCorrect** method.

```
private String autoCorrect(String value) {
    if (value == null) {
        return null;
    }
    value = value.trim();
    int length = value.length();
    StringBuilder temp = new StringBuilder();
    boolean lastCharWasSpace = false;
    for (int i = 0; i < length; i++) {
        char c = value.charAt(i);
        if (c == ' ') {
            if (!lastCharWasSpace) {
                temp.append(c);
            }
            lastCharWasSpace = true;
        } else {
            temp.append(c);
            lastCharWasSpace = false;
        }
    }
    return temp.toString();
}
```

You can test the filter using the **test1.jsp** and **test2.jsp** pages shown in
Listing 13.2 and Listing 13.3, respectively.

Listing 13.2: The test1.jsp page

```
<!DOCTYPE HTML>
<html>
<head>
<title>User Form</title>
</head>
<body>
<form action="test2.jsp" method="post">
    <table>
    <tr>
```

```
        <td>Name:</td>
        <td><input name="name"/></td>
    </tr>
    <tr>
        <td>Address:</td>
        <td><input name="address"/></td>
    </tr>
    <tr>
        <td colspan="2">
            <input type="submit" value="Login"/>
        </td>
    </tr>
    </table>
</form>
</body>
</html>
```

Listing 13.3: The test2.jsp page

```
<%@ taglib uri="http://java.sun.com/jsp/jstl/functions"
        prefix="fn"%>
<!DOCTYPE HTML>
<html>
<head>
<title>Form Values</title>
</head>
<body>
<table>
    <tr>
        <td>Name:</td>
        <td>
            ${param.name}
            (length:${fn:length(param.name)})
        </td>
    </tr>
    <tr>
        <td>Address:</td>
        <td>
            ${param.address}
            (length:${fn:length(param.address)})
        </td>
    </tr>
</table>
</body>
</html>
```

Call the **test1.jsp** page using this URL:

`http://localhost:8080/app13a/test1.jsp`

Enter a value with trailing or leading spaces or even extra spaces between words and click Submit. In the screen that follows you should see that the entered values have been auto-corrected.

Summary

The Servlet API comes with four wrapper classes (**ServletRequestWrapper**, **ServletResponseWrapper**, **HttpServletRequestWrapper**, and **HttpServletResponseWrapper**) that you can extend to decorate the servlet request and servlet response. A filter or a listener can then be used to create a wrapper and pass it to the servlet's **service** method, as shown in the **AutoCorrectFilter** example in this chapter.

Chapter 14
Asynchronous Processing

Servlet 3 introduces a new feature that enables servlets to process requests asynchronously. This chapter explains this new feature and presents examples on how to make use of it.

Overview

A computer has limited memory. The servlet/JSP container designer knew this and provided some configurable settings to make sure the container could run within the hosting computer's means. For instance, in Tomcat 7 the maximum number of threads for processing incoming requests is 200. If you have a multiprocessor server, then you can safely increase this number, but other than that it's recommended to use this default value.

A servlet or filter holds a request processing thread until it completes its task. If the task takes a long time to complete and the number of concurrent users exceeds the number of threads, the container may run the risk of running out of threads. If this happens, Tomcat will stack up the excess requests in an internal server socket (other containers may behave differently). If more requests are still coming, they will be refused until there are resources to handle them.

The asynchronous processing feature allows you to be frugal with container threads. You should use this feature for long-running operations. What this feature does is release the request processing thread while waiting for a task to complete so that the thread can be used by another request. Note that the asynchronous support is only suitable if you have a long running task AND you want to notify the user of the outcome of the task. If you only have a long running task but the user does not need to know the processing result, then you can just submit a **Runnable** to an **Executor** and return right away. For example, if you need to generate a report (which takes a while) and send the report by email when it's ready, then the servlet asynchronous processing feature is not the optimum solution. By contrast, if you need to generate a report and show it to the user when the report is ready, then asynchronous processing may be for you.

Writing Async Servlets and Filters

The **WebServlet** and **WebFilter** annotation types may contain the new **asyncSupport** attribute. To write a servlet or filter that supports asynchronous processing, set the **asyncSupported** attribute to true:

```
@WebServlet(asyncSupported=true ...)

@WebFilter(asyncSupported=true ...)
```

Alternatively, you can specify this in the deployment descriptor using the **async-supported** element within a **servlet** or **filter** element. For example, the following servlet is configured to support asynchronous processing.

```
<servlet>
    <servlet-name>AsyncServlet</servlet-name>
    <servlet-class>servlet.MyAsyncServlet</servlet-class>
    <async-supported>true</async-supported>
</servlet>
```

A servlet or filter that supports asynchronous processing can start a new thread by calling the **startAsync** method on the **ServletRequest**. There are two overloads of **startAsync**:

```
AsyncContext startAsync() throws java.lang.IllegalStateException

AsyncContext startAsync(ServletRequest servletRequest,
        ServletResponse servletResponse) throws
        java.lang.IllegalStateException
```

Both overloads return an instance of **AsyncContext**, which offer various methods and contains a **ServletRequest** and a **ServletResponse**. The first overload is straightforward and easy to use. The resulting **AsyncContext** will contain the original **ServletRequest** and **ServletResponse**. The second one allows you to wrap the original **ServletRequest** and **ServletResponse** and pass them to the **AsyncContext**. Note that you can only pass the original **ServletRequest** and **ServletResponse** or their wrappers to the second **startAsync** overload. Chapter 13, "Decorating Requests and Responses" discusses **ServletRequest** and **ServletResponse** wrapping.

Note that repeated invocation of **startAsync** will return the same **AsyncContext**. Calling **startAsync** in a servlet or filter that does not support asynchronous processing will throw a **java.lang.IllegalStateException**. Also note that the **start** method of **AsyncContext** does not block, so the next line of code will be executed even before the thread it dispatched starts.

Writing Async Servlets

Writing an asynchronous or async servlet or filter is relatively simple. You predominantly create an async servlet or filter if you have a task that takes a relatively long time to complete. Here is what you have to do in your asynchronous servlet or filter class.

1. Call the **startAsync** method on the **ServletRequest**. The **startAsync** returns an **AsyncContext**.
2. Call **setTimeout()** on the **AsyncContext**, passing the number of milliseconds the container has to wait for the specified task to complete. This step is optional, but if you don't set a timeout, the container's default will be used. An exception will be thrown if the task fails to complete within the specified timeout time.
3. Call **asyncContext.start**, passing a **Runnable** that executes a long-running task.
4. Call **asyncContext.complete** or **asyncContext.dispatch** from the **Runnable** at the completion of the task.

Here is the skeleton of an asynchronous servlet's **doGet** or **doPost** method.

```
final AsyncContext asyncContext = servletRequest.startAsync();
asyncContext.setTimeout( ... );
asyncContext.start(new Runnable() {
    @Override
    public void run() {

        // long running task
```

```
        asyncContext.complete() or asyncContext.dispatch()
    }
})
```

As an example, Listing 14.1 shows a servlet that supports asynchronous processing.

Listing 14.1: A simple asynchronous servlet with dispatch

```java
package servlet;
import java.io.IOException;
import javax.servlet.AsyncContext;
import javax.servlet.ServletException;
import javax.servlet.annotation.WebServlet;
import javax.servlet.http.HttpServlet;
import javax.servlet.http.HttpServletRequest;
import javax.servlet.http.HttpServletResponse;

@WebServlet(name = "AsyncDispatchServlet",
        urlPatterns = { "/asyncDispatch" },
        asyncSupported = true)
public class AsyncDispatchServlet extends HttpServlet {
    private static final long serialVersionUID = 222L;

    @Override
    public void doGet(final HttpServletRequest request,
            HttpServletResponse response)
            throws ServletException, IOException {
        final AsyncContext asyncContext = request.startAsync();
        request.setAttribute("mainThread",
                    Thread.currentThread().getName());
        asyncContext.setTimeout(5000);
        asyncContext.start(new Runnable() {
            @Override
            public void run() {
              // long-running task
                try {
                    Thread.sleep(3000);
                } catch (InterruptedException e) {
                }
                request.setAttribute("workerThread",
                        Thread.currentThread().getName());
                asyncContext.dispatch("/threadNames.jsp");
            }
        });
```

```
      }
  }
```

The servlet in Listing 14.1 supports asynchronous processing and its long-running task is simply to sleep for three seconds. To prove that the long-running task is executed in a different thread than the main thread (that executes the servlet's **doGet** method), it attaches the name of the main thread and that of the worker thread to the **ServletRequest** and dispatches to a **test.jsp** page. The **test.jsp** page (presented in Listing 14.2) displays the **mainThread** and **workerThread** variables. They should print different thread names.

Listing 14.2: The threadNames.jsp page

```
<!DOCTYPE HTML>
<html>
<head>
<title>Asynchronous servlet</title>
</head>
<body>
Main thread: ${mainThread}
<br/>
Worker thread: ${workerThread}
</body>
</html>
```

Note that you need to call the **dispatch** or **complete** method on the **AsyncContext** after the task ends so that it will not wait until it times out.

You can test the servlet by directing your browser to this URL:

```
http://localhost:8080/app14a/asyncDispatch
```

Figure 14.1 shows the name of the main thread and the name of the worker thread. What you see in your browser may be different, but the names will be different, proving that the worker thread is different from the main thread.

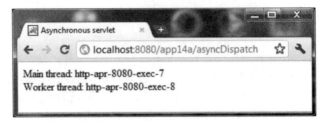

Figure 14.1: The AsyncDispatchServlet

Instead of dispatching to another resource at the completion of a task, you can also call the **complete** method on the **AsyncContext**. This method indicates to the servlet container that the task has completed.

As a second example, consider the servlet in Listing 14.3. The servlet sends a progress update every second so that the user can monitor progress. It sends HTML response and a simple JavaScript code to update an HTML **div** element.

Listing 14.3: An asynchronous servlet that sends progress updates

```
package servlet;
import java.io.IOException;
import java.io.PrintWriter;
import javax.servlet.AsyncContext;
import javax.servlet.ServletException;
import javax.servlet.annotation.WebServlet;
import javax.servlet.http.HttpServlet;
import javax.servlet.http.HttpServletRequest;
import javax.servlet.http.HttpServletResponse;

public class AsyncCompleteServlet extends HttpServlet {
    private static final long serialVersionUID = 78234L;

    @Override
    public void doGet(HttpServletRequest request,
            HttpServletResponse response)
            throws ServletException, IOException {
        response.setContentType("text/html");
        final PrintWriter writer = response.getWriter();
        writer.println("<html><head><title>" +
                "Async Servlet</title></head>");
        writer.println("<body><div id='progress'></div>");
        final AsyncContext asyncContext = request.startAsync();
        asyncContext.setTimeout(60000);
```

```
        asyncContext.start(new Runnable() {
            @Override
            public void run() {
                System.out.println("new thread:" +
                        Thread.currentThread());
                for (int i = 0; i < 10; i++) {
                    writer.println("<script>");
                    writer.println("document.getElementById(" +
                            "'progress').innerHTML = '" +
                            (i * 10) + "% complete'");
                    writer.println("</script>");
                    writer.flush();
                    try {
                        Thread.sleep(1000);
                    } catch (InterruptedException e) {
                    }
                }
                writer.println("<script>");
                writer.println("document.getElementById(" +
                        "'progress').innerHTML = 'DONE'");
                writer.println("</script>");
                writer.println("</body></html>");
                asyncContext.complete();
            }
        });
    }
}
```

This code fragment is responsible for sending progress updates:

```
                writer.println("<script>");
                writer.println("document.getElementById(" +
                        "'progress').innerHTML = '" +
                        (i * 10) + "% complete'");
                writer.println("</script>");
```

The browser will receive this string, where **x** is a number between 10 and 100.

```
<script>
document.getElementById('progress').innerHTML = 'x% complete'
</script>
```

To show how you can make a servlet asynchronous by declaring it in the deployment descriptor, the **AsyncCompleteServlet** class in Listing 14.3 is not annotated with **@WebServlet**. The deployment descriptor (**web.xml** file) is given in Listing 14.4.

Listing 14.4: The deployment descriptor

```xml
<?xml version="1.0" encoding="ISO-8859-1"?>
<web-app xmlns="http://java.sun.com/xml/ns/javaee"
    xmlns:xsi="http://www.w3.org/2001/XMLSchema-instance"
    xsi:schemaLocation="http://java.sun.com/xml/ns/javaee
  http://java.sun.com/xml/ns/javaee/web-app_3_0.xsd"
    version="3.0"
>
    <servlet>
        <servlet-name>AsyncComplete</servlet-name>
        <servlet-class>servlet.AsyncCompleteServlet</servlet-class>
        <async-supported>true</async-supported>
    </servlet>

    <servlet-mapping>
        <servlet-name>AsyncComplete</servlet-name>
        <url-pattern>/asyncComplete</url-pattern>
    </servlet-mapping>
</web-app>
```

You can test the **AsyncCompleteServlet** example by directing your browser to the following URL:

```
http://localhost:8080/app14a/asyncComplete
```

Figure 14.2 shows the result.

Figure 14.2: HTML page that receives progress updates

Async Listeners

In conjunction with support for servlets and filters that perform asynchronous operations, Servlet 3.0 also adds the **AsyncListener** interface so that you can be notified of what's happening during asynchronous processing. The **AsyncListener** interface defines the following methods that get called when certain event occurs.

`void onStartAsync(AsyncEvent event)`

This method gets called when an asynchronous operation has been initiated.

`void onComplete(AsyncEvent event)`

This method gets called when an asynchronous operation has completed.

`void onError(AsyncEvent event)`

This method gets called in the event an asynchronous operation has failed.

`void onTimeout(AsyncEvent event)`

This method gets called when an asynchronous has timed out, namely when it failed to finish within the specified timeout.

All the four methods receive an **AsyncEvent** from which you can retrieve the related **AsyncContext**, **ServletRequest**, and **ServletResponse** through its **getAsyncContext**, **getSuppliedRequest**, and **getSuppliedResponse**, respectively.

As an example, the **MyAsyncListener** class in Listing 14.5 implements the **AsyncListener** interface so that it can get notified when events in an asynchronous operation occur. Note that unlike other web listeners, you do not annotate an implementation of **AsyncListener** with **@WebListener**.

Listing 14.5: An asynchronous listener

```
package listener;
import java.io.IOException;
import javax.servlet.AsyncEvent;
import javax.servlet.AsyncListener;

// do not annotate with @WebListener
```

```
public class MyAsyncListener implements AsyncListener {

    @Override
    public void onComplete(AsyncEvent asyncEvent)
            throws IOException {
        System.out.println("onComplete");
    }

    @Override
    public void onError(AsyncEvent asyncEvent)
            throws IOException {
        System.out.println("onError");
    }

    @Override
    public void onStartAsync(AsyncEvent asyncEvent)
            throws IOException {
        System.out.println("onStartAsync");
    }

    @Override
    public void onTimeout(AsyncEvent asyncEvent)
            throws IOException {
        System.out.println("onTimeout");
    }
}
```

Since an **AsyncListener** class is not annotated with **@WebListener**, you have to register an **AsyncListener** manually to any **AsyncContext** that you are interested in getting event notifications from. You register an **AsyncListener** on an **AsyncContext** by calling the **addListener** method on the latter:

```
void addListener(AsyncListener listener)
```

The **AsyncListenerServlet** class in Listing 14.6 is an **async** servlet that utilizes the listener in Listing 14.5 to get event notifications.

Listing 14.6: Using AsyncListener

```
package servlet;
import java.io.IOException;
import javax.servlet.AsyncContext;
import javax.servlet.ServletException;
import javax.servlet.annotation.WebServlet;
import javax.servlet.http.HttpServlet;
```

```
import javax.servlet.http.HttpServletRequest;
import javax.servlet.http.HttpServletResponse;

import listener.MyAsyncListener;

@WebServlet(name = "AsyncListenerServlet",
        urlPatterns = { "/asyncListener" },
        asyncSupported = true)
public class AsyncListenerServlet extends HttpServlet {
    private static final long serialVersionUID = 62738L;

    @Override
    public void doGet(final HttpServletRequest request,
            HttpServletResponse response)
            throws ServletException, IOException {
        final AsyncContext asyncContext = request.startAsync();
        asyncContext.setTimeout(5000);

        asyncContext.addListener(new MyAsyncListener());
        asyncContext.start(new Runnable() {
            @Override
            public void run() {
                try {
                    Thread.sleep(3000);
                } catch (InterruptedException e) {
                }
                String greeting = "hi from listener";
                System.out.println("wait....");
                request.setAttribute("greeting", greeting);
                asyncContext.dispatch("/test.jsp");
            }
        });
    }
}
```

You can invoke the servlet by targeting this URL:

```
http://localhost:8080/app14a/asyncListener
```

Summary

Servlet 3.0 comes with a new feature for processing asynchronous operations. This is especially useful when your servlet/JSP application is a very busy one with one or more long-running operations. This feature works by assigning those operations to a new thread and thereby releasing the request processing thread back to the pool, ready to serve another request. In this chapter you learned how to write servlets that support asynchronous processing as well as listeners that get notified when certain events occur during the processing.

Chapter 15
Security

Security is a very important aspect in web application development and deployment. This is especially true because web applications are accessible to anyone with a browser and access to the world wide web. Securing an application can be done declaratively or programmatically. The following four issues are the cornerstones of web security: authentication, authorization, confidentiality, and data integrity.

Authentication is to do with verifying the identity of a web entity, especially a user trying to access an application. You normally authenticate a user by asking the user for a user name and password.

Authorization is normally done after authentication is successful and is concerned with the access level an authenticated user has. It attempts to answer the question "Should an authenticated user be allowed to enter a certain area of the application?"

Confidentiality is an important topic because sensitive data, such as as credit card details or social security numbers, should be protected. And, as you may know, data is relayed from one computer to another before reaching its destination on the Internet. Intercepting it is not technically difficult. As such, sensitive data should be encrypted when being transferred over the Internet.

Since data packets can be easily intercepted, tampering with them is almost as easy to those equipped with the right tools and knowledge. Fortunately, it is also possible to maintain data integrity by making sure sensitive data travel through a secure channel.

You'll learn about these aspects of security in this chapter. A lengthy discussion is also allocated for SSL, which is used as the protocol for creating secure channels over the Internet.

Authentication and Authorization

Authentication is the process of examining that someone is really who he/she claims to be. In a servlet/JSP application, authentication is normally done by asking the user for a user name and password.

Authorization is concerned with determining what level of access a user has. It applies to applications that consists of multiple zones where a user may have access to one section of an application but not to the others. For example, an online store may be divided into the general sections (for the general public to browse and search for products), the buyers section (for registered users to place orders), and the admin section (for administrators). Of the three, the admin section requires the highest level of access. Not only would admin users be required to authenticate themselves, they would also need to have been assigned access to the admin section.

Access levels are often called roles. At deployment a servlet/JSP application can be conveniently split into sections and configured so that each section can be accessed by users in a particular role. This is done by declaring security constraints in the deployment descriptor. In other words, declarative security. At the other end of spectrum, content restriction is also commonly achieved programmatically by trying to match pairs of user names and passwords with values stored in a database.

In the majority of servlet/JSP applications authentication and authorization are done programmatically by first authenticating the user name and password against a database table. Once authentication is successful, authorization can be done by checking another table or a field in the same table that stores user names and passwords. Using declarative security saves you some programming because the servlet/JSP container takes care of the authentication and authorization processes. In addition, the servlet/JSP container can be configured to authenticate against a database you're already using in the application. On top of that, with declarative authentication the user name and password can be encrypted by the browser prior to sending them to the server. The drawback of declarative security is that the authentication method that supports data encryption can only be used with a default login dialog whose look and feel cannot be customized. This reason alone is enough to make people walk away from declarative security. The only method of declarative security that allows a custom HTML form to be used unfortunately does not encrypt the data transmitted.

Some parts of a web application, such as the Admin module, are not customer facing, so the look of the login form is of little relevance. In this case, declarative security can still be used.

The interesting part of declarative security is of course the fact that security constraints are not programmed into servlets. Instead, they are declared in the deployment descriptor at the time the application is deployed. As such, it allows considerable flexibility in determining the users and roles that will have access to the application or sections of it.

To use declarative security, you start by defining users and roles. Depending on the container you're using, you can store user and role information in a file or database tables. Then, you impose constraints on a resource or a collection or resources in your application.

Now, how do you authenticate a user without programming? As you will find out later the answer lies in the HTTP and not in the Servlet specification.

Specifying Users and Roles

Every compliant servlet/JSP container must provide a way of defining users and roles. If you're using Tomcat you can create users and roles by editing the **tomcat-users.xml** file in the **conf** directory. An example **tomcat-users.xml** file is given in Listing 15.1.

Listing 15.1: The tomcat-users.xml file

```
<?xml version='1.0' encoding='utf-8'?>
<tomcat-users>
    <role rolename="manager"/>
    <role rolename="member"/>
    <user username="tom" password="secret" roles="manager,member"/>
    <user username="jerry" password="secret" roles="member"/>
</tomcat-users>
```

The **tomcat-users.xml** file is an XML document having the **tomcat-users** root element. Within it are **role** and **user** elements. The **role** element defines a role and the **user** element defines a user. The **role** element has a **rolename** attribute that specifies the name of the role. The **user** element has **username**, **password**, and **roles** attributes. The **username** attribute specifies the user name, the **password** attribute the password, and the **roles** attribute the role or roles the user belongs to.

The **tomcat-users.xml** file in Listing 15.1 declares two roles (**manager** and **member**) and two users (**tom** and **jerry**). User **tom** is a member of both the **member** and **manager** roles whereas **jerry** only belongs to the **member** role. It is obvious that tom has more access to the application than jerry.

Tomcat also supports matching roles and users against database tables. You can configure Tomcat to use JDBC to authenticate users.

Imposing Security Constraints

You have learned that you can hide static resources and JSP pages by storing them under **WEB-INF** or a directory under it. A resource placed here cannot be accessed directly by typing its URL, but can still be a forward target from a servlet or JSP page. While this approach is simple and straightforward, the drawback is resources hidden here are hidden forever. There's no way they can be accessed directly. If you simply want to protect resources from unauthorized users, you can put them in a directory under the application directory and declare a security constraint in the deployment descriptor.

The **security-constraint** element specifies a resource collection and the role or roles that can access the resources. This element can have two subelements, **web-resource-collection** and **auth-constraint**.

The **web-resource-collection** element specifies a collection of resources and can have any of these subelements: **web-resource-name**, **description**, **url-pattern**, **http-method**, and **http-method-ommission**.

The **web-resource-collection** element can have multiple **url-pattern** subelements, each of which refers to a URL pattern to which the containing security constraint applies. You can use an asterisk in the **url-pattern** element to refer to either a specific resource type (such as ***.jsp**) or all resources in a directory (such as **/*** or **/jsp/***). However, you cannot combine both, i.e. refer to a specific type in a specific directory. Therefore, the following URL pattern meant to refer to all JSP pages in the **jsp** directory is invalid: **/jsp/*.jsp**. Instead, use **/jsp/***, but this will also restrict any non-JSP pages in the jsp directory.

The **http-method** element names an HTTP method to which the enclosing security constraint applies. For example, a **web-resource-collection** element with a GET **http-method** element indicates that the **web-resource-collection** element applies only to the HTTP Get method. The security constraint that contains the resource collection does not protect against other HTTP methods such as Post and Put. The absence of the **http-method** element indicates the security constraint restricts access against all HTTP methods. You can have multiple **http-method** elements in the same **web-resource-collection** element.

The **http-method-omission** element specifies an HTTP method that is not included in the encompassing security constraint. Therefore, specifying **<http-method-omission>GET</http-method-omission>** restricts access to all HTTP methods except Get.

The **http-method** element and the **http-method-omission** element cannot appear in the same **web-resource-collection** element.

You can have multiple **security-constraint** elements in the deployment descriptor. If the **auth-constraint** element is missing from a security-constraint element, the resource collection is not protected. In addition, if you specify a role that is not defined by the container, no one will be able to access the resource collection directly. However, you can still forward to a resource in the collection from a servlet or JSP page.

As an example, the **security-constraint** elements in the **web.xml** file in Listing 15.2 restricts access to all JSP pages. As the **auth-constraint** element does not contain a **role-name** element, the resources are not accessible by their URLs.

Listing 15.2: Preventing access to resources in certain directories

```
<?xml version="1.0" encoding="ISO-8859-1"?>
<web-app xmlns="http://java.sun.com/xml/ns/javaee"
    xmlns:xsi="http://www.w3.org/2001/XMLSchema-instance"
    xsi:schemaLocation="http://java.sun.com/xml/ns/javaee
➥http://java.sun.com/xml/ns/javaee/web-app_3_0.xsd"
    version="3.0"
```

```
>
    <!-- restricts access to JSP pages -->
    <security-constraint>
        <web-resource-collection>
            <web-resource-name>JSP pages</web-resource-name>
            <url-pattern>*.jsp</url-pattern>
        </web-resource-collection>
        <!-- must have auth-constraint, otherwise the
            specified web resources will not be restricted -->
        <auth-constraint/>
    </security-constraint>
</web-app>
```

Now test it by directing your browser to this URL:

`http://localhost:8080/app15a/jsp/1.jsp`

The servlet container will gently tell you off by sending an HTTP 403 error: **Access to the requested resource has been denied**.

Now let's see how you can authenticate and authorize the user.

Authentication Methods

Now that you know how to impose security constraints on a resource collection, you should also learn how to authenticate users to access the resources. For resources that are secured declaratively, by using the **security-constraint** element in the deployment descriptor, authentication can be done by using the solutions that HTTP 1.1 offers: basic access authentication and digest access authentication. In addition, form-based access authentication can also be used.

HTTP authentication is defined in RFC 2617. You can download the specification here:

`http://www.ietf.org/rfc/rfc2617.txt`

Basic Access Authentication

Basic access authentication, or simply Basic authentication, is an HTTP authentication for accepting a user name and password. In Basic access authentication a user who accesses a protected resource will be rejected by the server, which will return a 401 (Unauthorized) response. The response includes a **WWW-Authenticate** header containing at least one challenge applicable to the requested resource. Here is an example of such response:

```
HTTP/1.1 401 Authorization Required
Server: Apache-Coyote/1.1
Date: Wed, 21 Dec 2011 11:32:09 GMT
WWW-Authenticate: Basic realm="Members Only"
```

The browser would then display a Login dialog for the user to enter a user name and a password. When the user clicks the Login button, the user name will be appended with a colon and concatenated with the password. The string will then be encoded with the Base64 algorithm before being sent to the server. Upon a successful login, the server will send the requested resource.

Base64 is a very weak algorithm and as such it is very easy to decrypt Base64 messages. Consider using Digest access authentication instead.

The **app15b** application shows how to use the Basic access authentication. Listing 15.3 presents the deployment descriptor of the application. The first **security-constraint** element protects the JSP pages from direct access. The second one restricts access to the **Servlet1** servlet to those in **manager** and **member** roles. The **Servlet1** class is a simple servlet that forwards to **1.jsp** and is presented in Listing 15.4.

Listing 15.3: The deployment descriptor of app15b

```
<?xml version="1.0" encoding="ISO-8859-1"?>
<web-app xmlns="http://java.sun.com/xml/ns/javaee"
    xmlns:xsi="http://www.w3.org/2001/XMLSchema-instance"
    xsi:schemaLocation="http://java.sun.com/xml/ns/javaee
➥http://java.sun.com/xml/ns/javaee/web-app_3_0.xsd"
    version="3.0"
>
    <!-- restricts access to JSP pages -->
    <security-constraint>
        <web-resource-collection>
            <web-resource-name>JSP pages</web-resource-name>
            <url-pattern>*.jsp</url-pattern>
        </web-resource-collection>
        <!-- must have auth-constraint, otherwise the
```

```
                specified web resources will not be restricted -->
        <auth-constraint/>
    </security-constraint>

    <security-constraint>
        <web-resource-collection>
            <web-resource-name>Servlet1</web-resource-name>
            <url-pattern>/servlet1</url-pattern>
        </web-resource-collection>
        <auth-constraint>
            <role-name>member</role-name>
            <role-name>manager</role-name>
        </auth-constraint>
    </security-constraint>

    <login-config>
        <auth-method>BASIC</auth-method>
        <realm-name>Members Only</realm-name>
    </login-config>
</web-app>
```

The most important element in the deployment descriptor in Listing 15.3 is the **login-config** element. It has two subelements, **auth-method** and **realm-name**. To use the Basic access authentication, you must give it the value **BASIC** (all capitals). The **realm-name** element should be given a name to be displayed in the browser Login dialog.

Listing 15.4: The Servlet1 class

```
package servlet;
import java.io.IOException;
import javax.servlet.RequestDispatcher;
import javax.servlet.ServletException;
import javax.servlet.annotation.WebServlet;
import javax.servlet.http.HttpServlet;
import javax.servlet.http.HttpServletRequest;
import javax.servlet.http.HttpServletResponse;

@WebServlet(urlPatterns = { "/servlet1" })
public class Servlet1 extends HttpServlet {

    private static final long serialVersionUID = -15560L;

    public void doGet(HttpServletRequest request,
            HttpServletResponse response) throws ServletException,
            IOException {
```

```
        RequestDispatcher dispatcher =
                request.getRequestDispatcher("/jsp/1.jsp");
        dispatcher.forward(request,  response);
    }
}
```

To test the Basic access authentication in **app15b**, try accessing the restricted resource in it using this URL.

```
http://localhost:8080/app15b/servlet1
```

Instead of seeing the output of **Servlet1**, you'll be prompted for a username and password like the screen shot in Figure 15.1.

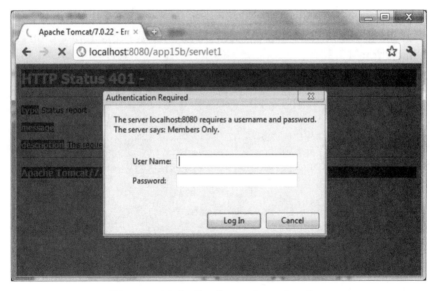

Figure 15.1: Basic authentication

Since the **auth-constraint** element mapped to **Servlet1** specifies both **manager** and **member** roles, you can use either tom or jerry to login.

Digest Access Authentication

Digest access authentication, or Digest authentication for short, is also an HTTP authentication and is similar to Basic access authentication. Instead of using the weak Base64 encryption algorithm, Digest access authentication uses the MD5 algorithm to create a hash of the combination of the user name, realm name, and the password and sends the hash to the server. Digest access authentication is meant to replace Basic access authentication as it offer a more secure environment.

Servlet/JSP containers are not obligated to support Digest access authentication but most do.

Configuring an application to use Digest access authentication is similar to using Basic access authentication. In fact, the only difference is the value of the **auth-method** element within the **login-config** element. For Digest access authentication, its value must be **DIGEST** (all uppercase).

As an example, the **app15c** application demonstrates the use of Digest access authentication. The deployment descriptor for this application is given in Listing 15.5.

Listing 15.5: The deployment descriptor for Digest authentication

```
<?xml version="1.0" encoding="ISO-8859-1"?>
<web-app xmlns="http://java.sun.com/xml/ns/javaee"
    xmlns:xsi="http://www.w3.org/2001/XMLSchema-instance"
    xsi:schemaLocation="http://java.sun.com/xml/ns/javaee
➥http://java.sun.com/xml/ns/javaee/web-app_3_0.xsd"
    version="3.0"
>
    <!-- restricts access to JSP pages -->
    <security-constraint>
        <web-resource-collection>
            <web-resource-name>JSP pages</web-resource-name>
            <url-pattern>*.jsp</url-pattern>
        </web-resource-collection>
        <!-- must have auth-constraint, otherwise the
            specified web resources will not be restricted -->
        <auth-constraint/>
    </security-constraint>

    <security-constraint>
        <web-resource-collection>
            <web-resource-name>Servlet1</web-resource-name>
            <url-pattern>/servlet1</url-pattern>
        </web-resource-collection>
        <auth-constraint>
            <role-name>member</role-name>
```

```
            <role-name>manager</role-name>
        </auth-constraint>
    </security-constraint>

    <login-config>
        <auth-method>DIGEST</auth-method>
        <realm-name>Digest authentication</realm-name>
    </login-config>
</web-app>
```

To test the application, direct your browser to this URL:

```
http://localhost:8080/app15c/servlet1
```

Figure 15.2 shows the Login dialog for Digest access authentication.

Figure 15.2: Digest authentication

Form-based Authentication

Basic and Digest access authentications do not allow you to use a customized login form. If you must have a custom form, then you can use form-based authentication. As the values transmitted are not encrypted, you should use this in conjunction with SSL.

With form-based authentication, you need to create a Login page and an Error page, which can be HTML or JSP pages. The first time a protected resource is requested, the servlet/JSP container will send the Login page. Upon a successful login, the requested resource will be sent. If login failed, however, the user will see the Error page.

To use form-based authentication, the **auth-method** element in your deployment descriptor must be given the value **FORM** (all upper case). In addition, the **login-config** element must have a **form-login-config** element with two subelements, **form-login-page** and **form-error-page**. Here is an example of the **login-config** element for form-based authentication.

```
<login-config>
    <auth-method>FORM</auth-method>
    <form-login-config>
        <form-login-page>/login.html</form-login-page>
        <form-error-page>/error.html</form-error-page>
    </form-login-config>
</login-config>
```

Listing 15.6 shows the deployment descriptor of **app15d**, an example that utilizes form-based authentication.

Listing 15.6: The deployment descriptor for form-based authentication

```
<?xml version="1.0" encoding="ISO-8859-1"?>
<web-app xmlns="http://java.sun.com/xml/ns/javaee"
    xmlns:xsi="http://www.w3.org/2001/XMLSchema-instance"
    xsi:schemaLocation="http://java.sun.com/xml/ns/javaee
➥http://java.sun.com/xml/ns/javaee/web-app_3_0.xsd"
    version="3.0"
>
    <!-- restricts access to JSP pages -->
    <security-constraint>
        <web-resource-collection>
            <web-resource-name>JSP pages</web-resource-name>
            <url-pattern>*.jsp</url-pattern>
        </web-resource-collection>
        <!-- must have auth-constraint, otherwise the
             specified web resources will not be restricted -->
        <auth-constraint/>
    </security-constraint>

    <security-constraint>
        <web-resource-collection>
```

```
                <web-resource-name>Servlet1</web-resource-name>
                <url-pattern>/servlet1</url-pattern>
        </web-resource-collection>
        <auth-constraint>
                <role-name>member</role-name>
                <role-name>manager</role-name>
        </auth-constraint>
    </security-constraint>

    <login-config>
        <auth-method>FORM</auth-method>
        <form-login-config>
                <form-login-page>/login.html</form-login-page>
                <form-error-page>/error.html</form-error-page>
        </form-login-config>
    </login-config>
</web-app>
```

The **form-login-page** element refers to the **login.html** page in Listing 15.7 and the **form-error-page** element references the **error.html** page in Listing 15.8.

Listing 15.7: The login.html page

```
<!DOCTYPE HTML>
<html>
<head>
    <title>Login</title>
</head>
<body>
<h1>Login Form</h1>
<form action='j_security_check' method='post'>
<div>
    User Name: <input name='j_username'/>
</div>
<div>
    Password: <input type='password' name='j_password'/>
</div>
<div>
    <input type='submit' value='Login'/>
</div>
</form>
</body>
</html>
```

Listing 15.8: The error.html page

```
<!DOCTYPE HTML>
<html>
<head>
<title>Login error</title>
</head>
<body>
Login failed.
</body>
</html>
```

To test the form-based authentication in **app15d**, direct your browser to this URL.

```
http://localhost:8080/app15d/servlet1
```

Figure 15.3 shows the **login.html** for the user to login.

Figure 15.3: Form-based authentication

Client Certificate Authentication

Also called the client-cert authentication, the client certificate authentication works over HTTPS (HTTP over SSL) and requires that every client have a client certificate. This is a very strong authentication mechanism but is not suitable for applications deployed over the Internet as it is impractical to demand that every user own a digital certificate. However, this authentication method can be used to access intranet applications within an organization.

Secure Sockets Layer (SSL)

Originally developed by Netscape, the SSL protocol enables secure communications over the Internet and at the same time ensures the confidentiality and data integrity.

To fully understand how SSL works, there are a number of technologies that you need to learn, from cryptography to private and public key pairs to certificates. This section discusses SSL and its components in detail.

Cryptography

From time to time there has always been a need for secure communication channels, i.e. where messages are safe and other parties cannot understand and tamper with the messages even if they can get access to them.

Historically, cryptography was only concerned with encryption and decryption, where two parties exchanging messages can be rest assured that only they can read the messages. In the beginning, people encrypted and decrypted messages using symmetric cryptography. In symmetric cryptography, you use the same key to encrypt and decrypt messages. Here is a very simple encryption/decryption technique.

Suppose, the encryption method uses a secret number to shift forward each character in the alphabet. Therefore, if the secret number is 2, the encrypted version of "ThisFriday" is "VjkuHtkfca". When you reach the end of the alphabet, you start from the beginning, therefore y becomes a. The receiver, knowing the key is 2, can easily decrypt the message.

However, symmetric cryptography requires that both parties know in advance the key for encryption/decryption. Symmetric cryptography is not suitable for the Internet for the following reasons

- Two people exchanging messages often do not know each other. For example, when buying a book at Amazon.com you need to send your particulars and credit card details. If symmetric cryptography was to be used, you would have to call Amazon.com prior to the transaction to agree on a key.

- Everyone wants to be able to communicate with many other parties. If symmetric cryptography was used, everyone would have to maintain different unique keys, each for a different party.
- Since you do not know the entity you are going to communicate with, you need to be sure that they are really who they claim to be.
- Messages over the Internet pass through many different computers. It is fairly trivial to tap other people's messages. Symmetric cryptography does not guarantee that a third party may not tamper with the data.

Therefore, today secure communication over the Internet uses asymmetric cryptography that offers these three features:

- encryption/decryption. Messages are encrypted to hide the messages from third parties. Only the intended receiver can decrypt them.
- authentication. Authentication verifies that an entity is who it claims to be.
- data integrity. Messages sent over the Internet pass many computers. It must be ensured that the data sent is unchanged and intact.

In asymmetric cryptography, public key encryption is used. With this type of encryption, data encryption and decryption is achieved through the use of a pair of asymmetric keys: a public key and a private key. A private key is private. The owner must keep it in a secure place and it must not fall into the possession of any other party. A public key is to be distributed to the public, usually downloadable by anyone who would like to communicate with the owner of the keys. You can use tools to generate pairs of public keys and private keys. These tools will be discussed later in this chapter.

The beauty of public key encryption is this: data encrypted using a public key can only be decrypted using the corresponding private key; at the same token data encrypted using a private key can only be decrypted using the corresponding public key. This elegant algorithm is based on very large prime numbers and was invented by Ron **R**ivest, Adi **S**hamir, and Len **A**dleman at Massachusetts Institute of Technology (MIT) in 1977. They simply called the algorithm RSA, based on the initials of their last names.

The RSA algorithm proves to be practical for use on the Internet, especially for e-commerce, because only the vendor is required to have a key pair for secure communications with all its buyers.

An illustration of how public key encryption works normally use two figures called Bob and Alice, so I'll use them too here.

Encryption/Decryption

One of the two parties who want to exchange messages must have a pair of keys. Suppose Alice wants to communicate with Bob and Bob has a public key and a private key. Bob will send Alice his public key and Alice can use it to encrypt messages sent to Bob. Only Bob can decrypt them because he owns the corresponding private key. To send a message to Alice, Bob encrypts it using his private key and Alice can decrypt it using Bob's public key.

However, unless Bob can meet with Alice in person to hand over his public key, this method is far from perfect. Anybody with a pair of keys can claim to be Bob and there is no way Alice can find out. On the Internet, where two parties exchanging messages often live half a globe away, meeting in person is often not possible.

Authentication

In SSL, authentication is addressed by introducing certificates. A certificate contains the following:

- a public key
- information about the subject, i.e. the owner of the public key.
- the certificate issuer's name.
- some timestamp to make the certificate expire after a certain period of time.

The crucial thing about a certificate is that it must be digitally signed by a trusted certificate issuer, such as VeriSign or Thawte. To digitally sign an electronic file (a document, a jar file, etc) is to add your signature to your document/file. The original file is not encrypted, and the real purpose of signing is to guarantee that the document/file has not been tampered with. Signing a document involves creating a digest of the document and encrypting the digest using the signer's private key. To check if the document is still in its still original condition, you perform these two steps.

1. Decrypt the digest accompanying the document using the signer's public key. You will soon learn that the public key of a trusted certificate issuer is widely available.
2. Create a digest of the document.
3. Compare the result of Step 1 and the result of Step 2. If the two match, then the file has not been tampered with.

Such authentication method works because only the holder of the private key can encrypt the document digest, and this digest can only be decrypted using the corresponding public key. Assuming you trust that you hold the original public key, then you know that the file has not been changed.

Note
Because certificates can be digitally signed by a trusted certificate issuer, people make their certificates publicly available, instead of their public keys.

There are a number of certificate issuers, including VeriSign and Thawte. A certificate issuer has a pair of public key and private key. To apply for a certificate, Bob has to generate a pair of keys and send his public key to a certificate issuer, who would later authenticate Bob by asking him to send a copy of his passport or other types of identification. Having verified Bob, a certificate issuer will sign the certificate using its private key. By 'signing' it means encrypting. Therefore, the certificate can only be read by using the certificate issuer's public key. The public key of a certificate issuer is normally distributed widely. For example, Internet Explorer, Netscape, FireFox and other browsers by default include several certificate issuers' public keys.

For example, in IE, click Tools --> Internet Options --> Content --> Certificates --> Trusted Root Certification Authorities tab to see the list of certificates. (See Figure 15.4).

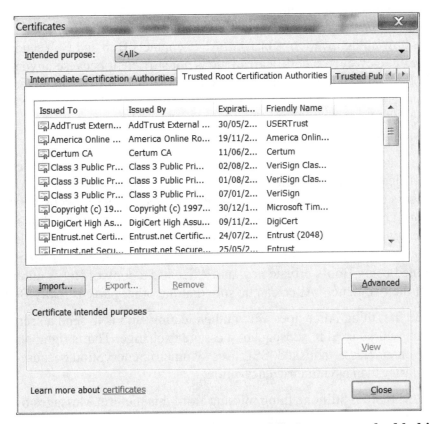

Figure 15.4: Certificate issuers whose public keys are embedded in Internet Explorer

Now, having a certificate, Bob will distribute the certificate instead of his public key before exchanging messages with another party.

Here is how it works.

A->B   Hi Bob, I'd like to speak with you, but first I need to make sure that you're really Bob.

B->A   Fair enough, here is my certificate

A->B   This is not sufficient, I need something else from you

B->A   Alice, it's really me + [message digest encrypted using Bob's private key]

In the last message from Bob to Alice, the message has been signed using Bob's private key, to convince Alice that the message is authentic. This is how authentication is proved. Alice contacts Bob and Bob sends his certificate. However, a certificate alone is not sufficient because anyone can get Bob's certificate. Remember that Bob sends his certificate to anyone who wants to exchange messages with him. Therefore, Bob sends her a message ("Alice, it's really me") and the digest of the same message encrypted using his private key.

Alice gets Bob's public key from the certificate. She can do it because the certificate is signed using the certificate issuer's private key and Alice has access to the certificate issuer's public key (her browser keeps a copy of it). Now, she also gets a message and the digest encrypted using Bob's private key. All Alice needs to do is digest the message and compare it with the decrypted digest Bob sent. Alice can decrypt it because it has been encrypted using Bob's private key, and Alice has a copy of Bob's public key. If the two match, Alice can be sure that the other party is really Bob.

The first thing Alice does after authenticating Bob is to send a secret key that will be used in subsequent message exchange. That's right, once a secure channel is established, SSL uses symmetric encryption because it is much faster than asymmetric encryption.

Now, there is still one thing missing from this picture. Messages over the Internet pass many computers. How do you make sure the integrity of those messages because anyone could intercept those messages on the way?

Data Integrity

Mallet, a malicious party, could be sitting between Alice and Bob, trying to decipher the messages being sent. Unfortunately for him, even though he could copy the messages, they are encrypted and Mallet does not know the key. However, Mallet could still destroy the messages or not relay some of them. To overcome this, SSL introduces a message authentication code (MAC). A MAC is a piece of data that is computed by using a secret key and some transmitted data. Because Mallet does not know the secret key, he cannot compute the right value for the digest. The message receiver can and therefore will discover if there is an attempt to tamper with the data, or if the data is not complete. If this happens, both parties can stop communicating.

One of such message digest algorithm is MD5. It is invented by RSA and is very secure. If 128-bit MAC values are employed, for example, the chance of a malicious party's of guessing the right value is about 1 in 18,446,744,073,709,551,616, or practically never.

How SSL Works

Now you know how SSL addresses the issues of encryption/decryption, authentication, and data integration, let's review how SSL works. This time, let's take Amazon.com as an example (in lieu of Bob) and a buyer (instead of Alice). Amazon.com, like any other bona fide e-commerce vendor has applied for a certificate from a trusted certificate issuer. The buyer is using Internet Explorer, which embeds the public keys of trusted certificate issuers. The buyer does not really need to know about how SSL works and does not need to have a public key or a private key. One thing he needs to ensure is that when entering important details, such as a credit card number, the protocol being used is HTTPS, instead of HTTP. This has to appear on the URL box. Therefore, instead of http://www.amazon.com, it has to start with https. For instance: https://secure.amazon.com. Some browsers also display a secure icon in the Address box. Figure 15.5 shows a secure sign in IE.

Figure 15.5: The secure icon in IE

When the buyer enters a secure page (when he has finished shopping), this is the sequence of events that happens in the background, between his browser and Amazon's server.

browser: Are you really Amazon.com?

server: Yes, here is my certificate.

The browser then checks the validity of the certificate using the certificate issuer's public key to decrypt it. If something is wrong, such as if the certificate has expired, the browser warns the user. If the user agrees to continue despite the certificate being expired, the browser will continue.

browser: A certificate alone is not sufficient, please send something else.

server: I'm really Amazon.com + [the digest of the same message encrypted using Amazon.com's private key].

The browser decrypts the digest using Amazon's public key and create a digest of "I'm Really Amazon.com". If the two match, authentication is successful. The browser will then generate a random key, encrypt it using Amazon's public key. This random key is to encrypt and decrypt subsequent messages. In other words, once Amazon is authenticated, symmetric encryption is used because it is faster then asymmetric cryptography. In addition to messages, both parties also send message digests for making sure that the messages are intact and unchanged.

Appendix C, "SSL Certificates," explains how you can create a digital certificate of your own and provides step-by-step instructions to generate a public/private key pair and have a trusted authority sign the public key as a certificate.

Programmatic Security

Even though declarative security is easy and straightforward, there are rare cases where you want to write code to secure your application. For this purpose, you can use the security annotation types and methods in the **HttpServletRequest** interface. Both are discussed in this section.

Security Annotation Types

In the previous section you learned how to restrict access to a collection of resources using the **security-constraint** element in the deployment descriptor. One aspect of this element is that you use a URL pattern that matches the URLs of the resources to be restricted. Servlet 3 comes with annotation types that can perform the same job on a servlet level. Using these annotation types, you can restrict access to a servlet without adding a **security-constraint** element in the deployment descriptor. However, you still need a **login-config** element in the deployment descriptor to choose an authentication method.

There are three annotation types in the **javax.servlet.annotation** package that are security related. They are **ServletSecurity**, **HttpConstraint**, and **HttpMethodConstraint**.

The **ServletSecurity** annotation type is used in a servlet class to impose security constraints on the servlet. A **ServletSecurity** annotation may have the **value** and **httpMethodConstraints** attributes.

The **HttpConstraint** annotation type defines a security constraint and can only be assigned to the **value** attribute of the **ServletSecurity** annotation. If the **httpMethodConstraints** attribute is not present in the enclosing **ServletSecurity** annotation, the security constraint imposed by the **HttpConstraint** annotation applies to all HTTP methods. Otherwise, the security constraint applies to the HTTP methods defined in the **httpMethodConstraints** attribute. For example, the following **HttpConstraint** annotation dictates that the annotated servlet can only be accessed by those in the **manager** role.

```
@ServletSecurity(value = @HttpConstraint(rolesAllowed = "manager"))
```

Of course, the annotations above can be rewritten as follows.

```
@ServletSecurity(@HttpConstraint(rolesAllowed = "manager"))
```

You still have to declare a **login-config** element in the deployment descriptor so that the container can authenticate the user.

Setting **TransportGuarantee.CONFIDENTIAL** to the **transportGuarantee** attribute of an **HttpConstraint** annotation will make the servlet only available through a confidential channel, such as SSL.

```
@ServletSecurity(@HttpConstraint(transportGuarantee =
TransportGuarantee.CONFIDENTIAL))
```

If the servlet/JSP container receives a request for such a servlet through HTTP, it will redirect the browser to the HTTPS version of the same URL.

The **HttpMethodConstraint** annotation type specifies an HTTP method to which a security constraint applies. It can only appear in the array assigned to the **httpMethodConstraints** attribute of a **ServletSecurity** annotation. For example, the following **HttpMethodConstraint** annotation restricts access to the annotated servlet via HTTP Get to the **manager** role. For other HTTP methods, no restriction exists.

```
@ServletSecurity(httpMethodConstraints = {
    @HttpMethodConstraint(value = "GET", rolesAllowed = "manager")
})
```

Note that if the **rolesAllowed** attribute is not present in an **HttpMethodConstraint** annotation, no restriction applies to the specified HTTP method. For example, the following **ServletSecurity** annotation employs both the **value** and **httpMethodConstraints** attributes. The **HttpConstraint** annotation defines roles that can access the annotated servlet and the **HttpMethodConstraint** annotation, which is written without the **rolesAllowed** attribute, overrides the constraint for the Get method. As such, the servlet can be accessed via Get by any user. On the other hand, access via all other HTTP methods can only be granted to users in the **manager** role.

```
@ServletSecurity(value = @HttpConstraint(rolesAllowed = "manager"),
    httpMethodConstraints = {@HttpMethodConstraint("GET")}
)
```

However, if the **emptyRoleSemantic** attribute of the **HttpMethodConstraint** annotation type is assigned **EmptyRoleSemantic.DENY**, then the method is restricted for all users. For example, the servlet annotated with the following **ServletSecurity** annotation prevents access via the Get method but allows access to all users in the **member** role via other HTTP methods.

```
@ServletSecurity(value = @HttpConstraint(rolesAllowed = "member"),
httpMethodConstraints = {@HttpMethodConstraint(value = "GET",
    emptyRoleSemantic = EmptyRoleSemantic.DENY)}
)
```

Servlet Security API

Besides the annotation types discussed in the previous section, programmatic security can also be achieved using the following methods in the **HttpServletRequest** interface.

`java.lang.String getAuthType()`

Returns the authentication scheme used to protect the servlet or null if no security constraint is being applied to the servlet.

`java.lang.String getRemoteUser()`

Returns the login of the user making this request or null if the user has not been authenticated.

`boolean isUserInRole(java.lang.String role)`

Returns a boolean indicating whether or not the user belongs to the specified role.

`java.lang.Principal getUserPrincipal()`

Returns a **java.security.Principal** containing the details of the current authenticated user or null if the user has not been authenticated.

`boolean authenticate(HttpServletResponse response) throws java.io.IOException`

Authenticates the user by instructing the browser to display a login form.

`void login(java.lang.String userName, java.lang.String password) throws javax.servlet.ServletException`

Attempts to log the user in using the supplied user name and password. The method does not return anything if login was successful. Otherwise, it will throw a **ServletException**.

`void logout() throws javax.servlet.ServletException`

Logs the user out.

As an example, the **ProgrammaticServlet** class in Listing 15.9 is part of the **app15e** sample application that shows how to authenticate the user programmatically. It is accompanied by the deployment descriptor in Listing 15.10 that declares a **login-config** element that employs Digest access authentication.

Listing 15.9: The ProgrammaticServlet class

```
package servlet;
import java.io.IOException;
import java.io.PrintWriter;

import javax.servlet.ServletException;
import javax.servlet.annotation.WebServlet;
import javax.servlet.http.HttpServlet;
import javax.servlet.http.HttpServletRequest;
import javax.servlet.http.HttpServletResponse;

@WebServlet(urlPatterns = { "/prog" })
public class ProgrammaticServlet extends HttpServlet {

    private static final long serialVersionUID = 87620L;

    public void doGet(HttpServletRequest request,
        HttpServletResponse response)
            throws ServletException, IOException {

      if (request.authenticate(response)) {
          response.setContentType("text/html");
          PrintWriter out = response.getWriter();
          out.println("Welcome");
      } else {
          // user not authenticated
          // do something
          System.out.println("User not authenticated");
      }
    }
}
```

Listing 15.10: The deployment descriptor for app15e

```xml
<?xml version="1.0" encoding="ISO-8859-1"?>
<web-app xmlns="http://java.sun.com/xml/ns/javaee"
    xmlns:xsi="http://www.w3.org/2001/XMLSchema-instance"
    xsi:schemaLocation="http://java.sun.com/xml/ns/javaee
  http://java.sun.com/xml/ns/javaee/web-app_3_0.xsd"
    version="3.0"
>
    <login-config>
        <auth-method>DIGEST</auth-method>
        <realm-name>Digest authentication</realm-name>
    </login-config>
</web-app>
```

When the user first requests the servlet, the user is not authenticated and the authenticate method returns false. As a result, the servlet/JSP container will send a **WWW-Authenticate** header, causing the browser to show a Login dialog for Digest access authentication. When the user submits the form with the correct user name and password, the **authenticate** method returns true and the Welcome message is shown.

You can test the application by using this URL:

```
http://localhost:8080/app15e/prog
```

Summary

In this chapter you have learned how to achieve the four pillars of web security: authentication, authorization, confidentiality, and data integrity. Servlet technology allows you to secure your applications declaratively and programmatically.

Chapter 16
Deployment

Deploying a Servlet 3 application is a breeze. Thanks to the servlet annotation types and depending on how complex your application is, you can deploy a servlet/JSP application without the deployment descriptor. Having said that, the deployment descriptor is still needed in many circumstances where more refined configuration is needed. When the deployment descriptor is present, it must be named **web.xml** and located under the **WEB-INF** directory. Java classes must reside in **WEB-INF/classes** and Java libraries in **WEB-INF/lib**. All application resources must then be packaged into a single file with war extension. A war file is basically a jar file.

This chapter discusses deployment and the deployment descriptor, which is an important component of an application.

Deployment Descriptor Overview

Before Servlet 3 deployment always involved a **web.xml** file, the deployment descriptor, in which you configured various aspects of your application. With Servlet 3 the deployment descriptor is optional because you can use annotations to map a resource with a URL pattern. However, the deployment descriptor is needed if one of these applies to you.

- You need to pass initial parameters to the **ServletContext**.
- You have multiple filters and you want to specify the order in which the filters are invoked.
- You need to change the session timeout.
- You want to restrict access to a resource collection and provide a way for the user to authenticate themselves.

Listing 16. 1 shows the skeleton of the deployment descriptor. It must be named **web.xml** and reside in the **WEB-INF** directory of the application directory.

Listing 16.1: The skeleton of the deployment descriptor

```
<?xml version="1.0" encoding="ISO-8859-1"?>
<web-app xmlns="http://java.sun.com/xml/ns/javaee"
    xmlns:xsi="http://www.w3.org/2001/XMLSchema-instance"
    xsi:schemaLocation="http://java.sun.com/xml/ns/javaee
➥http://java.sun.com/xml/ns/javaee/web-app_3_0.xsd"
    version="3.0"
    [metadata-complete="true|false"]
>

    ...

</web-app>
```

The **xsi:schemaLocation** attribute specifies the location of the schema against which the deployment descriptor can be validated. The **version** attribute specifies the version of the Servlet specification.

The optional **metadata-complete** attribute specifies whether the deployment descriptor is complete. If its value is true, the servlet/JSP container must ignore servlet-specific annotations. If this element is set to false or if it's not present, the container must examine the class files deployed with the application for servlet-specific annotations and scan for web fragments.

The **web-app** element is the root element and can have subelements for specifying:

- servlet declarations
- servlet mappings
- **ServletContext** initial parameters
- session configuration
- listener classes
- filter definitions and mappings
- MIME type mappings
- welcome file list
- error pages

- JSP-specific settings
- JNDI settings

The rules for each of the elements that may appear in a deployment descriptor are given in the **web-app_3_0.xsd** schema that can be downloaded from this site.

```
http://java.sun.com/xml/ns/javaee/web-app_3_0.xsd
```

The **web-app_3.0.xsd** schema includes another schema (**web-common_3_0.xsd**) that contains most of the information. The other schema can be found here.

```
http://java.sun.com/xml/ns/javaee/web-common_3_0.xsd
```

In turn, **web-common_3_0.xsd** includes two other schemas:

- **javaee_6.xsd**, which defines common elements shared by other Java EE 6 deployment types (EAR, JAR and RAR)
- **jsp_2_2.xsd**, which defines elements for configuring the JSP part of an application according to JSP 2.2 specification

The rest of this section lists servlet and JSP elements that may appear in the deployment descriptor. It does not include Java EE elements that are not in the Servlet or JSP specification.

Core Elements

This section discusses the more important elements in detail. Subelements of **<web-app>** can appear in any order. Certain elements, such as **session-config**, **jsp-config**, and **login-config**, can appear only once. Others, such as **servlet**, **filter**, and **welcome-file-list**, can appear many times.

The more important elements that can appear directly under **<web-app>** are given a separate subsection. To find the description of an element which is not directly under **<web-app>**, trace its parent element. For example, the **taglib** element can be found under the subsection "jsp-config" and the **load-on-startup** element under "servlet." The subsections under this section are presented in alphabetical order.

context-param

The **context-param** element passes values to the **ServletContext**. These values can be read from any servlet/JSP page. This element contains a name/value pair that can be retrieved by calling the **getInitParameter** method on the **ServletContext**. You can have multiple **context-param** elements as long as the parameter names are unique throughout the application. **ServletContext.getInitParameterNames()** returns all **ServletContext** parameter names.

The **context-param** element must contain a **param-name** element and a **param-value** element. The **param-name** element contains the parameter name, and the **param-value** element the parameter value. Optionally, a **description** element also can be present to describe the parameter.

The following are two example **context-param** elements.

```
<context-param>
    <param-name>location</param-name>
    <param-value>localhost</param-value>
</context-param>
<context-param>
    <param-name>port</param-name>
    <param-value>8080</param-value>
    <description>The port number used</description>
</context-param>
```

distributable

If present, the **distributable** element indicates that the application is written to be deployed into a distributed servlet/JSP container. The **distributable** element must be empty. For example, here is a **distributable** element.

```
<distributable/>
```

error-page

The **error-page** element contains a mapping between an HTTP error code to a resource path or between a Java exception type to a resource path. The **error-page** element dictates the container that the specified resource should be returned in the event of the HTTP error or if the specified exception is thrown.

This element must contain the following subelements.

- **error-code**, to specify an HTTP error code
- **exception-type**, to specify the fully-qualified name of the Java exception type to be captured
- **location**, to specify the location of the resource to be displayed in the event of an error or exception. The **location** element must start with a /.

For example, the following is an **error-page** element that tells the servlet/JSP container to display the **error.html** page located at the application directory every time an HTTP 404 error code occurs:

```
<error-page>
    <error-code>404</error-code>
    <location>/error.html</location>
</error-page>
```

The following is an **error-page** element that maps all servlet exceptions with the **exceptions.html** page.

```
<error-page>
    <exception-type>javax.servlet.ServletException</exception-type>
    <location>/exception.html</location>
</error-page>
```

filter

This element specifies a servlet filter. At the very minimum, this element must contain a **filter-name** element and a **filter-class** element. Optionally, it can also contain the following elements: **icon**, **display-name**, **description**, **init-param**, and **async-supported**.

The **filter-name** element defines the name of the filter. The filter name must be unique within the application. The **filter-class** element specifies the fully qualified name of the filter class. The **init-param** element is used to specify an initial parameter for the filter and has the same element descriptor as **<context-param>**. A **filter** element can have multiple **init-param** elements.

The following are two **filter** elements whose names are **Upper Case Filter** and **Image Filter**, respectively.

```
<filter>
    <filter-name>Upper Case Filter</filter-name>
    <filter-class>com.example.UpperCaseFilter</filter-class>
</filter>
<filter>
    <filter-name>Image Filter</filter-name>
    <filter-class>com.example.ImageFilter</filter-class>
    <init-param>
        <param-name>frequency</param-name>
        <param-value>1909</param-value>
     </init-param>
    <init-param>
        <param-name>resolution</param-name>
        <param-value>1024</param-value>
    </init-param>
</filter>
```

filter-mapping

The **filter-mapping** element specifies the resource or resources a filter is applied to. A filter can be applied to either a servlet or a URL pattern. Mapping a filter to a servlet causes the filter to work on the servlet. Mapping a filter to a URL pattern makes filtering occur to any resource whose URL matches the URL pattern. Filtering is performed in the same order as the appearance of the **filter-mapping** elements in the deployment descriptor.

The **filter-mapping** element contains a **filter-name** element and a **url-pattern** element or a **servlet-name** element.

The **filter-name** value must match one of the filter names declared using the **filter** elements.

The following are two **filter** elements and two **filter-mapping** elements:

```
<filter>
    <filter-name>Logging Filter</filter-name>
    <filter-class>com.example.LoggingFilter</filter-class>
</filter>
<filter>
    <filter-name>Security Filter</filter-name>
    <filter-class>com.example.SecurityFilter</filter-class>
```

```
</filter>

<filter-mapping>
    <filter-name>Logging Filter</filter-name>
    <servlet-name>FirstServlet</servlet-name>
</filter-mapping>
<filter-mapping>
    <filter-name>Security Filter</filter-name>
    <url-pattern>/*</url-pattern>
</filter-mapping>
```

listener

The **listener** element registers a listener. It contains a **listener-class** element, which defines the fully qualified name of the listener class. Here is an example.

```
<listener>
    <listener-class>com.example.AppListener</listener-class>
</listener>
```

locale-encoding-mapping-list and locale-encoding-mapping

The **locale-encoding-mapping-list** element contains one or more **locale-encoding-mapping** elements. A **locale-encoding-mapping** element maps a locale name with an encoding and contains a **locale** element and an **encoding** element. The value for **<locale>** must be either a language-code defined in ISO 639, such as "en", or a language-code_country-code, such as "en_US". When a language-code_country-code is used, the country-code part must be one of the country codes defined in ISO 3166.

For instance, here is a **locale-encoding-mapping-list** that contains a **locale-encoding-mapping** element that maps the Japanese language to Shift_JIS encoding.

```
<locale-encoding-mapping-list>
    <locale-encoding-mapping>
        <locale>ja</locale>
        <encoding>Shift_JIS</encoding>
    </locale-encoding-mapping>
</locale-encoding-mapping-list>
```

login-config

The **login-config** element is used to specify the authentication method used to authenticate the user, the realm name, and the attributes needed by the form login mechanism if form-based authentication is used. A **login-config** element has an optional **auth-method** element, an optional **realm-name** element, and an optional **form-login-config** element.

The **auth-method** element specifies the access authentication method. Its value is one of the following: **BASIC**, **DIGEST**, **FORM**, or **CLIENT-CERT**.

The **realm-name** element specifies the realm name to use in Basic access authentication and Digest access authentication.

The **form-login-config** element specifies the login and error pages that should be used in form-based authentication. If form-based authentication is not used, these elements are ignored.

The **form-login-config** element has a **form-login-page** element and a **form-error-page** element. The **form-login-page** element specifies the path to a resource that displays a Login page. The path must start with a / and is relative to the application directory.

The **form-error-page** element specifies the path to a resource that displays an error page when login fails. The path must begin with a / and is relative to the application directory.

As an example, here is an example of the **login-config** element.

```
<login-config>
    <auth-method>DIGEST</auth-method>
    <realm-name>Members Only</realm-name>
</login-config>
```

And, here is another example.

```
<login-config>
    <auth-method>FORM</auth-method>
    <form-login-config>
        <form-login-page>/loginForm.jsp</form-login-page>
        <form-error-page>/errorPage.jsp</form-error-page>
    </form-login-config>
</login-config>
```

mime-mapping

The **mime-mapping** element maps a MIME type to an extension. It contains an **extension** element and a **mime-type** element. The **extension** element describes the extension and the **mime-type** element specifies the MIME type. For example, here is a **mime-mapping** element.

```
<mime-mapping>
    <extension>txt</extension>
    <mime-type>text/plain</mime-type>
</mime-mapping>
```

security-constraint

The **security-constraint** element allows you to restrict access to a collection of resources declaratively.

The **security-constraint** element contains an optional **display-name** element, one or more **web-resource-collection** elements, an optional **auth-constraint** element, and an optional **user-data-constraint** element.

The **web-resource-collection** element identifies a collection of resources to which access needs to be restricted. In it you can define the URL pattern(s) and the restricted HTTP method or methods. If no HTTP method is present, the security constraint applies to all HTTP methods.

The **auth-constraint** element specifies the user roles that should have access to the resource collection. If no **auth-constraint** element is specified, the security constraint applies to all roles.

The **user-data-constraint** element is used to indicate how data transmitted between the client and servlet/JSP container must be protected.

A **web-resource-collection** element contains a **web-resource-name** element, an optional **description** element, zero or more **url-pattern** elements, and zero or more **http-method** elements.

The **web-resource-name** element contains a name associated with the protected resource.

The **http-method** element can be assigned one of the HTTP methods, such as GET, POST, or TRACE.

The **auth-constraint** element contains an optional **description** element and zero or more **role-name** element. The **role-name** element contains the name of a security role.

The **user-data-constraint** element contains an optional **description** element and a **transport-guarantee** element. The **transport-guarantee** element must have one of the following values: **NONE, INTEGRAL**, or **CONFIDENTIAL. NONE** indicates that the application does not require transport guarantees. **INTEGRAL** means that the data between the server and the client should be sent in such a way that it can't be changed in transit. **CONFIDENTIAL** means that the data transmitted must be encrypted. In most cases, Secure Sockets Layer (SSL) is used for either **INTEGRAL** or **CONFIDENTIAL**.

The following example uses a **security-constraint** element to restrict access to any resource with a URL matching the pattern **/members/***. Only a user in the **payingMember** role will be allowed access. The **login-config** element requires the user to log in and the Digest access authentication method is used.

```
<security-constraint>
    <web-resource-collection>
        <web-resource-name>Members Only</web-resource-name>
        <url-pattern>/members/*</url-pattern>
    </web-resource-collection>
    <auth-constraint>
        <role-name>payingMember</role-name>
    </auth-constraint>
</security-constraint>

<login-config>
    <auth-method>Digest</auth-method>
    <realm-name>Digest Access Authentication</realm-name>
</login-config>
```

security-role

The **security-role** element specifies the declaration of a security role used in security constraints. This element has an optional **description** element and a **role-name** element. The following is an example **security-role** element.

```
<security-role>
    <role-name>payingMember</role-name>
</security-role>
```

servlet

The **servlet** element is used to declare a servlet. It can contain the following elements.

- an optional **icon** element
- an optional **description** element
- an optional **display-name** element
- a **servlet-name** element
- a **servlet-class** element or a **jsp-file** element
- zero or more **init-param** elements
- an optional **load-on-startup** element
- an optional **run-as** element
- an optional **enabled** element
- an optional **async-supported** element
- an optional **multipart-config** element
- zero or more **security-role-ref** elements

At a minimum a **servlet** element must contain a **servlet-name** element and a **servlet-class** element, or a **servlet-name** element and a **jsp-file** element. The **servlet-name** element defines the name for that servlet and must be unique throughout the application.

The **servlet-class** element specifies the fully qualified class name of the servlet.

The **jsp-file** element specifies the full path to a JSP page within the application. The full path must begin with a /.

The **init-param** subelement can be used to pass an initial parameter name and value to the servlet. The element descriptor of **init-param** is the same as **context-param**.

You use the **load-on-startup** element to load the servlet automatically into memory when the servlet/JSP container starts up. Loading a servlet means instantiating the servlet and calling its **init** method. You use this element to avoid delay in the response for the first request to the servlet, caused by the servlet loading to memory. If this element is present and a **jsp-file** element is specified, the JSP file is precompiled into a servlet and the resulting servlet is loaded.

load-on-startup is either empty or has an integer value. The value indicates the order of loading this servlet when there are multiple servlets in the same application. For example, if there are two **servlet** elements and both contain a **load-on-startup** element, the servlet with the lower **load-on-startup** value is loaded first. If the value of the **load-on-startup** is empty or is a negative number, it is up to the web container to decide when to load the servlet. If two servlets have the same **load-on-startup** value, the loading order between the two servlets cannot be determined.

Defining **run-as** overrides the security identity for calling an Enterprise JavaBean by that servlet in this application. The role name is one of the security roles defined for the current web application.

The **security-role-ref** element maps the name of the role called from a servlet using **isUserInRole(*name*)** to the name of a security role defined for the application. The **security-role-ref** element contains an optional **description** element, a **role-name** element, and a **role-link** element.

The **role-link** element is used to link a security role reference to a defined security role. The **role-link** element must contain the name of one of the security roles defined in the **security-role** elements.

The **async-supported** element is an optional element that can have a true or false value. It indicates whether or not this servlet supports asynchronous processing.

The **enabled** element is also an optional element whose value can be true or false. Setting this element to false disables this servlet.

For example, to map the security role reference "PM" to the security role with role-name "payingMember," the syntax would be as follows.

```
<security-role-ref>
    <role-name>PM</role-name>
    <role-link>payingMember</role-link>
</security-role-ref>
```

In this case, if the servlet invoked by a user belonging to the "payingMember" security role calls **isUserInRole("payingMember")**, the result would be true.

The following are two example **servlet** elements:

```
<servlet>
    <servlet-name>UploadServlet</servlet-name>
    <servlet-class>com.brainysoftware.UploadServlet</servlet-class>
    <load-on-startup>10</load-on-startup>
</servlet>
<servlet>
    <servlet-name>SecureServlet</servlet-name>
    <servlet-class>com.brainysoftware.SecureServlet</servlet-class>
    <load-on-startup>20</load-on-startup>
</servlet>
```

servlet-mapping

The **servlet-mapping** element maps a servlet to a URL pattern. The **servlet-mapping** element must have a **servlet-name** element and a **url-pattern** element.

The following **servlet-mapping** element maps a servlet with the URL pattern **/first**.

```
<servlet>
    <servlet-name>FirstServlet</servlet-name>
    <servlet-class>com.brainysoftware.FirstServlet</servlet-class>
</servlet>
<servlet-mapping>
    <servlet-name>FirstServlet</servlet-name>
    <url-pattern>/first</url-pattern>
</servlet-mapping>
```

session-config

The **session-config** element defines parameters for **javax.servlet.http.HttpSession** instances. This element may contain one or more of the following elements: **session-timeout**, **cookie-config**, or **tracking-mode**.

The **session-timeout** element specifies the default session timeout interval in minutes. This value must be an integer. If the value of the **session-timeout** element is zero or a negative number, the session will never time out.

The **cookie-config** element defines the configuration of the session tracking cookies created by this servlet/JSP application.

The **tracking-mode** element defines the tracking mode for sessions created by this web application. Valid values are **COOKIE**, **URL**, or **SSL**.

The following **session-config** element causes the **HttpSession** objects in the current application to be invalidated after twelve minutes of inactivity.

```
<session-config>
    <session-timeout>12</session-timeout>
</session-config>
```

welcome-file-list

The **welcome-file-list** element specifies the file or servlet that is displayed when the URL entered by the user in the browser does not contain a servlet name or a JSP page or a static resource.

The **welcome-file-list** element contains one or more **welcome-file** elements. The **welcome-file** element contains the default file name. If the file specified in the first **welcome-file** element is not found, the web container will try to display the second one, and so on.

Here is an example **welcome-file-list** element.

```
<welcome-file-list>
    <welcome-file>index.htm</welcome-file>
    <welcome-file>index.html</welcome-file>
    <welcome-file>index.jsp</welcome-file>
</welcome-file-list>
```

The following example uses a **welcome-file-list** element that contains two **welcome-file** elements. The first **welcome-file** element specifies a file in the application directory called **index.html**; the second defines the welcome servlet under the servlet directory, which is under the application directory:

```
<welcome-file-list>
    <welcome-file>index.html</welcome-file>
```

```
    <welcome-file>servlet/welcome</welcome-file>
</welcome-file-list>
```

JSP-Specific Elements

The **jsp-config** element under **<web-app>** contains elements specific to JSP. It can have zero or more **taglib** elements and zero or more **jsp-property-group** elements. The **taglib** element is explained in the first subsection of this section and the **jsp-property-group** element in the second subsection.

taglib

The **taglib** element describes a JSP custom tag library. The **taglib** element contains a **taglib-uri** element and a **taglib-location** element.

The **taglib-uri** element specifies the URI of the tag library used in the servlet/JSP application. The value for **<taglib-uri>** is relative to the location of the deployment descriptor.

The **taglib-location** element specifies the location of the TLD file for the tag library.

The following is an example **taglib** element.

```
<jsp-config>
    <taglib>
        <taglib-uri>
            http://brainysoftware.com/taglib/complex
        </taglib-uri>
        <taglib-location>/WEB-INF/jsp/complex.tld
    </taglib-location>
    </taglib>
</jsp-config>
```

jsp-property-group

The **jsp-property-group** element groups a number of JSP files so they can be given global property information. You can use subelements under **<jsp-property-group>** to do the following.

- Indicate whether EL is ignored
- Indicate whether scripting elements are allowed
- Indicate page encoding information
- Indicate that a resource is a JSP document (written in XML)
- Prelude and code automatic includes

The **jsp-property-group** element has the following subelements.

- an optional **description** element
- an optional **display-name** element
- an optional **icon** element
- one or more **url-pattern** elements
- an optional **el-ignored** element
- an optional **page-encoding** element
- an optional **scripting-invalid** element
- an optional **is-xml** element
- zero or more **include-prelude** elements
- zero or more **include-code** elements

The **url-pattern** element is used to specify a URL pattern that will be affected by the property settings.

The **el-ignored** element can have a boolean value of true or false. A value of true means that the EL expressions will not evaluated in the JSP pages whose URL match the specified URL pattern(s). The default value of this element is false.

The **page-encoding** element specifies the encoding for the JSP pages whose URL match the specified URL pattern(s). The valid value for **page-encoding** is the same as the value of the **pageEncoding** attribute of the **page** directive used in a matching JSP page. There will be a translation-time error to name a different encoding in the **pageEncoding** attribute of the **page** directive of a JSP page and in a JSP configuration element matching the page. It is also a translation-time error to name a different encoding in the prolog or text declaration of a document in XML syntax and in a JSP configuration element matching the document. It is legal to name the same encoding through multiple mechanisms.

The **scripting-invalid** element accepts a boolean value. A value of true means that **scripting** is not allowed in the JSP pages whose URLs match the specified pattern(s). By default, the value of the **scripting-invalid** element is false.

The **is-xml** element accepts a boolean value and true indicates that the JSP pages whose URLs match the specified pattern(s) are JSP documents.

The **include-prelude** element is a context-relative path that must correspond to an element in the servlet/JSP application. When the element is present, the given path will be automatically included (as in an **include** directive) at the beginning of each JSP page whose URL matches the specified pattern(s).

The **include-coda** element is a context-relative path that must correspond to an element in the application. When the element is present, the given path will be automatically included (as in the **include** directive) at the end of each JSP page in this **jsp-property-group** element.

For example, here is a **jsp-property-group** element that causes EL evaluation in all JSP pages to be ignored.

```
<jsp-config>
    <jsp-property-group>
        <url-pattern>*.jsp</url-pattern>
        <el-ignored>true</el-ignored>
    </jsp-property-group>
</jsp-config>
```

And, here is a **jsp-property-group** element that is used to enforce script-free JSP pages throughout the application.

```
<jsp-config>
    <jsp-property-group>
        <url-pattern>*.jsp</url-pattern>
        <scripting-invalid>true</scripting-invalid>
    </jsp-property-group>
</jsp-config>
```

Deployment

Deploying a Servlet/JSP application has always been easy since the first version of Servlet. It has just been a matter of zipping all application resources in its original directory structure into a war file. You can either use the jar tool in the JDK or a popular tool such as WinZip. All you need is make sure the zipped file has war extension. If you're using WinZip, rename the result once it's done.

You must include in your war file all libraries and class files as well as HTML files, JSP pages, images, copyright notices (if any), and so on. Do not include Java source files. Anyone who needs your application can simply get a copy of your war file and deploy it in a servlet/JSP container.

Web Fragments

Servlet 3 adds web fragments, a new feature for deploying plug-ins or frameworks in an existing web application. Web fragments are designed to complement the deployment descriptor without having to edit the **web.xml** file. A web fragment is basically a package (jar file) containing the usual web objects, such as servlets, filter, and listeners, and other resources, such as JSP pages and static images. A web fragment can also have a descriptor, which is an XML document similar to the deployment descriptor. The web fragment descriptor must be named **web-fragment.xml** and reside in the **META-INF** directory of the package. A web fragment descriptor may contain any elements that may appear under the **web-app** element in the deployment descriptor, plus some web fragment-specific elements. An application can have multiple web fragments.

Listing 16.2 shows the skeleton of the web fragment descriptor. The text printed in bold highlights the difference between it and the deployment descriptor. The root element in a web fragment is, unsurprisingly, **web-fragment**. The **web-fragment** element can even have the **metadata-complete** attribute. If the value of the **metadata-complete** attribute is true, annotations in the classes contained by the web fragment will be skipped.

Listing 16.2: The skeleton of a web-fragment.xml file

```
<?xml version="1.0" encoding="ISO-8859-1"?>
<web-fragment xmlns="http://java.sun.com/xml/ns/javaee"
    xmlns:xsi="http://www.w3.org/2001/XMLSchema-instance"
    xsi:schemaLocation="http://java.sun.com/xml/ns/javaee
➡http://java.sun.com/xml/ns/javaee/web-fragment_3_0.xsd"
    version="3.0"
    [metadata-complete="true|false"]
>

    ...

</web-fragment>
```

As an example, the **app16a** application contains a web fragment in a jar file named **fragment.jar**. The jar file has been imported to the **WEB-INF/lib** directory of **app16a**. The focus of this example is not on **app16a** but rather on the **webfragment** project, which contains a servlet (**fragment.servlet.FragmentServlet**, printed in Listing 16.3) and a **web-fragment.xml** file (given in Listing 16.4).

Listing 16.3: The FragmentServlet class

```
package fragment.servlet;
import java.io.IOException;
import java.io.PrintWriter;
import javax.servlet.ServletException;
import javax.servlet.http.HttpServlet;
import javax.servlet.http.HttpServletRequest;
import javax.servlet.http.HttpServletResponse;

public class FragmentServlet extends HttpServlet {

    private static final long serialVersionUID = 940L;

    public void doGet(HttpServletRequest request,
        HttpServletResponse response)
            throws ServletException, IOException {

        response.setContentType("text/html");
        PrintWriter out = response.getWriter();
        out.println("A plug-in");
    }
}
```

Listing 16.4: The web fragment descriptor in project webfragment

```
<?xml version="1.0" encoding="ISO-8859-1"?>
<web-fragment xmlns="http://java.sun.com/xml/ns/javaee"
    xmlns:xsi="http://www.w3.org/2001/XMLSchema-instance"
    xsi:schemaLocation="http://java.sun.com/xml/ns/javaee
�th.ttp://java.sun.com/xml/ns/javaee/web-fragment_3_0.xsd"
    version="3.0"
>

    <servlet>
        <servlet-name>FragmentServlet</servlet-name>
        <servlet-class>fragment.servlet.FragmentServlet</servlet-
        class>
    </servlet>
    <servlet-mapping>
        <servlet-name>FragmentServlet</servlet-name>
        <url-pattern>/fragment</url-pattern>
    </servlet-mapping>
</web-fragment>
```

FragmentServlet is a simple servlet that sends a string to the browser. The **web-fragment.xml** file registers and maps the servlet. The structure of the **fragment.jar** file is depicted in Figure 16.1.

📂 fragment
　　◢ 📂 servlet
　　　　🔹 FragmentServlet.class
📂 META-INF
　　🅇 web-fragment.xml

Figure 16.1: The structure of the fragment.jar file

You can test the **Fragment** servlet by invoking using this URL:

```
http://localhost:8080/app16a/fragment
```

You should see the output from the **Fragment** servlet.

Summary

This chapter explained how you can configure and deploy your servlet/JSP applications. The chapter started by introducing the directory structure of a typical application and then moved to an explanation of the deployment descriptor.

After the application is ready for deployment, you can deploy it by retaining the files and directory structure of your application. Alternatively, you can package the application into a WAR file and deploy the whole application as a single file.

Chapter 17
Dynamic Registration and
Servlet Container Initializers

Dynamic registration is a new feature in Servlet 3 for installing new web objects (servlets, filters, listeners) without reloading the application. The servlet container initializer is also a new addition in Servlet 3 that is especially useful for framework developers. This chapter discusses both features and presents examples.

Dynamic Registration

To make dynamic registration possible, the **ServletContext** interface has added these methods to dynamically create a web object.

```
<T extends Filter> createFilter(java.lang.Class<T> clazz)

<T extends java.util.EventListener> createListener(
        java.lang.Class<T> clazz)

<T extends Servlet> createServlet(java.lang.Class<T> clazz)
```

For example, if **MyServlet** is a class that directly or indirectly implements **javax.servlet.Servlet**, you can instantiate **MyServlet** by calling **createServlet**:

```
Servlet myServlet = createServlet(MyServlet.class);
```

After you create a web object, you can add it to the **ServletContext** using one of these methods, also new in Servlet 3.

```
FilterRegistration.Dynamic addFilter(java.lang.String filterName,
        Filter filter)
```

```
<T extends java.util.EventListener> void addListener(T t)

ServletRegistration.Dynamic addServlet(java.lang.String
        servletName, Servlet servlet)
```

Alternatively, you can simultaneously create and add a web object to the **ServletContext** by calling one of these methods on the **ServletContext**.

```
FilterRegistration.Dynamic addFilter(java.lang.String filterName,
        java.lang.Class<? extends Filter> filterClass)

FilterRegistration.Dynamic addFilter(java.lang.String filterName,
        java.lang.String className)

void addListener(java.lang.Class<? extends java.util.EventListener>
        listenerClass)

void addListener(java.lang.String className)

ServletRegistration.Dynamic addServlet(java.lang.String
        servletName, java.lang.String className)

ServletRegistration.Dynamic addServlet(java.lang.String
        servletName, java.lang.String className)
```

To create or add a listener, the class passed to the first **addListener** method override must implement one or more of the following interfaces:

- **ServletContextAttributeListener**
- **ServletRequestListener**
- **ServletRequestAttributeListener**
- **HttpSessionListener**
- **HttpSessionAttributeListener**

If the **ServletContext** was passed to a **ServletContextInitializer**'s **onStartup** method, the listener class may also implement **ServletContextListener**. For information about the on **startUp** method and the **ServletContextInitializer** interface, see the section below.

The return value of the **addFilter** or **addServlet** method is either a **FilterRegistration.Dynamic** or a **ServletRegistration.Dynamic**.

Both **FilterRegistration.Dynamic** and **ServletRegistration.Dynamic** are subinterfaces of **Registration.Dynamic**. **FilterRegistration.Dynamic** allows you to configure a filter and **ServletRegistration.Dynamic** a servlet.

As an example, consider the **app17a** application that contains a servlet named **FirstServlet** and a listener called **DynRegListener**. The servlet is not annotated with **@WebServlet**, nor is it declared in the deployment descriptor. The listener registers the servlet dynamically and put it into use.

The **FirstServlet** class is given in Listing 17.1 and the **DynRegListener** class in Listing 17.2.

Listing 17.1: The FirstServlet class

```
package servlet;
import java.io.IOException;
import java.io.PrintWriter;
import javax.servlet.ServletException;
import javax.servlet.http.HttpServlet;
import javax.servlet.http.HttpServletRequest;
import javax.servlet.http.HttpServletResponse;

public class FirstServlet extends HttpServlet {
    private static final long serialVersionUID = -6045338L;

    private String name;

    @Override
    public void doGet(HttpServletRequest request,
            HttpServletResponse response)
            throws ServletException, IOException {
        response.setContentType("text/html");
        PrintWriter writer = response.getWriter();
        writer.println("<html><head><title>First servlet" +
                "</title></head><body>" + name);
        writer.println("</body></head>");
    }

    public void setName(String name) {
        this.name = name;
    }
}
```

Listing 17.2: The DynRegListener class

```
package listener;
import javax.servlet.Servlet;
```

```
import javax.servlet.ServletContext;
import javax.servlet.ServletContextEvent;
import javax.servlet.ServletContextListener;
import javax.servlet.ServletRegistration;
import javax.servlet.annotation.WebListener;
import servlet.FirstServlet;

@WebListener
public class DynRegListener implements ServletContextListener {

    @Override
    public void contextDestroyed(ServletContextEvent sce) {
    }

    // use createServlet to obtain a Servlet instance that can be
    // configured prior to being added to ServletContext
    @Override
    public void contextInitialized(ServletContextEvent sce) {
        ServletContext servletContext = sce.getServletContext();

        Servlet firstServlet = null;
        try {
            firstServlet =
                servletContext.createServlet(FirstServlet.class);
        } catch (Exception e) {
            e.printStackTrace();
        }

        if (firstServlet != null && firstServlet instanceof
                FirstServlet) {
            ((FirstServlet) firstServlet).setName(
                    "Dynamically registered servlet");
        }

        // the servlet may not be annotated with @WebServlet
        ServletRegistration.Dynamic dynamic = servletContext.
                addServlet("firstServlet", firstServlet);
        dynamic.addMapping("/dynamic");
    }
}
```

When the application starts, the container calls the listener's
contextInitialized method. As a result, an instance of **FirstServlet** gets
created and registered and mapped to **/dynamic**. If everything goes well,
you should be able to invoke **FirstServlet** with this URL.

```
Http://localhost:8080/app17a/dynamic
```

Servlet Container Initializers

If you have used a Java web framework, such as Struts or Struts 2, you know that you need to configure your application before you can use the framework. Typically, you will need to tell the servlet container that you're using a framework by modifying the deployment descriptor. For example, to use Struts 2 in your application, you add the following tags to the deployment descriptor:

```
<filter>
    <filter-name>struts2</filter-name>
    <filter-class>
        org.apache.struts2.dispatcher.ng.filter.
➡ StrutsPrepareAndExecuteFilter
    </filter-class>
</filter>

<filter-mapping>
    <filter-name>struts2</filter-name>
    <url-pattern>/*</url-pattern>
</filter-mapping>
```

In Servlet 3, this is no longer necessary. A framework can be packaged in such a way that initial registration of web objects happens automatically.

The brain of servlet container initialization is the **javax.servlet.ServletContainerInitializer** interface. This is a simple interface with only one method, **onStartup**. This method is called by the servlet container before any **ServletContext** listener is given the opportunity to execute.

The signature of **onStartup** is as follows.

```
void onStartup(java.util.Set<java.lang.Class<?>> klazz,
        ServletContext servletContext)
```

Classes implementing **ServletContainerInitializer** must be annotated with **@HandleTypes** to declare the class types the initializer can handle.

As an example, the **initializer.jar** library accompanying this book contains a servlet container initializer that registers a servlet named **UsefulServlet**. Figure 17.1 shows the structure of **initializer.jar**.

Figure 17.1: The structure of initializer.jar

This library is a pluggable framework. There are two resources that are of importance here, the initializer class (**initializer.MyServletContainerInitializer**, printed in Listing 17.3) and a metadata text file named **javax.servlet.ServletContainerInitializer**. This text file must be placed under **META-INF/services** in the jar file. The text file consists of only one line, which is the name of the class implementing **ServletContainerInitializer**, and is given in Listing 17.4.

Listing 17.3: A ServletContainerInitializer

```
package initializer;
import java.util.Set;
import javax.servlet.ServletContainerInitializer;
import javax.servlet.ServletContext;
import javax.servlet.ServletException;
import javax.servlet.ServletRegistration;
import javax.servlet.annotation.HandlesTypes;
import servlet.UsefulServlet;

@HandlesTypes({UsefulServlet.class})
public class MyServletContainerInitializer implements
        ServletContainerInitializer {

    @Override
    public void onStartup(Set<Class<?>> classes, ServletContext
            servletContext) throws ServletException {

        System.out.println("onStartup");
        ServletRegistration registration =
                servletContext.addServlet("usefulServlet",
                "servlet.UsefulServlet");
```

```
        registration.addMapping("/useful");
        System.out.println("leaving onStartup");
    }
}
```

Listing 17.4: The javax.servlet.ServletContainerInitializer file

```
initializer.MyServletContainerInitializer
```

The main job of the **onStartup** method in **MyServletContainerInitializer** is to register web objects. In this example, there is only one such object, a servlet named **UsefulServlet**, which is mapped to the **/useful** pattern. In a large framework, registration instructions can come from an XML document, as in Struts and Struts 2.

The **app17b** application accompanying this chapter already contains a copy of **initializer.jar** in the **WEB-INF/lib** directory. To confirm that **UsefulServlet** is registered successfully when the application starts, direct your browser to this URL and see if you see some output from the servlet:

```
http://localhost:8080/app17b/useful
```

It is not hard to imagine that one day all frameworks will be deployed as a plug-in.

Summary

In this chapter you have learned two new features for deploying applications and plug-ins on the fly. The first feature is dynamic registration, which allows you to dynamically add servlets, filters, and listeners without application restart. The second one is the servlet container initializer, which allows you to deploy plug-ins without changing the deployment descriptor of the user application. The servlet container initializer is particularly useful to framework developers.

Chapter 18
Introduction to Struts 2

In Chapter 10, "Application Design" you learned about the advantages of the Model 2 architecture and how to build applications based on that model. This chapter introduces Struts 2 as a framework for rapid Model 2 application development, starting with a discussion of the benefits of Struts 2 and how it expedites Model 2 application development. It also explains the basic components of Struts 2: the filter dispatcher, actions, results, and interceptors.

Introducing Struts 2 configuration is another objective of this chapter. Most Struts application will have a **struts.xml** and a **struts.properties** files. The former is the more important as it is where you configure your actions. The latter is optional as there exists a **default.properties** file that contains standard settings that work for most applications. At the end of this chapter, you will rewrite the **app10b** application and witness how Struts 2 reduces the amount of code you need to write.

If after reading this chapter you're interested to learn more about Struts 2, I recommend my own *Struts 2 Design and Programming: A Tutorial* (ISBN 978-0980331608).

The Benefits of Struts 2

Struts 2 is an MVC framework that employs a filter dispatcher as the controller. When writing a Model 2 application without a framework, it is your responsibility to provide a controller as well as write action classes. Your controller must be able to do these:

1. Determine from the URI what action to invoke.

2. Instantiate the action class.
3. If an action object exists, populate the action's properties with request parameters.
4. If an action object exists, call the action method.
5. Forward the request to a view (JSP page).

The first benefit of using Struts is that you don't have to write a controller and can concentrate on writing business logic in action classes. Here is the list of features that Struts is equipped with to make development more rapid and enjoyable:

- Struts provides a filter dispatcher, saving you writing one.
- Struts employs an XML-based configuration file to match URIs with actions. Since XML documents are text files, many changes can be made to the application without recompilation.
- Struts instantiates the action class and populates action properties with user inputs. If you don't specify an action class, a default action class will be instantiated.
- Struts validates user input and redirects user back to the input form if validation failed. Input validation is optional and can be done programmatically or declaratively. On top of that, Struts provides built-in validators for most of the tasks you may encounter when building a web application.
- Struts invokes the action method and you can change the method for an action through the configuration file.
- Struts examines the action result and executes the result. The most common result type, Dispatcher, forwards control to a JSP page. However, Struts 2 comes with various result types that allow you to do things differently, such as generate a PDF, redirect to an external resource, send an error message, etc.

The list shows how Struts 2 can help you with the tasks you did when developing the Model 2 applications in Chapter 10, "Application Design." There is much more. Custom tags for displaying data, data conversion, support for AJAX, support for internationalization and localization, and extension through plug-ins are some of them.

How Struts 2 Works

Struts 2 has a filter dispatcher similar to that in **app10b**. Its fully qualified name in Struts 2.3 is **org.apache.struts2.dispatcher.ng.filter.-StrutsPrepareAndExectureFilter**. (Earlier versions of Struts 2 used a different class.) To use the filter, register it in the deployment descriptor (**web.xml** file) using this **filter** and **filter-mapping** elements.

```
<filter>
    <filter-name>struts2</filter-name>
    <filter-class>
        org.apache.struts2.dispatcher.ng.filter.
➡StrutsPrepareAndExecuteFilter
    </filter-class>
</filter>
<filter-mapping>
    <filter-name>struts2</filter-name>
    <url-pattern>/*</url-pattern>
</filter-mapping>
```

There's a lot that a filter dispatcher in a Model 2 application has to do and Struts 2's filter dispatcher is by no means an exception. Since Struts 2 has much more features to support, its filter dispatcher could grow infinitely in complexity. However, Struts 2 approaches this by splitting task processing in its filter dispatcher into subcomponents called interceptors. The first interceptor you'll notice is the one that populates the action object with request parameters. You'll learn more about interceptors in the section "Interceptors" later in this chapter.

In a Struts 2 application the action method is executed after the action's properties are populated. An action method can have any name as long as it is a valid Java method name.

An action method returns a **String** value. This value indicates to Struts 2 where control should be forwarded to. A successful action method execution will forward to a different view than a failed one. For instance, the **String** "success" indicates a successful action method execution and "error" indicates that there's been an error during processing and an error message should be displayed. Most of the time a **RequestDispatcher** will be used to forward to a JSP page, however JSP pages are not the only valid destination. A result that returns a file for download does not need a JSP page. Neither does a result that simply sends a redirection command or sends a chart to be rendered. Even if an action needs to be forwarded to a view, the view may not necessarily be a JSP page. A Velocity template or a FreeMarker template can also be used.

Now that you know all the basic components in Struts 2, I'll continue by explaining how Struts 2 works. Since Struts 2 uses a filter dispatcher as its controller, all activities start from this object.

The Case for Velocity and FreeMarker

JSP programmers would probably mumble, "Why introduce new view technologies and not stick with JSP?" Good question. The answer is, while you can get away with just JSP, there's a compelling reason to learn Velocity and/or FreeMarker. Velocity and FreeMarker templates can be packaged in a JAR, which is how Struts 2 plug-ins are distributed. You cannot distribute JSP pages in a JAR, at least not easily, although you'll find a way to do so if you're determined enough. In addition, there are claims that Velocity is faster than JSP.

The first thing that a filter dispatcher does is verify the request URI and determine what action to invoke and which Java action class to instantiate. The filter dispatcher in **app10b** did this by using a string manipulation method. However, this is impractical since during development the URI may change several times and you will have to recompile the filter each time the URI or something else changes.

For matching URIs with action classes, Struts 2 uses a configuration file named **struts.xml**. Basically, you need to create a **struts.xml** file and place it under **WEB-INF/classes**. You define all actions in the application in this file. Each action has a name that directly corresponds to the URI used to invoke the action. Each action declaration may specify the fully qualified name of an action class, if any. You have to specify the action method name unless its name is **execute**, the default method name Struts 2 will assume in the absence of an explicit one.

An action class must have at least one result to tell Struts 2 what to do after it executes the action method. There may be multiple results if the action method may return different results depending on, say, user inputs.

The **struts.xml** file is read when Struts 2 starts. In development mode, Struts 2 checks the timestamp of this file every time it processes a request and will reload it if it has changed since the last time it was loaded. As a result, if you are in development mode and you tell Struts 2 that, you don't need to restart your web container every time your application changes. Saving you time.

Configuration file loading will fail if you don't comply with the rules that govern the **struts.xml** file. If, or should I say when, this happens, Struts 2 will fail to start and you must restart your container. Sometimes it's hard to decipher what you've done wrong due to unclear error messages. If this happens, try commenting out actions that you suspect are causing it, until you isolate and fix the one that is impending development.

Note

I discuss Struts 2 development mode when discussing the Struts configuration files in the section "Configuration Files" later in this chapter.

Figure 18.1 shows how Struts processes action invocation. It does not include the reading of the configuration file, which only happens once during application launch.

For every action invocation the filter dispatcher does the following:

1. Consult the Configuration Manager to determine what action to invoke based on the request URI.
2. Run each of the interceptors registered for this action. One of the interceptors will populate the action's properties.
3. Execute the action method.
4. Execute the result.

Note that some interceptors run again after action method execution, before the result is executed.

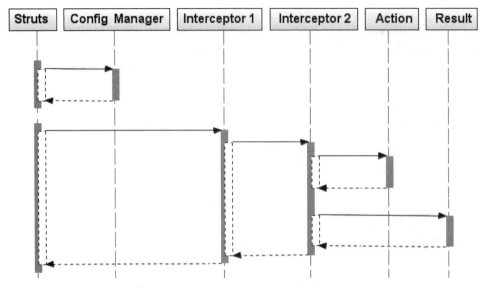

Figure 18.1: How Struts 2 works

Interceptors

As mentioned earlier, there are a lot of things a filter dispatcher must do. Code that would otherwise reside in the filter dispatcher class is modularized into interceptors. The beauty of interceptors is they can be plugged in and out by editing the Struts 2 configuration file. In fact, Struts 2 achieves a high degree of modularity using this strategy. New code for action processing can be added without recompiling the main framework.

Table 18.1 lists Struts 2's default interceptors. The words in brackets in the Interceptor column are the names used to register the interceptors in the configuration file. Yes, as you will see shortly, you need to register an interceptor in the configuration file before you can use it. For example, the registered name for the Alias interceptor is **alias**.

There are quite a number of interceptors, and this can be confusing to a beginner. The thing is you don't have to know about interceptors intimately before you can write a Struts 2 application. Just know that interceptors play a vital role in Struts.

Most of the time the default interceptors are good enough. However, if you need non-standard action processing, you can write your own interceptor. Writing custom interceptors is discussed in Chapter 18, "Custom Interceptors" of *Struts 2 Design and Programming: A Tutorial*.

Interceptor	Description
Alias (alias)	Converts similar parameters that may have different names between requests.
Chaining (chain)	When used with the Chain result type, this interceptor makes the previous action's properties available to the current action.
Checkbox (checkbox)	Handles check boxes in a form so that unchecked check boxes can be detected.
Cookie (cookie)	Adds a cookie to the current action.
Conversion Error (conversionError)	Adds conversion errors to the action's field errors.
Create Session (createSession)	Creates an **HttpSession** object if one does not yet exist for the current user.
Debugging (debugging)	Supports debugging.
Execute and Wait (execAndWait)	Executes a long-processing action in the background and sends the user to an intermediate waiting page.
Exception (exception)	Maps exceptions to a result.
File Upload (fileUpload)	Supports file upload.
I18n (i18n)	Supports internationalization and localization.
Logger (logger)	Outputs the action name.
Message Store (store)	Stores and retrieves action messages or action errors or field errors for action objects whose classes implement **ValidationAware**.
Model Driven (modelDriven)	Supports for the model driven pattern for action classes that implement **ModelDriven**.
Scoped Model Driven (scopedModelDriven)	Similar to the Model Driven interceptor but works for classes that implement **ScopedModelDriven**.
Parameters (params)	Populates the action's properties with the request parameters.
Prepare (prepare)	Supports action classes that implement the **Preparable** interface.

Scope (scope)	Provides a mechanism for storing action state in the session or application scope.
Servlet Config (servletConfig)	Provides access to the **Maps** representing **HttpServletRequest** and **HttpServletResponse**.
Static Parameters (staticParams)	Maps static properties to action properties.
Roles (roles)	Supports role-based action.
Timer (timer)	Outputs the time needed to execute an action.
Token (token)	Verifies that a valid token is present.
Token Session (tokenSession)	Verifies that a valid token is present.
Validation (validation)	Supports input validation.
Workflow (workflow)	Calls the **validate** method in the action class.
Parameter Filter (n/a)	Removes parameters from the list of those available to the action.
Profiling (profiling)	Supports action profiling.

Table 18.1: Struts 2's default interceptors

Struts 2's Configuration Files

A Struts 2 application uses a number of configuration files. The primary two are **struts.xml** and **struts.properties**, but there can be other configuration files. For instance, a Struts plug-in comes with a **struts-plugin.xml** configuration file. And if you're using Velocity as your view technology, expect to have a **velocity.properties** file. This chapter briefly explains the **struts.xml** and **struts.properties** files.

In **struts.xml** you define almost all aspects of your application, including the actions, the interceptors that need to be called for each action, and the possible results for each action.

Interceptors and result types used in an action must be registered before they can be used. Happily, Struts 2 configuration files support inheritance and default configuration files are included in the **struts2-core-VERSION.jar** file. The **struts-default.xml** file, one of such default configuration files, registers the default result types and interceptors. As such, you can use the default result types and interceptors without registering them in your own **struts.xml** file, making it cleaner and shorter.

The **default.properties** file, packaged in the same JAR, contains settings that apply to all Struts applications. As a result, unless you need to override the default values, you don't need to have a **struts.properties** file.

Let's now look at **struts.xml** and **struts.properties** in more detail.

The struts.xml File

The **struts.xml** file is an XML file with a **struts** root element. You define all the actions in your Struts 2 application in this file. Here is the skeleton of a **struts.xml** file.

```
<?xml version="1.0" encoding="UTF-8" ?>
<!DOCTYPE struts PUBLIC
    "-//Apache Software Foundation//DTD Struts Configuration 2.0//EN"
    "http://struts.apache.org/dtds/struts-2.0.dtd">
<struts>

...

</struts>
```

The more important elements that can appear between **<struts>** and **</struts>** are discussed next.

The package Element

Since Struts has been designed with modularity in mind, actions are grouped into packages. Think packages as modules. A typical **struts.xml** file can have one or many packages:

```
<struts>
    <package name="package-1" namespace="namespace-1"
            extends="struts-default">
        <action name="..."/>
        <action name="..."/>
            ...
    </package>
    <package name="package-2" namespace="namespace-2">
```

```
        extends="struts-default">
    <action name="..."/>
     <action name="..."/>
           ...
    </package>


    ...


    <package name="package-n" namespace="namespace-n">
          extends="struts-default">
      <action name="..."/>
      <action name="..."/>
           ...
    </package>
</struts>
```

A **package** element must have the **name** attribute. The **namespace** attribute
is optional and if it is not present, the default value "/" is assumed. If the
namespace attribute has a non-default value, the namespace must be added
to the URI that invokes the actions in the package. For example, the URI for
invoking an action in a package with a default namespace is this:

`/context/actionName.action`

To invoke an action in a package with a non-default namespace, you use
this URI:

`/context/namespace/actionName.action`

A **package** element almost always extends the **struts-default** package
defined in **struts-default.xml**. By doing so, all actions in the package can
use the result types and interceptors registered in **struts-default.xml**. Here
is the skeleton of the **struts-default** package. The interceptors have been
omitted to save space.

```
<?xml version="1.0" encoding="UTF-8" ?>
<!DOCTYPE struts PUBLIC
    "-//Apache Software Foundation//DTD Struts Configuration 2.0//EN"
    "http://struts.apache.org/dtds/struts-2.0.dtd">

<struts>
    <package name="struts-default">
        <result-types>
            <result-type name="chain" class="com.opensymphony.
                ➥xwork2.ActionChainResult"/>
```

```
            <result-type name="dispatcher" class="org.apache.
               ➡struts2.dispatcher.ServletDispatcherResult"
               default="true"/>
            <result-type name="freemarker" class="org.apache.
               ➡struts2.views.freemarker.FreemarkerResult"/>
            <result-type name="httpheader" class="org.apache.
               ➡struts2.dispatcher.HttpHeaderResult"/>
            <result-type name="redirect" class="org.apache.struts2.
               ➡dispatcher.ServletRedirectResult"/>
            <result-type name="redirect-action" class="org.apache.
               ➡struts2.dispatcher.ServletActionRedirectResult"/>
            <result-type name="stream" class="org.apache.struts2.
               ➡dispatcher.StreamResult"/>
            <result-type name="velocity" class="org.apache.struts2.
               ➡dispatcher.VelocityResult"/>
            <result-type name="xslt" class="org.apache.struts2.
               ➡views.xslt.XSLTResult"/>
            <result-type name="plaintext" class="org.apache.struts2.
               ➡dispatcher.PlainTextResult"/>
        </result-types>

        <interceptors>

            [all interceptors]

        </interceptors>
    </package>
</struts>
```

The include Element

A large application may have many packages. In order to make the
struts.xml file easier to manage for a large application, it is advisable to
divide it into smaller files and use **include** elements to reference the files.
Each file would ideally include a package or related packages.

A **struts.xml** file with multiple **include** elements would look like this.

```
<?xml version="1.0" encoding="UTF-8" ?>
<!DOCTYPE struts PUBLIC
    "-//Apache Software Foundation//DTD Struts Configuration 2.0//EN"
    "http://struts.apache.org/dtds/struts-2.0.dtd">

<struts>
```

```
    <include file="module-1.xml" />
    <include file="module-2.xml" />
    ...
    <include file="module-n.xml" />

</struts>
```

Each **module.xml** file would have the same **DOCTYPE** element and a **struts** root element. Here is an example:

```
<?xml version="1.0" encoding="UTF-8"?>
<!DOCTYPE struts PUBLIC
    "-//Apache Software Foundation//DTD Struts Configuration 2.0//EN"
    "http://struts.apache.org/dtds/struts-2.0.dtd">

<!-- file module-n.xml -->
<struts>
    <package name="test" extends="struts-default">
        <action name="Test1" class="test.Test1Action">
            <result>/jsp/Result1.jsp</result>
        </action>
        <action name="Test2" class="test.Test2Action">
            <result>/ajax/Result2.jsp</result>
        </action>
    </package>
</struts>
```

The action Element

An **action** element is nested within a **package** element and represents an action. An action must have a name and you may choose any name for it. A good name reflects what the action does. For instance, an action that displays a form for entering a product's details may be called **displayAddProductForm**. By convention, you are encouraged to use the combination of a noun and a verb. For example, instead of calling an action **displayAddProductForm**, name it **Product_input**. However, it is totally up to you.

An action may or may not specify an action class. Therefore, an **action** element may be as simple as this.

```
<action name="MyAction">
```

An action that does not specify an action class will be given an instance of the default action class. The **ActionSupport** class is the default action class.

If an action has a non-default action class, however, you must specify the fully qualified class name using the **class** attribute. In addition, you must also specify the name of the action method, which is the method in the action class that will be executed when the action is invoked. Here is an example.

```
<action name="Address_save" class="app.Address" method="save">
```

If the **class** attribute is present but the **method** attribute is not, **execute** is assumed for the method name. In other words, the following **action** elements mean the same thing.

```
<action name="Employee_save" class="app.Employee" method="execute">
<action name="Employee_save" class="app.Employee">
```

The result Element

<result> is a subelement of **<action>** and tells Struts 2 where you want the action to be forwarded to. A **result** element corresponds to the return value of an action method. Because an action method may return different values for different situations, an **action** element may have several **result** elements, each of which corresponds to a possible return value of the action method. This is to say, if a method may return "success" and "input," you must have two **result** elements. The **name** attribute of the **result** element maps a result with a method return value.

Note

If a method returns a value without a matching **result** element, Struts will try to find a matching result under the **global-results** element (See the discussion of this element below). If no corresponding **result** element is found under **global-results**, an exception will be thrown.

For example, the following **action** element contains two **result** elements.

```
<action name="Product_save" class="app.Product" method="save">
    <result name="success" type="dispatcher">
        /jsp/Confirm.jsp
```

```
    </result>
    <result name="input" type="dispatcher">
        /jsp/Product.jsp
    </result>
</action>
```

The first result will be executed if the action method **save** returns "success," in which case the **Confirm.jsp** page will be displayed. The second result will be executed if the method returns "input," in which case the **Product.jsp** page will be sent to the browser.

By the way, the **type** attribute of the **result** element specifies the result type. The value of the **type** attribute must be a result type that is registered in the containing package or a parent package extended by the containing package. Assuming that the action **Product_save** is in a package that extends **struts-default**, it is safe to use a Dispatcher result for this action because the Dispatcher result type is defined in **struts-default**.

If you omit the **name** attribute in a **result** element, "success" is implied. In addition, if the **type** attribute is not present, the default result type **Dispatcher** is assumed. Therefore, these two **result** elements are the same.

```
<result name="success" type="dispatcher">/jsp/Confirm.jsp</result>

<result>/jsp/Confirm.jsp</result>
```

An alternative syntax that employs the **param** element exists for the Dispatcher **result** element. In this case, the parameter name to be used with the **param** element is **location**. In other words, this **result** element

```
<result>/test.jsp</result>
```

is the same as this:

```
<result>
    <param name="location">/test.jsp</param>
</result>
```

You'll learn more about the **param** element later in this section.

The global-results Element

A **package** element may contain a **global-results** element that contains results that act as general results. If an action cannot find a matching result under its action declaration, it will search the **global-results** element, if any.

Here is an example of the **global-results** element.

```
<global-results>
    <result name="error">/jsp/GenericErrorPage.jsp</result>
    <result name="login" type="redirect-action">Login</result>
</global-results>
```

The Interceptor-related Elements

There are five interceptor-related elements that may appear in a **struts.xml** file: **interceptors**, **interceptor**, **interceptor-ref**, **interceptor-stack**, and **default-interceptor-ref**. They are explained in this section.

An **action** element must contain a list of interceptors that will process the action object. Before you can use an interceptor, however, you have to register it using an **interceptor** element under **<interceptors>**. Interceptors defined in a package can be used by all actions in the package.

For example, the following **package** element registers two interceptors, **validation** and **logger**.

```
<package name="main" extends="struts-default">
    <interceptors>
        <interceptor name="validation" class="..."/>
        <interceptor name="logger" class="..."/>
    </interceptors>
</package>
```

To apply an interceptor to an action, use the **interceptor-ref** element under the **action** element of that action. For instance, the following configuration registers four interceptors and apply them to the **Product_delete** and **Product_save** actions.

```
<package name="main" extends="struts-default">
    <interceptors>
        <interceptor name="alias" class="..."/>
        <interceptor name="i18n" class="..."/>
```

```
            <interceptor name="validation" class="..."/>
            <interceptor name="logger" class="..."/>
    </interceptors>

    <action name="Product_delete" class="...">
        <interceptor-ref name="alias"/>
        <interceptor-ref name="i18n"/>
        <interceptor-ref name="validation"/>
        <interceptor-ref name="logger"/>
        <result>/jsp/main.jsp</result>
    </action>

    <action name="Product_save" class="...">
        <interceptor-ref name="alias"/>
        <interceptor-ref name="i18n"/>
        <interceptor-ref name="validation"/>
        <interceptor-ref name="logger"/>
        <result name="input">/jsp/Product.jsp</result>
        <result>/jsp/ProductDetails.jsp</result>
    </action>
</package>
```

With these settings every time the **Product_delete** or **Product_save** actions are invoked, the four interceptors will be given a chance to process the actions. Note that the order of appearance of the **interceptor-ref** element is important as it determines the order of invocation of registered interceptors for that action. In this example, the **alias** interceptor will be invoked first, followed by the **i18n** interceptor, the **validation** interceptor, and the **logger** interceptor.

With most Struts 2 application having multiple **action** elements, repeating the list of interceptors for each action can be a daunting task. In order to alleviate this problem, Struts allows you to create interceptor stacks that group required interceptors. Instead of referencing interceptors from within each **action** element, you can reference the interceptor stack instead.

For instance, six interceptors are often used in the following orders: **exception**, **servletConfig**, **prepare**, **checkbox**, **params**, and **conversionError**. Rather than referencing them again and again in your action declarations, you can create an interceptor stack like this:

```
<interceptor-stack name="basicStack">
    <interceptor-ref name="exception"/>
    <interceptor-ref name="servlet-config"/>
```

```
    <interceptor-ref name="prepare"/>
    <interceptor-ref name="checkbox"/>
    <interceptor-ref name="params"/>
    <interceptor-ref name="conversionError"/>
</interceptor-stack>
```

To use these interceptors, you just need to reference the stack:

```
<action name="..." class="...">
    <interceptor-ref name="basicStack"/>
    <result name="input">/jsp/Product.jsp</result>
    <result>/jsp/ProductDetails.jsp</result>
</action>
```

The **struts-default** package defines several stacks. In addition, it defines a **default-interceptor-ref** element that specifies the default interceptor or interceptor stack to use if no interceptor is defined for an action:

```
<default-interceptor-ref name="defaultStack"/>
```

If an action needs a combination of other interceptors and the default stack, you must redefine the default stack as the **default-interceptor-ref** element will be ignored if an **interceptor** element can be found within an **action** element.

The param Element

The **param** element can be nested within another element such as **action**, **result-type**, and **interceptor** to pass a value to the enclosing object.

The **param** element has a **name** attribute that specifies the name of the parameter. The format is as follows:

```
<param name="property">value</param>
```

Used within an **action** element, **param** can be used to set an action property. For example, the following **param** element sets the **siteId** property of the action.

```
<action name="customer" class="…">
    <param name="siteId">california01</param>
</action>
```

And the following **param** element sets the **excludeMethod** of the validation **interceptor-ref**:

```
<interceptor-ref name="validation">
    <param name="excludeMethods">input,back,cancel</param>
</interceptor-ref>
```

The **excludeMethods** parameter is used to exclude certain methods from invoking the enclosing interceptor.

The constant Element

In addition to the **struts.xml** file, you can have a **struts.properties** file. You create the latter if you need to override one or more key/value pairs defined in the **default.properties** file, which is included in the **struts2-core-VERSION.jar** file. Most of the time you won't need a **struts.properties** file as the **default.properties** file is good enough. Besides, you can override a setting in the **default.properties** file using the **constant** element in the **struts.xml** file.

The **constant** element has a **name** attribute and a **value** attribute. For example, the **struts.devMode** setting determines whether or not the Struts application is in development mode. By default, the value is **false**, meaning the application is not in development mode.

The following **constant** element sets **struts.devMode** to **true**.

```
<struts>
    <constant name="struts.devMode" value="true"/>

    ...
</struts>
```

The struts.properties File

You create a **struts.properties** file if you need to override settings in the **default.properties** file. For example, the following **struts.properties** file overrides the value of **struts.devMode** in **default.properties**.

```
struts.devMode = true
```

A **struts.properties** file must reside in the classpath or in **WEB-INF/classes**.

To avoid having to create a new file, you can use **constant** elements in the **struts.xml** file. Alternatively, you can use the **init-param** element in the filter declaration of the Struts filter dispatcher:

```
<filter>
    <filter-name>struts</filter-name>
    <filter-class>
        org.apache.struts2.dispatcher.FilterDispatcher
    </filter-class>
    <init-param>
        <param-name>struts.devMode</param-name>
        <param-value>true</param-value>
    </init-param>
</filter>
```

A Simple Struts Application

Let's now rewrite **app10b** using Struts 2 and call the new application **app18a**. You will use similar JSP pages and an action class called **Product**.

The directory structure of **app18a** is given in Figure 18.2. Each component of the application is discussed in the next sub-sections.

The Deployment Descriptor and the Struts Configuration File

The deployment descriptor is given in Listing 18.1 and the Struts 2 configuration file in Listing 18.2.

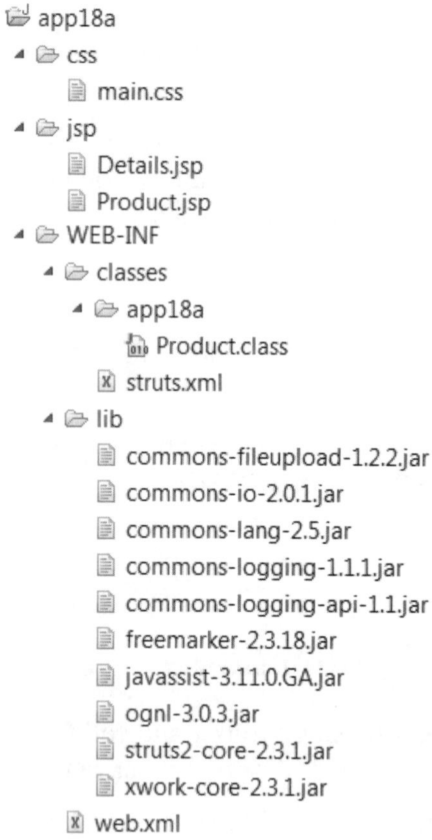

```
app18a
  css
    main.css
  jsp
    Details.jsp
    Product.jsp
  WEB-INF
    classes
      app18a
        Product.class
      struts.xml
    lib
      commons-fileupload-1.2.2.jar
      commons-io-2.0.1.jar
      commons-lang-2.5.jar
      commons-logging-1.1.1.jar
      commons-logging-api-1.1.jar
      freemarker-2.3.18.jar
      javassist-3.11.0.GA.jar
      ognl-3.0.3.jar
      struts2-core-2.3.1.jar
      xwork-core-2.3.1.jar
    web.xml
```

Figure 18.2: The directory structure of app18a

Listing 18.1: The deployment descriptor (web.xml file)

```xml
<?xml version="1.0" encoding="ISO-8859-1"?>
<web-app xmlns="http://java.sun.com/xml/ns/javaee"
    xmlns:xsi="http://www.w3.org/2001/XMLSchema-instance"
    xsi:schemaLocation="http://java.sun.com/xml/ns/javaee
      http://java.sun.com/xml/ns/javaee/web-app_3_0.xsd"
    version="3.0"
>
    <filter>
        <filter-name>struts2</filter-name>
        <filter-class>
            org.apache.struts2.dispatcher.ng.filter.
StrutsPrepareAndExecuteFilter
        </filter-class>
    </filter>
```

```
    <filter-mapping>
        <filter-name>struts2</filter-name>
        <url-pattern>/*</url-pattern>
    </filter-mapping>

    <!-- Restrict direct access to JSPs.
        For the security constraint to work, the auth-constraint
        and login-config elements must be present -->
    <security-constraint>
        <web-resource-collection>
            <web-resource-name>JSPs</web-resource-name>
            <url-pattern>/jsp/*</url-pattern>
        </web-resource-collection>
        <auth-constraint/>
    </security-constraint>

    <login-config>
        <auth-method>BASIC</auth-method>
    </login-config>
</web-app>
```

Listing 18.2: The struts.xml

```
<?xml version="1.0" encoding="UTF-8" ?>
<!DOCTYPE struts PUBLIC
    "-//Apache Software Foundation//DTD Struts Configuration 2.0//EN"
    "http://struts.apache.org/dtds/struts-2.0.dtd">

<struts>
    <package name="app18a" namespace="/" extends="struts-default">
        <action name="Product_input">
            <result>/jsp/ProductForm.jsp</result>
        </action>

        <action name="Product_save" class="app18a.Product">
            <result>/jsp/ProductDetails.jsp</result>
        </action>
    </package>
</struts>
```

The **struts.xml** file defines a package (**app18a**) that has two actions,
Product_input and **Product_save**. The **Product_input** action does not
have an action class. Invoking **Product_input** simply forwards control to
the **ProductForm.jsp** page. This page contains an entry form for entering
product information.

The **Product_save** action has a non-default action class (**app18.Product**). Since no **method** attribute is present in the action declaration, the **execute** method in the **Product** class will be invoked.

Note

During development you can add this **constant** element on top of your package element to switch Struts 2 to development mode.

```
<constant name="struts.devMode" value="true" />
```

The Action Class

The **Product** class in Listing 18.3 is the action class for action **Product_save**. The class has three properties (**productName, description,** and **price**) and one action method, **execute**.

Listing 18.3: The Product action class

```
package app18a;
import java.io.Serializable;

public class Product implements Serializable {
    private static final long serialVersionUID = 1000L;

    private String name;
    private String description;
    private String price;

    public String getName() {
        return name;
    }

    public void setName(String name) {
        this.name = name;
    }

    public String getDescription() {
        return description;
    }

    public void setDescription(String description) {
        this.description = description;
    }
```

```
    public String getPrice() {
        return price;
    }

    public void setPrice(String price) {
        this.price = price;
    }
    public String execute() {
        return "success";
    }
}
```

Running the Application

The app18a application is a Struts 2 replica of the app10b application in Chapter 10. To invoke the first action, use the following URL.

```
http://localhost:8080/app18a/Product_input.action
```

You will see something like Figure 10.2 in your browser. Enter values in the fields and submit the form. Your browser will display a confirmation message similar to Figure 10.3.

Congratulations. You've just seen Struts 2 in action!

Summary

In this chapter you have learned about what Struts 2 offers to speed up Model 2 application development. You have also learned how to configure Struts applications and you have written your first Struts application.

Appendix A
Tomcat

Tomcat is the most popular servlet/JSP container today. It's free, mature, and open-sourced. You need Tomcat 7 or another compliant servlet/JSP container to run the sample applications accompanying this book. This appendix provides a quick installation and configuration guide and is by no means a comprehensive tutorial.

Downloading and Configuring Tomcat

You should first download the latest version of Tomcat from http://tomcat.apache.org. You should get the latest binary distribution in either zip or gz. Tomcat 7 requires Java 6 to run.

After you download the zip or gz file, unpack the file. You will see several directories under the installation directory.

In the **bin** directory, you will find programs to start and stop Tomcat. The **webapps** directory is important because you can deploy your applications there. In addition, the **conf** directory contains configuration files, including the **server.xml** and **tomcat-users.xml** files. The **lib** directory is also of interest since it contains the Servlet and JSP APIs that you need to compile your servlets and custom tags.

After extracting the zip or gz file, set the **JAVA_HOME** environment variable to the JDK installation directory.

For Windows users, it is a good idea to download the Windows installer for easier installation.

Starting and Stopping Tomcat

Once you've downloaded and extracted a Tomcat binary, you can start Tomcat by running the **startup.bat** (on Windows) or the **startup.sh** file (on Unix/Linux/Mac OS). Both files reside under the **bin** directory of Tomcat's installation directory. By default, Tomcat runs on port 8080, so you can test Tomcat by directing your browser to this address:

```
http://localhost:8080
```

To stop Tomcat, run the **shutdown.bat** (on Windows) or **shutdown.sh** file (on Unix/Linux/Mac OS) in the **bin** directory.

Defining A Context

To deploy a servlet/JSP application to Tomcat, you need to define a Tomcat context either explicitly or implicitly. Each Tomcat context represents a web application in Tomcat.

There are several ways of defining a Tomcat context explicitly, including

- Creating an XML file in Tomcat's **conf/Catalina/localhost** directory.
- Adding a **Context** element in Tomcat's **conf/server.xml** file.

If you decide to create an XML file for each context, the file name is important as the context path is derived from it. For example, if you place a **commerce.xml** file in the **conf/Catalina/localhost** directory, the context path of your application will be **commerce** and a resource can be invoked using this URL:

```
http://localhost:8080/commerce/resourceName
```

A context file must contain a **Context** element as its root element. Most of the times the element does not have child elements and is the only element in the file. For example, here is an example context file, consisting of a single line.

```
<Context docBase="C:/apps/commerce" reloadable="true"/>
```

The only required attribute is **docBase**, which specifies the location of the application. The **reloadable** attribute is optional, but if it is present and its value is set to true, Tomcat will monitor the application for any addition, deletion, or update of a Java class file and other resources. When such a change is detected, Tomcat will reload the application. Setting **reloadable** to **true** is recommended during development but not in production.

When you add a context file to the specified directory, Tomcat will automatically load the application. When you delete it, Tomcat will unload the application.

Another way of defining a context is by adding a **Context** element in the **conf/server.xml** file. To do this, open the file and create a **Context** element under the **Host** element. Unlike the previous method, defining a context here requires that you specify the **path** attribute for your context path. Here is an example:

```
<Host name="localhost"  appBase="webapps" unpackWARs="true"
      autoDeploy="true">

   <Context path="/commerce"
         docBase="C:/apps/commerce"
         reloadable="true"
   />
</Host>
```

Generally, managing contexts through **server.xml** is not recommended as updates will only take effect after you restart Tomcat. However, if you have a bunch of applications that you need to test quickly, like when you are learning to write servlets and JSP pages, you may find working with **server.xml** almost ideal as you can manage all your applications in a single file.

Finally, you can also deploy an application implicitly by copying a war file or the whole application to Tomcat's **webapps** directory.

More information on Tomcat contexts can be found here:

```
http://tomcat.apache.org/tomcat-7.0-doc/config/context.html
```

Defining A Resource

You can define a JNDI resource that your application can use in your Tomcat context definition. A resource is represented by the **Resource** element under the **Context** element.

For instance, to add a **DataSource** resource that opens connections to a MySQL database, add this **Resource** element.

```
<Context [path="/appName"] docBase="...">
    <Resource name="jdbc/dataSourceName"
        auth="Container"
        type="javax.sql.DataSource"
        username="..."
        password="..."
        driverClassName="com.mysql.jdbc.Driver"
        url="..."
    />
</Context>
```

More information on the **Resource** element can be found here.

http://tomcat.apache.org/tomcat-7.0-doc/jndi-resources-howto.html

Installing SSL Certificates

Tomcat supports SSL and you should use it to secure transfer of confidential data such as social security numbers and credit card details. You can generate a public/private key pair using the KeyTool program and pay a trusted authority to create and sign a digital certificate for you. The process of generating the key pair and having it signed is discussed in Appendix C, "SSL Certificates."

Once you receive your certificate and import it into your keystore, the next step will be to install it on your server. If you're using Tomcat, simply copy your keystore in a location on the server and configure Tomcat. Then, open your **conf/server.xml** file and add the following **Connector** element under **<service>**.

```
<Connector port="443"
    minSpareThreads="5"
```

```
maxSpareThreads="75"
enableLookups="true"
disableUploadTimeout="true"
acceptCount="100"
maxThreads="200"

scheme="https"
secure="true"
SSLEnabled="true"
keystoreFile="/path/to/keystore"
keyAlias="example.com"
keystorePass="01secret02%%%"
clientAuth="false"
sslProtocol="TLS"
/>
```

The lines in bold are related to SSL.

Appendix B
Web Annotations

Servlet 3 comes with a set of annotation types in the **javax.servlet.annotation** package for annotating web objects such as servlets, filters, and listeners. This Appendix lists the annotation types.

HandlesTypes

This annotation type is used to declare the class types that a **ServletContainerInitializer** can handle. It has one attribute, value, that is used to declare the class types. For example, the following **ServletContainerInitializer** is annotated with **@HandleTypes** that declares that the initializer can handle **UsefulServlet**.

```
@HandlesTypes({UsefulServlet.class})
public class MyInitializer implements ServletContainerInitializer {
    ...
}
```

HttpConstraint

The **HttpConstraint** annotation type represents the security constraints applied to all HTTP protocol methods for which a corresponding **HttpMethodConstraint** element is not present. This annotation type must reside within the **ServletSecurity** annotation.

The attributes of **HttpConstraint** are given in Table B.1.

Attribute	Description
rolesAllowed	A string array representing the authorized roles.
transportGuarantee	Indicates whether or not there is a data protection requirement that must be met. The valid value is a member of the **ServletSecurity.TransportGuarantee** enum (CONFIDENTIAL or NONE).
value	The default authorization semantic.

Table B.1: HttpConstraint attributes

For example, the following **HttpConstraint** annotation declares that the annotated servlet can only be accessed by users that are part of the **manager** role. Since no **HttpMethodConstraint** annotation is present, the constraint applies to all HTTP methods.

```
@ServletSecurity(@HttpConstraint(rolesAllowed = "manager"))
```

HttpMethodConstraint

This annotation type represents a security constraint on a specific HTTP method. The **HttpMethodConstraint** annotation can only appear within the **ServletSecurity** annotation.

The attributes of **HttpMethodConstraint** are given in Table B.2.

Attribute	Description
emptyRoleSemantic	The default authorization semantic. The value must be one of the members of the **ServletSecurity.EmptyRoleSemantic** enum (**DENY** or **PERMIT**).
rolesAllowed	A string array representing the authorized roles.
transportGuarantee	Indicates whether or not there is a data protection requirement that must be met. The valid value is a member of the **ServletSecurity.TransportGuarantee** enum (**CONFIDENTIAL** or **NONE**).
value	The HTTP method affected.

Table B.2: HttpMethodConstraint attributes

For example, the following **ServletSecurity** annotation employs both the **value** and **httpMethodConstraints** attributes. The **HttpConstraint** annotation defines roles that can access the annotated servlet and the **HttpMethodConstraint** annotation, which is written without the **rolesAllowed** attribute, overrides the constraint for the Get method. As such, the servlet can be accessed via Get by any user. On the other hand, access via all other HTTP methods can only be granted to users in the **manager** role.

```
@ServletSecurity(value = @HttpConstraint(rolesAllowed = "manager"),
    httpMethodConstraints = {@HttpMethodConstraint("GET")}
)
```

However, if the **emptyRoleSemantic** attribute of the **HttpMethodConstraint** annotation type is assigned **EmptyRoleSemantic.DENY**, then the method is restricted for all users. For example, the servlet annotated with the following **ServletSecurity** annotation prevents access via the Get method but allows access to all users in the **member** role via other HTTP methods.

```
@ServletSecurity(value = @HttpConstraint(rolesAllowed = "member"),
httpMethodConstraints = {@HttpMethodConstraint(value = "GET",
    emptyRoleSemantic = EmptyRoleSemantic.DENY)}
)
```

MultipartConfig

The **MultipartConfig** annotation type is used to annotate a servlet to indicate that instances of the servlet is capable of handling the multipart/form-data MIME type, which is commonly used when uploading files.

Table B.3 lists the attributes of **MultipartConfig**.

For example, the following **MultipartConfig** annotation specifies that the maximum file size that can be uploaded is a million bytes.

```
@MultipartConfig(maxFileSize = 1000000)
```

Attribute	Description
fileSizeThreshold	The size threshold after which the uploaded file will be written to disk.
location	The save location when the uploaded file is saved to disk.
maxFileSize	The maximum size for uploaded files. Files larger than the specified value will be rejected. By default, the value of **maxFileSize** is -1, which means unlimited.
maxRequestSize	The maximum size allowed for multipart HTTP requests. By default, the value is -1, which translates into unlimited.

Table B.3: MultipartConfig attributes

ServletSecurity

The **ServletSecurity** annotation type is used to annotate a servlet class to apply security constraints on the servlet. The attributes that can appear in the **ServletSecurity** annotation are given in Table B.4.

Attribute	Description
httpMethodConstrains	An array of **HttpMethodConstraints** specifying HTTP method specific constraints.
value	The **HttpConstraint** annotation that defines the protection to be applied to all HTTP methods for which a corresponding **HttpMethodConstraint** is not found.

Table B.4: ServletSecurity attributes

For example, the following **ServletSecurity** annotation contains an **HttpConstraint** annotation that dictates that the annotated servlet can only be accessed by those in the **manager** role.

```
@ServletSecurity(value = @HttpConstraint(rolesAllowed = "manager"))
```

WebFilter

The **WebFilter** annotation type is used to annotate a filter. Table B.5 shows attributes that may appear in the **WebFilter** annotation. All attributes are optional.

Attribute	Description
asyncSupported	Indicates whether the filter supports asynchronous processing.
description	The filter description.
dispatcherTypes	An array of **DispatcherType**s to which the filter applies.
displayName	The display name of the filter.
filterName	The name of the filter.
initParams	The init parameters of the filter.
largeIcon	The large icon of the filter
servletNames	The names of the servlets to which the filter applies.
smallIcon	The small icon of the filter.
urlPatterns	The URL patterns to which the filter applies
value	The URL patterns to which the filter applies

Table B.5: WebFilter attributes

WebInitParam

This annotation type is used to pass initialization parameters to a servlet or a filter. The attributes that may appear in a **WebInitParam** annotation are given in Table B.6. The asterisk to the right of the attribute name indicates that the attribute is required.

Attribute	Description
description	The description of the initialization parameter.
name*	The name of the initialization parameter.
value*	The value of the initialization parameter.

Table B.6: WebInitParam attributes

WebListener

This annotation type is used to annotate a listener. Its only attribute, **value**, is optional and contains the description of the listener.

WebServlet

This annotation type is used to annotate a servlet. Its attributes are listed in Table B.7. All attributes are optional.

Attribute	Description
asyncSupported	Indicates whether the servlet supports asynchronous processing.
description	The servlet description.
displayName	The display name of the servlet.
initParams	The init parameters of the servlet.
largeIcon	The large icon of the servlet.
loadOnStartup	The loading order for the servlet in an application that consists of multiple servlets.
name	The name of the servlet.
smallIcon	The small icon of the servlet
urlPatterns	The URL patterns to invoke the servlet.
value	The URL patterns to invoke the servlet.

Table B.7: WebServlet attributes

Appendix C
SSL Certificates

SSL certificates are a tool for securing communications over the Internet as well as maintaining data security. It is a widespread misunderstanding to assume that only e-commerce sites and online banking must use an SSL certificate. In fact, most web sites that employ some kind of login page should also use an SSL certificate so that passwords will not be transferred as plain text.

In this appendix you will learn how to generate a public/private key pair using the KeyTool program and have the public key signed by a trusted authority as a certificate. See Appendix A, "Tomcat" for information on installing SSL certificates in Tomcat.

Certificate Overview

SSL is based on both symmetric and asymmetric cryptography. The latter involves a pair of keys, one private and one public. This is explained in Chapter 15, "Security."

A public key is normally wrapped in a certificate since a certificate is a more trusted way of distributing a public key. The certificate is signed using the private key that corresponds to the public key contained in the certificate. It is called a self-signed certificate. In other words, a self-signed certificate is one for which the signer is the same as the subject described in the certificate.

A self-signed certificate is good enough for people to authenticate the sender of a signed document if those people already know the sender. For better acceptance, you need a certificate signed by a Certificate Authority, such as VeriSign and Thawte. You need to send them your self-signed certificate.

After a CA authenticates you, they will issue you a certificate that replaces the self-signed certificate. This new certificate may also be a chain of certificates. At the top of the chain is the 'root', which is the self-signed certificate. Next in the chain is the certificate from a CA that authenticates you. If the CA is not well known, they will send it to a bigger CA that will authenticate the first CA's public key. The last CA will also send the certificate, hence forming a chain of certificates. This bigger CA normally has their public keys widely distributed so people can easily authenticate certificates they sign.

Java provides a set of tools and APIs that can be used to work with asymmetric cryptography explained in the previous section. With them you can do the following:

- Generate pairs of public and private keys. You can then send the public key generated to a certificate issuer to obtain your own certificate. For a fee, of course.
- Store your private and public keys in a database called keystore. A keystore has a name and is password protected.
- Store other people's certificates in the same keystore.
- Create your own certificate by signing it with your own private key. However, such certificates will have limited use. For testing, self-signed certificates are good enough.
- Digitally sign a file. This is particularly important because browsers will only allow applets access to resources if the applets are stored in a jar file that has been signed. Signed Java code guarantee the user that you are really the developer of the class. If they trust you they may have less doubt in running the Java class.

Let's now review the tool.

The KeyTool Program

The KeyTool program is a utility to create and maintain public and private keys and certificates. It comes with the JDK and is located in the **bin** directory of the JDK. Keytool is a command-line program. To check the correct syntax, simply type keytool at the command prompt. The following will provide examples of some important functions.

Generating Key Pairs

Before you start, there are a few things to notice with regard to key generation in Java.

1. Keytool generates a public/private key pair and creates a certificate signed using the private key (self-signed certificate). Among others, the certificate contains the public key and the identity of the entity whose key it is. Therefore, you need to supply your name and other information. This name is called a distinguished name and contains the following information:

```
CN= common name, e.g. Joe Sample
OU=organizational unit, e.g. Information Technology
O=organization name, e.g. Brainy Software Corp
L=locality name, e.g. Vancouver
S=state name, e.g. BC
C=country, (two letter country code) e.g. CA
```

2. Your keys will be stored in a database called keystore. A keystore is file-based and password-protected so that no unauthorized persons can access the private keys stored in it.
3. If no keystore is specified when generating keys or when performing other functions, the default keystore is assumed. The default keystore is named **.keystore** in the user's home directory (i.e. in the directory defined by the **user.home** system property. For example, for Windows XP the default keystore is located under C:\Documents and Settings*userName* directory in Windows.
4. There are two types of entries in a keystore:
   a. Key entries, each of which is a private key accompanies by the certificate chain of the corresponding public key.
   b. Trusted certificate entries, each of which contains the public key of an entity you trust.

   Each entry is also password-protected, therefore there are two types of passwords, the one that protects the keystore and one that protects an entry.

5. Each entry in a keystore is identified by a unique name or an alias. You must specify an alias when generating a key pair or doing other activities with keytool.
6. If when generating a key pair you don't specify an alias, **mykey** is used as an alias.

The shortest command to generate a key pair is this.

```
keytool -genkeypair
```

Using this command, the default keystore will be used or one will be created if none exists in the user's home directory. The generated key will have the alias **mykey**. You will then be prompted to enter a password for the keystore and supply information for your distinguished name. Finally, you will be prompted for a password for the entry.

Invoking **keytool –genkeypair** again will result in an error because it will attempt to create a pair key and use the alias **mykey** again.

To specify an alias, use the –alias argument. For example, the following command creates a key pair identified using the keyword **email**.

```
keytool -genkeypair -alias email
```

Again, the default keystore is used.

To specify a keystore, use the **–keystore** argument. For example, this command generate a key pair and store it in the keystore named **myKeystore** in the C:\javakeys directory.

```
keytool -genkeypair -keystore C:\javakeys\myKeyStore
```

After you invoke the program, you will be asked to enter mission information.

A complete command for generating a key pair is one that uses the genkeypair, alias, keypass, storepass and dname arguments. For example.

```
keytool -genkeypair -alias email4 -keypass myPassword -dname
"CN=JoeSample, OU=IT, O=Brain Software Corp, L=Surrey, S=BC, C=CA"
-storepass myPassword
```

Getting Certified

While you can use Keytool to generate pairs of public and private keys and self-signed certificates, your certificates will only be trusted by people who already know you. To get more acceptance, you need your certificates signed by a certificate authority (CA), such as VeriSign, Entrust or Thawte.

If you intend to do this, you need to generate a Certificate Signing Request (CSR) by using the –certreq argument of Keytool. Here is the syntax:

```
keytool -certreg -alias alias -file certregFile
```

The input of this command is the certificate referenced by *alias* and the output is a CSR, which is the file whose path is specified by *certregFile*. Send the CSR to a CA and they will authenticate you offline, normally by asking you to provide valid identification details, such as a copy of your passport or driver's license.

If the CA is satisfied with your credentials, they will send you a new certificate or a certificate chain that contains your public key. This new certificate is used to replace the existing certificate chain you sent (which was self-signed). Once you receive the reply, you can import your new certificate into a keystore by using the **importcert** argument of Keytool.

Importing a Certificate into the Keystore

If you receive a signed document from a third party or a reply from a CA, you can store it in a keystore. You need to assign an alias you can easily remember to this certificate.

To import or store a certificate into a keystore, use the **importcert** argument. Here is the syntax.

```
keytool -importcert -alias anAlias -file filename
```

As an example, to import the certificate in the file joeCertificate.cer into the keystore and give it the alias brotherJoe, you use this:

```
keytool -importcert -alias brotherJoe -file joeCertificate.cer
```

The advantages of storing a certificate in a keystore is twofold. First, you have a centralized store that is password protected. Second, you can easily authenticate a signed document from a third party if you have imported their certificate in a keystore.

Exporting a Certificate from the Keystore

With your private key you can sign a document. When you sign the document, you make a digest of the document and then encrypt the digest with your private key. You then distribute the document as well as the encrypted digest.

For others to authenticate the document, they must have your public key. For security, your public key needs to be signed too. You can self-sign it or you can get a trusted certificate issuer to sign it.

The first thing to do is extract your certificate from a keystore and save it as a file. Then, you can easily distribute the file. To extract a certificate from a keystore, you need to use the **–exportcert** argument and pass the alias and the name of the file to contain your certificate. Here is the syntax:

```
keytool -exportcert -alias anAlias -file filename
```

A file containing a certificate is typically given the .cer extension. For example, to extract a certificate whose alias is Meredith and save it to the meredithcertificate.cer file, you use this command:

```
keytool -exportcert -alias Meredith -file meredithcertificate.cer
```

Listing Keystore Entries

Now that you have a keystore to store your private keys and the certificates of parties you trust, you can enquiry its content by listing it using the keytool program. You do it by using the **list** argument.

```
keytool -list -keystore myKeyStore -storepass myPassword
```

Again, the default keystore is assumed if the keystore argument is missing.

Index